LERWICK HARBOUR

LERWICK HARBOUR

by

James R. Nicolson

Published by Lerwick Harbour Trust.
1877 - 1977

First published by Lerwick Harbour Trust,
1/2 Alexandra Buildings, Lerwick,
May, 1977.

ILLUSTRATIONS

Photographs were supplied by:
Harry Jamieson collection — Nos. 1, 2, 3, 4, 8, 11.
Erling J. F. Clausen collection — Nos. 5, 13.
Shetland Library and Museum collection — Nos. 6, 7, 9, 10, 12, 15, 16.
Dennis Coutts — Nos. 17, 18, 19, 20, 21, 22, 23, 25, 26, 27, 28, 29, 30.
Martin Smith — No. 24.

Printed in Shetland by The Shetland Times Ltd.,
Lerwick, Shetland.

CONTENTS

	Acknowledgements	vi
	Foreword	vii
1	The Early Days	1
2	The Growth of Trade	8
3	Lerwick Harbour Trust	22
4	The Difficult Years	31
5	Changes in the Fishing Industry	44
6	Alexandra Wharf	53
7	Changes Along the Seafront	63
8	The Dominance of the Steam Drifter	70
9	The Small Boat Harbour	83
10	Lerwick at War	92
11	Between the Wars	107
12	World War Two	126
13	Post-War Reconstruction	136
14	Economic Recovery	155
15	The Oil Boom	171
16	The Harbour in 1977	186
	Index	195

ACKNOWLEDGEMENTS

Although this book is based largely on the Minute Books of Lerwick Harbour Trust a great deal of extra information has come from the files of "The Shetland Times" which was founded in 1872 and still continues to thrive and from those of "The Shetland News" which was published between 1885 and 1963. I am grateful to Mr Basil Wishart, Editor of "The Shetland Times," and to Dr T. M. Y. Manson, formerly Editor of "The Shetland News," for their co-operation in allowing me to use this material. In writing the opening chapter I relied heavily on Mr Thomas Manson's "Lerwick During the Last Half Century" which was published in 1923 and which is still recognised as the most authoritative work on the history of Lerwick.

In covering more recent times a great deal of information came from men with an intimate knowledge of the harbour — men such as Mr Arthur B. Laurenson, Mr Magnus Shearer, Mr Francis Garriock and Capt. William Inkster. The Trustees themselves read my manuscript and pointed out several errors and omissions. It was extremely difficult to obtain accurate information about World War II but this lack was overcome through the assistance of Mr Tom Henry and indeed Chapter 12 of this book is based largely upon his knowledge and recollections.

Most of all I am indebted to Mr Erling J. F. Clausen for his advice and assistance at every stage. Mr Clausen read my manuscript, pointed out several errors and provided much additional information.

FOREWORD

To a much greater extent than other local authorities, port authorities serve the outside world as well as their own localities and hinterlands through the untold thousands of seamen and fishermen and the innumerable shipping companies that use their facilities for import and export trade and the flow of seaborne passengers.

Of no port authority is this more true than it is of the Trust governing the cosmopolitan port of Lerwick. It would in any event have been fitting that a history of that body should be published in the hundredth year of its existence. What adds zest to this centenary history is the fact that owing both to the natural growth of sea traffic and the startling rise of the North Sea oil industry, the Trust in its centenary year is grappling with change as great as and faster than the changes which led to its formation in 1877.

The rise and fall of the great herring fishing industry; the financial problems in times of stalemate; the strains, stresses and excitements of two world wars impinging on the "stopper" in the North Sea bottleneck which Lerwick really is; and the current wild uprush of developments, combine to make the centenary history of Lerwick Harbour Trust an enthralling one.

The Trust have been fortunate in the author they have found to write that history. A Shetlander, a native not of Lerwick but of rural Aith, resident in the ancient capital of Scalloway, James R. Nicolson is able to take an objective view of his subject-matter.

Starting out in life with two university degrees, working as a geologist in Sierra Leone before returning to Shetland to become first a fisherman and then a geologist in the oil industry, Mr Nicolson has been led by his literary tendencies gradually to settle down to the life of a whole-time writer. In five years his production included four valuable books: "Shetland" (the last full description of the islands before the emergence of oil); "The Tent and the Simbek"; Beyond the Great Glen", and "Shetland and Oil".

Along with an intensely practical outlook Mr Nicolson has a reverence for the past and descriptive powers to portray both past and present. He does more than just memorialise Lerwick Harbour Trust. He outlines the history of Lerwick itself from its first beginnings, and describes fishery and other developments in a way adequate to explain the Trust's activities. Lerwegians and others will find a new interest in familiar buildings and roadways after reading his account of the 18th century town and the concluding chapter in which he ties past and present together.

Lerwick Harbour Trust were always admirable for their single-minded devotion to their unending task of maintaining and developing the harbour works and for the remarkable degree of unanimity which characterised their discussions.

Mr Nicolson's detailed history, the product of much painstaking research, not only confirms this general impression, but throws light on several obscure questions and provides many essential details either not known to the average citizen or long forgotten.

Above all it is a chronicle of most commendable enterprise, from the venture in faith of the local merchants whose personal financial guarantees enabled the Trust to come into being a hundred years ago, to the keen-sighted action of the Trust only a few years ago in purchasing the Gremista estate north of the town in order to keep control of the harbour in face of the coming oil industry.

Whatever lies in the future, Lerwick Harbour Trust can be proud of their first hundred years' achievement, and they can be satisfied with this record of it.

Of special interest in the book as it unfolds itself is the roll of names of the men who have worked for and in the Trust, names which, particularly for the older generation of readers, will evoke endless personal memories.

T. M. Y. MANSON.

Chapter One

THE EARLY DAYS

Although Lerwick is an old town with a rich and fascinating history it is young compared to other settlements in Shetland. The land here is relatively infertile and throughout the entire period of Norse rule the site was largely ignored. Lerwick's great asset is its harbour, big enough to accommodate a whole fleet of ships. But the early Norse settlers did not need this. They required land to till and a beach where their small open boats could be hauled ashore. So they settled along the shores of Bressay — the island opposite — at Sound and Gulberwick to the South and at Grimista, Dale and Califf farther north. But at least they gave a name to the little bay on the eastern side of the scattald of Sound where a swift-flowing stream entered the sea through an estuary of soft mud. They called it Leir Vik — the muddy bay.

Although long unused Bressay Sound may not have been unknown to the Norsemen. Many people believe that this was the "Breideyjar Sund" where King Haakon Haakonson broke his journey in 1263. It must have been a magnificent sight as 200 great war galleys swept in past the Bard and the Knab and into Bressay Sound itself. But the watchers on Bressay and on the heights above Leir Vik were not alarmed since they too owed their allegiance to Norway and had no part in the southern nation of Scotland whose rising power King Haakon had set out to crush. The ensuing Battle of Largs was inconclusive yet it marked the end of Norse rule in the west. Nevertheless for another 200 years Shetland was to remain part of the Norse earldom of Orkney and Shetland.

Shetland's transfer to Scotland in 1469 made no difference to Bressay Sound. Scottish earls replaced the Norse jarls and they built their mansions at Sumburgh and Scalloway in the more thickly populated South and West of Shetland. But while the Norse and the Scots had virtually ignored this magnificent harbour a third European power was soon to realise its potential.

This nation was Holland whose hardy fishermen venturing ever farther northwards had discovered a silver mine of herring a few miles east of Shetland and with their new-found wealth had proceeded to build the city of Amsterdam and a fleet of warships to challenge the naval power of England.

The Dutch herring fishery was bound by numerous regulations, one of the most important being that fishing must not start before June 24, the Feast of St. John the Baptist. But weeks beforehand the large, lumbering busses set sail from Holland making their way slowly northwards. The fishermen found the broad waters of Bressay Sound an ideal place to assemble and wait for the coming of Johnsmas and the accepted date for starting to fish.

They were glad to get their feet on dry land after their long journey and soon the little bay of Lerwick was recognised as the landing place for those seeking recreation ashore. Some historians suggest that the rock known as the Cockstool served as a natural jetty and that the Dutch carved steps to help them climb the green slimy face of the rock.

Shetlanders soon realised that the arrival of the Dutch afforded an opportunity for trade and the site of the early market place, midway between Lerwick and Scalloway, is still known as the Hollanders' Knowe. In exchange for brandy, gin and tobacco the Shetlanders sold or bartered eggs, chickens and the woollen garments for which Shetland even then was famous.

It was not long before some enterprising islander found it to his advantage to set up his stall on the shore of Bressay Sound itself near the landing place of the Dutch on the south side of Lerwick. Success is infectious and soon a collection of huts sprang up along the shore.

Meanwhile over at the Earl's castle at Scalloway a new name, Lerwick, was on everyone's lips. Rumours filtered over the hill of the growing activity. The inevitable moral lapses were magnified and there were reports of much immorality and drunkenness. In 1625 the Court of Scalloway ordered the huts at Lerwick to be 'utterlie dimolished and downe cassin to the ground'. Perhaps the ancient capital feared this threat to its hitherto unchallenged supremacy.

The building of the upstart village was only temporarily delayed and the Dutch continued to assemble at Lerwick every summer. But they did not have it all their own way for on

13th June 1640 a Dutch warship and three armed vessels of the East India company lying in Bressay Sound were surprised by ten armed Spanish ships. A terrific battle ensued, the Dutch warship surrendered, two of the Indiamen, the "De Haan" and "De Reiger" were sunk on the western side of the sound while the third, the "Jonas", escaped through the north entrance but being pursued by two Spanish frigates, was run ashore at Brunthamarsland and blown up.

At this time the settlement at Lerwick was purely seasonal. Pont's map of Orkney and Shetland, published in 1654 by Blaeu of Amsterdam, does not show Lerwick although it shows Grimista and Sound. But the tremendous potential of Bressay Sound in peace and war had by this time been realised by the English government and it was in a time of war that Lerwick was put on the map. Again the Dutch were associated — this time as enemies of England. In 1652 Robert Blake, one of the generals at sea, lay with his fleet of 80 ships in Bressay Sound sheltering from the gale which sank many of the Dutch fleet under the command of Admiral van Tromp then on the west side of Shetland. In 1653 94 English ships commanded by Admirals Deans and Monk anchored in Bressay Sound; troops were landed to garrison Scalloway Castle and the building of a fort was commenced at Lerwick — the first permanent building in this area.

Cromwell's troops stayed for only three years but between 1665 and 1668 the fort was again garrisoned against a possible Dutch invasion and the present ramparts were erected. When peace was temporarily restored building operations came to a halt and the soldiers departed taking with them the cannon. Then in 1673 Dutch sailors landed at Lerwick and burned the barracks and several of the houses in the town.

The Dutch resumed fishing after the wars and again visited Lerwick for trade and recreation. By this time Lerwick was a permanent settlement south of Cromwell's fort and no longer dependent on the Dutch for its prosperity although their arrival each summer was certainly a boost to trade.

In 1700 the Rev. John Brand visited Shetland and found between 200 and 300 families in this prosperous little town. The people had built a church at their own expense but it was visited only rarely by the minister of Tingwall who had three other churches under his charge. It was on the recommendation of John Brand that Lerwick and the neighbouring district was disjoined from Tingwall in 1701 and made into a separate parish —a considerable rise in status for the town.

In 1702 the Dutch suffered another reverse — this time at the hands of the French. Four French warships attacked the Dutch frigate "Wolfswinkel" and some poorly armed merchant vessels that were protecting the herring fleet. After a heroic fight lasting four hours the captain of the "Wolfswinkel" blew up his ship rather than surrender. The French warships then proceeded to Lerwick where they lit up the whole harbour with the burning of 150 busses.

It took a long time for the fleet to recover. In 1736 300 Dutch vessels fished off Shetland and by 1761 their numbers had dwindled to only 152; but by 1784 the fleet had recovered and there were said to arrive annually at Lerwick between 200 and 300 Dutch 'Iceland Ships' and a similar number of herring busses. In addition to these herring fishers came from Dunkirk, Prussia and Denmark, while a large number of Dutch and English 'Greenland Ships', or whalers, passed through Bressay Sound.

THE EARLY MERCHANTS

By this time Lerwick had become the home of several of the landed gentry of Shetland who throughout the 18th century were to become increasingly involved in the commerce of the islands. Shetland's main industry was the summer fishing for ling, tusk and cod caught by long lines from small open boats that fished at considerable distances from land. The fish were purchased by the merchants who cured them on their drying beaches in many parts of the islands. In autumn and early winter the dried fish were exported to the Continent.

One of the best known of Lerwick's early merchants was William Nicolson of Lochend, whose dwelling house — Lochend House — still stands on south Commercial Street. On his death in 1758 his business was managed by his cousin, Arthur, and we are fortunate that the latter's day book for the year 1762 still survives. It is described in detail by W. Sandison whose book "A Shetland Merchant's Day-book in 1762" gives a marvellous insight into the working of a fairly large business at that time. Woollen stockings were purchased from the country people; gin, rum and brandy were imported from the continent, and fish, oil and hides were purchased for export. He had a trading

centre at Heogan and another at Fetlar and regularly, once a
month, his 'large' boat took to Fetlar food, lines and other
supplies for his fishermen, returning with cured or partly cured
ling. Then in autumn cargoes of dried fish, oil, hides, beef,
mutton and woollen garments were shipped to the Continent.

There was another drying beach at Grimista on the shore
of Lerwick's North Harbour, and the merchant's booth or
trading centre still stands as a memorial to the period. It was
at the Böd of Gremista that Shetland's most famous son, Arthur
Anderson, was born in 1792, and spent the short childhood then
considered sufficient for a boy. At the age of ten he entered
the employment of yet another merchant, Thomas Bolt of
Cruister in Bressay, first as a beach boy then as a clerk. The
parting advice of Thomas Bolt to young Anderson when he
eventually left Shetland to "Doe weel and persevere" became
the motto of Lerwick's Anderson Educational Institute. The
school was gifted to the people of Shetland by Arthur Anderson
many years after he had put this advice into practice. For Arthur
Anderson is better known as the co-founder of the great P
& O Line.

In addition to the laird-merchants there was a great number
of lesser businessmen all of whom played their part in the
growth of trade. Such was the importance of Lerwick that
customs officers were stationed to supervise the trade of the
port. Some of them settled permanently in Lerwick to become
businessmen and property owners in their own right.

LERWICK IN 1766

The oldest existing plan of Lerwick is the "Perspective
View" drawn by William Aberdeen in 1766 which gives a
marvellous opportunity to study the growth of the town in the
first 100 years of its existence. It is interesting too, because it
reveals the line of the natural coastline, only glimpses of which
are visible today.

The bight that had given its name to the town was a wide-
angled bay having its apex near the spot where the Market
Cross now stands. Here a burn entered the sea — a swift flowing
stream rising from one of the numerous springs in the hill
above and running down a valley now occupied by Mounthooly
Street. Rounding the headland of the Knab the steep cliffs gave
way to low banks continuing past the promontory of the Deuk's

Neb, becoming lower still as the shoreline curved inwards past the Cockstool Rock to the burn mouth at the head of the bay.

While the south arm of the bay had a rocky shoreline the north arm was entirely different with a long wide beach running northwards until it met the cliffs even then dominated by the mass of the fort. It was a low sandy beach typical of many in Shetland today and we can surmise that it would be frequented by wading seabirds and that the ordinary people of Lerwick would come down to dig for "spoots" when the tide was out.

Lerwick was basically a small village of about 100 buildings, although some of those shown in the perspective drawing probably housed several families. Most of them were strung along the shore facing the sound, with a footpath, the origin of Cross Street, later to become known as Commercial Street, between them and the edge of the sea. Several of the merchants had noosts below the footpath and occasionally steps led down to small landing places.

It is surprising how many of the houses shown in William Aberdeen's drawing are still inhabited today. The Old Manse is there and Lochend House and most of the buildings on the upper side of south Commercial Street. But even in 1766 space on the upper side of the street was limited and a move had begun to erect buildings across the footpath on the very edge of the sea on land reclaimed by a process of infilling and levelling —Lerwick's seaward extension had already begun.

The first building to be erected on the seaward side of the street was the Tolbooth or town house. The building shown in Aberdeen's drawing standing proudly beside the Cockstool rock was actually the new Tolbooth — a handsome building with a spire, built on the site of the old Tolbooth and completed in 1766. The second building to be erected on the seaward side was the house built at the South End by the merchant, Patrick Scollay, about 1730. Scollay's house was later purchased by Patrick Torrie who in 1764 inaugurated Morton Lodge of Freemasons in Lerwick. The perspective drawing shows Patrick Torrie's house and it also shows another innovation — a store house built into the sea. This was the very first of the lodberries that soon became such an integral part of the seascape of Lerwick. But between Patrick Torrie's house and the Tolbooth the shoreline was still in its natural state. Opposite the gable of Lochend House a flight of steps led down the banks into the sea and William Aberdeen actually shows a small boat lying in readiness at the Lochend steps.

North of the Tolbooth another house stood on the seaward side of the street — a small house where Messrs P. Solotti & Son's shop now stands — and behind it was a small jetty. North of this house there was a slight curvature of the shore that was later to become known as Sinclair's Beach and which is now entirely hidden by the Post Office.

From the burn mouth northwards the shoreline as shown by William Aberdeen bears even less resemblance to that of the present day. There were already several houses on the lower side of the street and the origins of many of the lanes can be seen. The town's people were desperately short of space and between the building later to be occupied by Robert Goudie & Sons and the house opposite a portion of the street had been roofed over to support a building. This device was known as a "trance" and William Aberdeen depicts a total of three in the northern half of Commercial Street.

The building occupied today by R. & C. Robertson was even in 1766 a landmark but in the perspective drawing it is shown as a trading centre close to the beach with its own small jetty behind it. North of this building the shore continued as a sandy beach until in the lee of the fort there was another trading nucleus and on a spur of rock protruding from below the cliffs stood the most northerly landing jetty of old Lerwick— the North Lodberry. But here the street ended for there was not even a footpath around the fort to the bare and unused North Ness beyond.

Chapter Two

THE GROWTH OF TRADE

The end of the 18th century was a momentous period in the history of Shetland. Britain was at war both in Europe and America and the strategic importance of these islands once again ensured their involvement. It was a time of violence and piracy at sea, a time of uncertainty when men were seized by the Press Gang for enforced service in the Royal Navy.

For Lerwick too, it was a time of uncertainty but it was also a time of great activity when the harbour was constantly crowded with ships. In 1781 the fort, from then on to become known as Fort Charlotte, was repaired and regarrisoned, mainly to defend Lerwick from American ships. At the same time a road was laid between the fort and the Knab for the conveyance of guns to the battery there.

It must have been about this time that the heavy iron rings were set into rocks on both sides of the sound. There were six on the Lerwick side between the North Ness and the Knab and six along the Bressay shore. The purpose of these rings became forgotten and theories were put forward in later years as to their function. It was suggested that between those rings and their counterparts on the Bressay shore ropes were tied as a sort of boom defence. However it is almost certain that the real purpose was to make it easier for vessels to get ready for sailing, especially when the harbour was crowded. A rope could be run out from the ship to the most conveniently situated ring and on the signal being given a person stationed beside the ring would let the rope go.

For Lerwick it was also a time of opportunity since the presence of so many ships and men gave a boost to the commerce of the town and several new firms started in business. One of the new merchants who arrived at this time was a man named Clark who in 1796 erected the building later to become known as the Seamen's Home. Another incomer was James Bain, joiner and auctioneer, who came from Cunningsburgh and

bought houses from Nicolson of Lochend. His name is perpetuated today in Bain's Beach and in the Gilbert Bain Hospital
named in honour of his son.

James Copeland was an Orcadian who farmed the island
of Noss and is said to have kept 24 milking cows, whose milk
he sold daily in Lerwick. In 1817 he built the most southerly
house and pier on Lerwick's foreshore. This pier is known as
Gillie's pier after George Gillie, a blacksmith, who occupied
the older house of rough stone that forms the back of the pier.

Each merchant had to have a portion of the foreshore
as his access to the sea independently of all his neighbours
and as they jostled for a position the entire shoreline between
Gillie's Pier and Fort Charlotte was quickly lined with piers
and lodberries. Smuggling played a great part in the life of
the town and an important feature of each of these erections
was a compartment or even a secret tunnel where Dutch gin
and tobacco could be deposited safe from the prying eyes of
the Revenue Officers.

Perhaps the most unfortunate of these early merchants
was Morrison who reclaimed his portion of land on the north
side of the burn mouth near where the Market Cross now
stands. Here he built a house and a substantial pier projecting
from the eastern gable. Unfortunately he was chosen by representatives of the Crown for a test case to establish the Crown's
right in the foreshore and he was charged with having encroached
on land below the high water mark.

Morrison contended that he had merely done what Copeland and many others had done, but the representatives of the
Crown maintained that no matter what others had done, whether
in ignorance or not, the time had come to put a stop to the infringement of the Act anent the Scottish foreshores. Morrison
lost his case and he died in 1820, it is said of a broken heart.
It is doubly tragic that Morrison did not live to see his pier
become, as it did by stages, the main landing place for the
town of Lerwick.

THE DOCKS

While these developments were taking place in the old
part of Lerwick even more ambitious schemes were under way
in the northern part of the harbour. The area north and west
of the North Ness was in many ways far more desirable from

B

the point of view of development. The area was far more sheltered than the little bay of Lerwick and it had the advantage of a vast amount of level unused land.

Men responsible for these projects were William Hay (1787-1858) and Charles Ogilvy (1802 - 1844) under the partnership known as Hay & Ogilvy. In the 1820s the whole region of Free-field was opened up with docks and warehouses, curing yards for herring and white fish and a boat-building yard with car-penters' shops and sailmakers' and ship riggers' lofts. Here they built the schooners "Janet Hay" and "North Britain", the largest vessels ever to be built in Shetland.

The most important of Hay & Ogilvy's activities was herring curing. Hitherto the local herring industry had been virtually non-existent, remaining the monopoly of the Dutch. But under the guidance of Hay & Ogilvy improved vessels known as half-deckers were brought from the Scottish mainland and curing stations were set up at several places in Shetland. The islands' catch rose from 10,000 crans in 1830 to 36,000 barrels in 1833 and in 1834 55,000 barrels of herring were exported to southern markets and the West Indies.

Such was the success of Shetland's fishing industry at this period that it began to attract the attention of Faroese business-men anxious to develop their own island group. One day in 1839 the Danish trading schooner "Hector" called at Lerwick with a party of visitors. They included Christian Ployen, a Danish official resident in Faroe. The "Hector" did not even drop anchor — she was met by a rowing boat into which the three passengers and their luggage were loaded and while the "Hector" continued towards the north mouth the visitors were rowed to the landing place at Morrison's Pier. Mr Ployen later described this as "a flight of stairs of hewn stone, nicely constructed, which at once gives one a pleasant notion of the town".

Mr Ployen's host was the Danish Consul, Mr Charles Ogilvy, who made sure that the visitors benefited from their visit. Ler-wick was enjoying a period of unprecedented prosperity, thanks to the development of the herring industry, and the man largely responsible for this was the same Charles Ogilvy, partner in the firm of Hay & Ogilvy.

But neither Mr Ployen nor Mr Ogilvy realised that the herring boom of that period had passed its peak. The 1839 season was unsuccessful and so was that of 1840, while in 1841 a September gale wreacked havoc among the fleet causing the loss of many boats and heavy loss of nets among those that survived. Hay & Ogilvy, their funds already overstretched, could not stand such a succession of disasters. The crash came in 1842 —the biggest financial disaster ever suffered in Shetland. It was not only the shareholders who lost money. Hundreds of fishermen lost their savings and a promising herring fishery came to an abrupt end.

Fortunately for Lerwick, William Hay was soon able to recover his fortunes and he formed the company known as Hay & Co., that was to play such a prominent part in the development of Lerwick. But his partner Charles Ogilvy did not recover from his sad experience. He died in 1844 at the early age of 42.

THE FAROE SMACKS

It was fortunate for Shetland that the herring fishery was only one sector of the economy. The trade in dried fish continued to expand during most of the 19th century and it received an added boost with the development of cod fishing in large fully-decked smacks able to make trips of several weeks' duration to distant waters.

Lerwick's involvement in the smack fishery began in the 1820s when Hay & Ogilvy began building sloops at Freefield. At first fishing was confined to the home cod banks west of Shetland, then in 1833 Hay & Ogilvy sent three vessels to fish at Faroe where good catches were taken. In the 1840s Shetland smacks made several trips to the Davis Straits where the cod were plentiful but of poor quality. Thereafter fishing was confined mainly to the Faroe Banks but with frequent trips to Iceland and Rockall.

A prominent businessman of this period was Joseph Leask who had a shop on the site occupied today by the Pearl Assurance Company's offices. He also had a shop in Pitt Lane which at that time was known as Leask's Closs. In 1852 Mr Leask purchased the docks at Garthspool, formerly owned by Hay & Ogilvy, and added fish curing, ship chandlery, sail making and carpentry to his list of interests. He was the owner of several smacks including the "Novice" and the "Royal Tar" and the schooners "Destiny", "Anaconda" and "Venus".

Another merchant deeply involved in cod fishing was Laurence Tait, draper, whose first vessel the 'Sage'', a sloop of 48 tons, was brought to Lerwick about 1852. In 1857 his son George Reid Tait purchased the large Danish built ketch "Sir Colin Campbell" and he later added the "Sentinel" and "Robert" to his fleet.

The Harrison family were deeply involved in the cod boom. In 1863 Gilbert Harrison & Son purchased the ketch "Cynthia", then John Harrison acquired the "Onward", "Whymper" and "Fair Maid". By 1869 Mr Harrison had added another five vessels — the "Danish Rose", "Foam", "White Squall", "Cyclone", and "'Telegraph" to his large fleet. In 1871 W. Stevenson Smith purchased the "Lily of the Valley", one of the best known of Lerwick's cod fleet. He later purchased the "Ino" and the "Contest", both of them successful fishers under a succession of capable skippers.

THE GREENLAND WHALERS

The merchants of Lerwick had still another iron in the fire since many of them acted as agents for the whaling companies that operated from Peterhead, Aberdeen, Dundee, Hull and numerous other ports throughout most of the 19th century. Many of these vessels visited Lerwick each spring to complete their crews for there was no lack of able-bodied men in Shetland eager to find employment.

The arrival of these ships each year caused a great deal of activity as their crews sought amusement ashore and the offices of local agents were flooded with applicants for berths. After a long season in northern latitudes the whalers returned to Shetland in November to disembark local crew members before continuing south to their home ports.

On 9th March 1859 there were no fewer than 50 of these vessels at anchor in Lerwick harbour. Each left for the Arctic with 20 to 30 Shetlanders on board. Among the best known of local agents were Joseph Leask and George Reid Tait, already mentioned as owners of cod smacks. Mr Tait retired in 1871 and sold his business to his two young assistants, John Leisk and Alex Sandison, who carried it on under the name of Leisk & Sandison and continued to act as agents for whalers. Mr Leisk was later to play a leading part in the development of Lerwick harbour.

But undoubtedly the most important agent was Mr William Spence Smith who started this line of business in 1874. In 1890 Mr Smith began business as a clothier although still remaining a shipping agent, and in 1892 he went into partnership with Mr Hugh J. Robertson and so the well known firm of Smith & Robertson was born.

Like the cod fishing at Faroe, the Greenland whaling industry has left many tales of hardship, bravery and tragedy. It is a period that is remembered with admiration and pride on account of the contribution made by Shetlanders. Most famous of these whaling ships was the "Diana" of Hull which in 1867 more or less drifted into Ronas Voe after fourteen months absence from Britain. She had been trapped in the ice for six months when there remained adequate provision for only two. Thirteen of her crew, including nine Shetlanders, had died during that terrible winter but it was considered almost a miracle that so many of her crew survived. Their return is commemorated in the Diana Fountain which was erected on Lerwick's harbour front in 1890.

COMMUNICATIONS

One of the most interesting chapters in the history of Lerwick is the development of communications with the mainland of Scotland. There was a Post Office at Lerwick as early as 1736, letters being carried by the masters of trading vessels, while the small vessel "Isabella" of Lerwick made a voyage south once a year for mail and general cargo.

In 1760 the Government awarded to a trading consortium in Leith an annual subsidy of £60 to carry mail to Lerwick five times a year. The grant was inadequate so the mail became of secondary importance and the sloop called at several Scottish ports, often taking six months to reach Shetland. In 1794 a firm in Aberdeen offered to take over this service and increase the number of sailings to ten a year if it was granted an annual subsidy of £120. The Postmaster General refused to grant more than £60 but a similar sum was contributed by the clergy, heritors and other "principal inhabitants" of the islands.

In the next few years a whole succession of sailing vessels carried the mails to Lerwick. One of the most famous was the "Lord Fife", an armed mail carrier and a record breaker in her day. On August 8th 1811 she arrived at Leith roads,

having taken 37 hours from Lerwick, and four years later
she completed the journey from Leith to Lerwick in 39 hours.
All the uncertainty and danger of travel at this time is epitomised
in the little sailing vessel "Doris" which disappeared with all
hands on her way to Lerwick in 1813. Many important islanders
were lost with her and the name was long remembered in
Shetland.

The champion of Shetland at this time was the former beach
boy from Grimista, Arthur Anderson, who had risen to promin-
ence in commercial circles in London and yet never forgot
his native islands. He long advocated the establishment of a
mail service to Shetland by steamship and in 1837 he offered
to provide a regular service by one of his company's own vessels.
His offer was rejected but the suggestion was adopted and the
following year the mail contract was given to the Aberdeen,
Leith, Clyde and Tay Shipping Company.

The company had been formed in 1810, its fleet consisting
of sailing vessels. Its interest in steam propulsion began in 1825
with a paddle steamer running between Aberdeen and Leith.
Gradually the service was extended around the North of Scotland and in 1836 the new paddle steamer "Sovereign" included
in her itinerary a fortnightly call at Lerwick during the summer.
Built at Port Glasgow, the "Sovereign" was a vessel of 378
gross tons. She was 158 feet long and her engines generated
240 h.p. From the beginning Aberdeen was the headquarters of
the firm while Leith occupied the secondary position of southern
terminus.

In 1838 the company was awarded a government contract
to carry mail to Orkney and Shetland by steamer once a week
between April and October. The "Sovereign" continued on this
run assisted by the "Bonnie Dundee" which on one occasion
in 1841 completed the journey from Lerwick to Aberdeen in
the remarkable time of 20½ hours. During the rest of the year
the mail was carried by the company's schooners "William
Hogarth" and "Fairy". Although more satisfactory than the
previous smacks they too were unreliable and on 2nd January,
1852, the "William Hogarth" was lost with all hands in a storm
east of Shetland.

In 1858 a fortnightly winter run was started by paddle
steamer but paddles proved unsuitable for winter conditions
in this area and only when the screw-driven s.s. "Queen" of

448 tons was acquired in 1861 was a reliable weekly winter service begun. A further improvement took place in 1866 when a mid-week call at Lerwick was added during the summer.

During this main period of expansion the tradition began of naming the ships after saints with northern connections. The s.s. "St. Magnus" appeared in 1867, the s.s. "St. Clair" in 1868 and the s.s. "St. Nicholas" in 1871. With the older s.s. "Queen" these vessels constituted a first class fleet. In 1875 the company changed its name to the North of Scotland & Orkney & Shetland Steam Navigation Company.

The coming of the steamship did not mean that the age of sail was over. Several local companies and individuals operated sailing vessels commanded by skilled and highly respected captains. Best known of these was Robert Nisbet who in 1859 was given his first command — the schooner "Novice" belonging to Joseph Leask. In 1865 he took command of the well-known clipper "Matchless" belonging to the Zetland New Shipping Company and sailed in her until 1875 when he acquired his own vessel "Queen of the Isles". In 1881 he joined the "North of Scotland" Company and in 1909, 50 years after receiving his first command, he was still an active captain in charge of the s.s. "St. Nicholas".

These vessels operated a more or less regular service to Leith and Aberdeen but in addition Lerwick firms owned a large number of coasting vessels. Hay & Co. owned the "Prince of Wales", the "Janet Hay" and the "Ariel" which was still going strong in 1908; and the schooner "Columbine" which operated until 1914. This vessel must not be confused with the smack "Columbine" in which Betty Mouat drifted to Norway in 1886. There were also a number of smaller firms, some operating only one vessel. J. & A. Sutherland, merchants of Charlotte Place, owned the "Vivacious" and the "Courier", while Mr William Spence Smith had the schooner "Fairy" plying between Shetland and the Firth of Forth in the 1870s.

The first vessel to ply regularly between Lerwick and Unst was the "Janet" which began sailing in 1839. She was merely the first of a large number of trading smacks that operated a more or less regular service from Lerwick to ports in the North Mainland and North Isles of Shetland. In the 1860s there were attempts to improve this service by introducing the larger vessel "Imogen". She was put in charge of Captain Robert Nisbet but he commanded her for barely a year, leaving her in 1865 to command the schooner "Matchless".

Steam came to the North Isles run in 1868 when the Shetland Islands Steam Navigation Company introduced the small steamship "Chieftain's Bride". In 1876 the company was reorganised and a better service was provided by the s.s. "Lady Ambrosine" but she did not operate for long, being replaced in 1877 by the s.s. "Earl of Zetland" which served this route for a remarkable 68 years.

THE VENICE OF THE NORTH

To a visitor entering Lerwick harbour in the 1870s the shoreline presented an entirely different aspect from what it does today. There was no breakwater and small boat harbour, no Victoria Pier and Esplanade, no Alexandra Wharf and Fish Market. Commercial Street was then fully developed with buildings all along the seaward side but behind these buildings the sea still rolled on shingly beaches and lapped against the private piers and store houses of the various merchants. This was the feature of Lerwick that gave it such a distinctive appearance throughout most of the 19th century and earned for it (rather euphemistically) the title of "Venice of the North". From Leog to Fort Charlotte the entire shoreline was broken by piers and lodberries, little fingers projecting into Bressay Sound marking the culmination of a hundred years of progress under private enterprise. Fortunately those at the South End are still with us in 1977 just as they were 100 years ago.

The store long used by the "North of Scotland" shipping company was the lodberry that can still be seen on the south side of Craigie's Stane. In the seawall of this store there is a door and in the courtyard at the shore end of the lodberry there is a large door facing north and opening on to Craigie's Stane. The steamers anchored in the harbour and goods were loaded into flit boats which unloaded at either of these doors, depending on weather conditions. The office of the shipping company was housed in a little building below Quendale House until 1875 when the company moved to new premises on Commercial Street opposite the Grand Hotel.

To the north of Craigie's Stane stands Robertson's Lodberry, named after Bailie John Robertson who was joint agent with

Charles Merrylees for the shipping company until he retired leaving Mr Merrylees as sole agent. North of Bain's Beach stands Yate's Lodberry and another building that has not changed much since the 1870s. This is the Queen's Hotel, built in the 1860s although extended much later by incorporating houses on either side. Later still a wing was added to the south-east corner. Here in the 1870s Hay & Co. had a shop and offices.

From here northwards the shoreline has altered beyond recognition in the last 100 years. In the 1870s the Tolbooth with the Cockstool Rock at its base overlooked a little jetty known as Hay's Pier, now swallowed up in the breakwater. Farther north was Mouat's Lodberry, taking its name from James Mouat, shipping agent, who died in 1852, and next to it was Clark's Lodberry at the back of the Seamen's Home.

The space now occupied by the Post Office was then a piece of vacant ground known as Sinclair's Beach. It was reached by steps running down from Commercial Street in a line with the Nort Kirk Closs. On the north side of the beach, opposite the Commercial Bank, stood a large house built in 1866 by William and Robert Sinclair, two brothers from Dunrossness, who carried on a general merchant's business. William was lost in the "Doris" tragedy of 1813. Behind this house there stood a lodberry and a high-sided pier and immediately to the south of this lodberry, low down on Sinclair's Beach, stood a small house occupied by Mr Ollason, a shoemaker. South of this house stood a little pier usually known as Sinclair's Pier.

In spite of the many changes since 1766 the original bay of Lerwick was still recognisable a hundred years ago. It was dominated by Morrison's Pier, projecting from the gable of the building that is now known as Victoria Warehouse. Over a period of 40 years Morrison's Beach had been gradually reclaimed by the dumping of rubbish on the south side of the pier. This became a nuisance and in 1866 the nuisance was overcome when a retaining wall was built southwards from the pier. The work was carried out by public subscription and thereafter Morrison's Pier became a public pier, largely due to the efforts of Bailie John Robertson.

It was a modest pier by present day standards, extending to a point near where the Diana fountain now stands, but it was big enough to accommodate the "Chieftain's Bride", the small steamer that had brought an improved service to the North Isles. Following its extension the pier rejoiced in the name of Victoria Wharf.

On the North side of Victoria Wharf stood an old building occupied by John Robertson, merchant, a nephew of Bailie John Robertson. Both these gentlemen were soon to be closely associated with the development of the port. Several improvements had been carried out to this building since 1766. The trance had been removed in 1836 and Messrs Goudie's building had been set back into line with the buildings on either side.

Extending northwards from Victoria Wharf was another succession of piers and lodberries, including such long forgotten structures as Irvine's Pier, Grierson's Lodberry (where the shipping office now stands), Tait's Lodberry (now the Thule Bar), and the North Lodberry which disappeared when the building now occupied by Tods was rebuilt but which in the 1870s stood fronted on three sides by the sea.

Fort Charlotte a hundred years ago was far more imposing than it is now since the cliffs were real sea cliffs dropping steeply into the sea. There was, however, a footpath leading to the North Ness since a considerable amount of development had taken place there. Once a bare headland it had been transformed into a dairy farm through the efforts of its proprietor, Captain Peter Leslie Smith, a native of Dunrossness. A substantial house had been built and two stone piers used as fish curing stations. There were in addition two boat building yards, one occupied by Mr Laurence Arcus, the other by Mr Laurence Goodlad. The latter had been given the name, Malakoff, at the time of the Crimean War.

At the south end of the headland stood the Gas Pier and its neighbour, Stove's Pier. The former had been built between 1853 and 1856 for the landing of coal for the gasworks above but it was also used by the shipping company for the transfer of cattle by flitboat to steamers anchored in the harbour. Stove's Pier was built by the Stove brothers who owned a nearby sawmill which stood where the present car park stands. Norwegian vessels used to unload timber at Stove's Pier through a hatch in the bow because they could not come alongside. Between these piers lay the Tarry Beach, so named because of the tarry waste exuded by the gasworks and released into the sea.

LERWICK'S YEAR

Just as the shoreline of Lerwick a hundred years ago bore little resemblance to that of the present day so the events that marked each season were entirely different from those of the 1970s. In March came the Greenland ships and the busy scenes at the agents' offices. Then soon after the departure of the whalers it was time for the Faroe smacks to be fitted out for their own season in northern waters.

June saw the arrival of the Dutch herring fleet and the harbour again full of broad bluff-bowed sailing vessels. A great change had come over the Dutch fleet since the 1860s, since with the introduction of light weight cotton drift nets to replace those made of hemp a lighter type of vessel was required. So the heavy buss was gradually being replaced by the smaller and lighter bomschuit — a fantastic vessel, almost as broad as she was long, and built to float in three or four feet of water. Most of them came from Katwyk and Scheveningen where the low sandy shores and shallow seas made it impossible for deep-draughted vessels to land. The bom sailed well before the wind but in tacking or beating she would have been useless had it not been for the help of lee boards which were let down when needed and gave stability to the vessel. She was both a herring catcher and a floating curing station, as well as home for nine or ten men. When she left home she was full of barrels, some of them containing salt, and as the salt became used up more barrels became available to be filled with herring.

It was a beautiful sight to see Lerwick harbour crowded with bomschuits with their brightly painted woodwork and their brown sails patched with red and yellow. The Dutchmen were an indispensible feature of the summer scene as with hands stuffed deep in pockets they strolled along Commercial Street in their homely dress consisting of a jersey, wide baggy breeches and wooden clogs.

In the latter half of the 19th century the stipulation was removed whereby fishing could not start before 24th June, but still Johnsmas was recognised as a holiday and the Dutchmen congregated at Lerwick as their forefathers had done for centuries. In the first few weeks of the season, Dutch boats called at Lerwick to tranship their catches in other vessels to Holland since the first herring of the season were considered a delicacy and fetched very high prices. Indeed a sample of the very first landing was sent to the Royal Palace.

In the early part of the 19th century two mother ships accompanied the herring fleet to Shetland but about the middle of the century the practice was abandoned. One of Lerwick's most illustrious medical men first came to Shetland as surgeon on a mother ship. This was Dr Petrus Dorotheus Loeterbagh who in 1863 decided to settle in Lerwick. He started in business as a pharmacist in what is now known as the Medical Hall and studied for a time in Edinburgh to become qualified to practise as a doctor in this country. He built up a large practice before his death in 1871.

The arrival of the Dutch was the signal for the start of Lerwick's favourite summer pastime — trading or bartering. Unfortunately H.M. Customs Officers frowned on this practice, calling it smuggling, and their attempts to stamp it out gave an extra touch of glamour to the game. A favourite prank was the teasing of these officials. A group of boys would row off to the anchored boms then return slowly to give the impression that they carried contraband. They would land stealthily at some secluded pier along the South End and would invariably be grabbed by the customs officers. Immediately the boys would protest their innocence and ask in indignant tones "what was Lerwick coming to when innocent boys could not even go for a row without being molested?" The officials could not afford to take chances for they knew full well that these innocent look-ing boys were as capable of being smugglers as were their elders.

Lerwick's own summer fishing was still the ling and cod fishing from open sixerns. Then in September the crews put on a few herring nets and sought a share of what the Dutch had left. And all the time the smacks returned regularly with cargoes of wet salted cod which were dried at Freefield and Garthspool and on the beaches at Heogan and Gremista.

Boat building was confined to the construction of small vessels but a large number of men were employed on this activity. Foremost of the builders was Hay & Co., at Freefield, who continued the tradition started by Hay & Ogilvy. It is astonish-ing to consider how much Lerwick owes to that development of the 1820s. Hay & Ogilvy's foreman was Thomas Smith and under him Laurence Arcus (1822-1905) served his apprentice-ship as a carpenter and boatbuilder. He in turn became a builder of boats in the lodberry later purchased by George Reid Tait and from Mr Arcus Laurence Goodlad acquired the skill that enabled him to start his own yard at the Malakoff.

October saw the beaching of the sixerns, and the laying up of the smacks for the winter except those that spent the winter in the coasting trade. For the ordinary townspeople October was the month for laying in supplies for the winter and in the days before refrigeration the traditional standby was a bullock salted in tubs. In the absence of a public slaughterhouse the people had to do the best they could so the lodberries were pressed into service as abattoirs and for weeks at a time the shoreline of Lerwick was red with the blood of slaughtered cattle.

In those days the festive season was prolonged — Christmas, New Year's Day and Up-Helly-Aa commemorated by both old and new styles in a way that was unique in Britain. On Christmas Eve the "peerie guizers" ruled the streets from five o'clock to eight, letting off such a fusillade of squibs, crackers and pistol shots that a stranger might have imagined the town was under siege. By 11 p.m. the bigger guizers had begun to appear accompanied by fiddlers and accordionists, and by midnight the street would be thronged with people singing and dancing and waiting for the main spectacle of the evening. Then suddenly it would appear — a large sled towed by a gang of youths and supporting tubs of tar all blazing furiously. This was the famous "tar barrel", an indispensible feature of Christmas Eve celebrations at Lerwick for most of the 19th century. Sometimes rival tar barrels would appear in the street at the same time — that of the "Southerners" heading north and the "Northerners" heading south. If they happened to meet head on in the narrow part of the street named the Roost, which even one tar barrel could negotiate with difficulty, the result was utter confusion.

Tar barrels appeared again on New Year's Eve and on Up-Helly-Aa on 29th January. It is little wonder that shopkeepers boarded up their windows on those three occasions and that tar barrels were eventually banned by the magistrates in 1874. But the fire festival was not suppressed for long. It was to reappear again in a new guise with a far more elaborate ritual and with the blessing of the law.

Chapter Three

LERWICK HARBOUR TRUST

However attractive the old shoreline of Lerwick its in-adequacies were obvious. There was a large number of private piers but not even Morrison's Pier could accommodate the small steamer that then plied between Lerwick and the South. She had to anchor in the harbour while goods, passengers and live-stock were unloaded and loaded by flitboat. It was an alarming prospect for travellers, especially female passengers, to discover that after a long and uncomfortable journey, they had an even more uncomfortable and a frequently dangerous journey in an open boat before they could reach dry land. The idea of a proper pier had long been discussed by Lerwick's business com-munity, while from 1872, when the newspaper was founded, the columns of "The Shetland Times" contained numerous references to the question. In 1875 the shipping company were discussing the possibility of providing a better pier themselves and this may have awakened public opinion to the urgency of the situation.

In May 1876 a conference was held between Lerwick Town Council and a committee appointed for this purpose by the Commissioners of Supply (forerunners of the County Council), and it was agreed that a proper steamer's pier could be con-structed in the region of Victoria Wharf. A public meeting was held to outline the proposals and a committee of promoters was formed. Next a sum of £715 was guaranteed by 52 local business-men and others as a guarantee fund for the preliminary expenses that would be incurred in promoting either a Provisional Order or a Private Bill.

Mr Dyce Cay, then employed on Aberdeen Harbour Works, was engaged as consulting engineer and he proceeded to draw up plans along the lines suggested. The central part of the scheme was a mole 200 feet long connected to Victoria Wharf by an 80 ft. long bridge. The existing roads and streets leading to Victoria Wharf were obviously too narrow for transporting goods or driving livestock, therefore a wide esplanade, with a spending slope on the seaward slope, was proposed from Victoria Wharf northwards to the Gas Pier and from Victoria Wharf south to Hay's Pier.

The new pier was planned mainly as a facility for the steamers of the "North of Scotland" company but there were in addition numerous smaller sailing vessels that called regularly with coal, timber and other materials. For these vessels it was proposed that the spending slope of the esplanade would be interrupted in three places by wharves. The largest on the north side of the new pier would be 230 feet long, while on the south side there would be a 100 feet long wharf and a smaller one at Hays Pier.

The final part of Mr Cay's scheme was a branch road from the north end of Commercial Street, at Charlotte Place, proceeding in a north-easterly direction for 310 feet to meet the northern section of the esplanade.

Next the question of the scheme's viability was raised. The estimated cost of the project was £15,000, while on the best possible advice available the income of the proposed works would not be more than £1750 a year. The outlook was far from bright but the promoters had faith that the new works would attract increased trade to the port and bring the increased revenue that was desired.

The Bill was drafted and presented to Parliament, Mr Sandison, part time Town Clerk, doing a great deal of work in his employment with Messrs Sievewright & MacGregor, solicitors. Then opposition came from an unexpected quarter— the "North of Scotland" shipping company. Although they were in favour of a pier being built they considered that the proposals if passed into law would be "injurious and oppressive to them". They were especially critical of the proposed esplanade which, if constructed, would merely beautify the town without earning a single penny towards the cost of the scheme. They also argued that a better site for the new pier would be found below Fort Charlotte. Their greatest concern, however, was the high tonnage charges which it was proposed to levy on vessels using the works.

Other objections came from Mr G. H. B. Hay representing residents at the south end of Lerwick. Mr Hay attacked the scheme in general, maintaining that it would be of very little benefit to the town owing to the exposed nature of the site chosen. He also feared that the promoters might build only the parts of the scheme that suited them and fail to provide replacements for the many piers to be swallowed up in the esplanade. These objections were easily overcome by agreeing to build the wharves on the south side of Victoria Wharf before or simultaneously with the other works and to execute the work at Hay's Pier in such a way that the property on the south side would not be damaged.

The opposition of the shipping company was far more serious but it too was overcome when a committee of the promoters proceeded to Aberdeen for a meeting with directors of the shipping company. There the tonnage rates were fixed while the company was promised several concessions. It was agreed that until the pier was built the company would pay only half rates on goods and livestock while goods in transit would be charged only once. Moreover it was agreed that a special clause would be inserted into the Bill whereby the company's vessels would be charged on only the first 40 voyages made to Lerwick each year.

This was still not the end of the shipping company's objections. Although the Bill had now passed the committee stage in the House of Commons the promoters decided to attach a passenger rate whereby each passenger would pay a charge of sixpence for the use of the proposed pier. But the shipping company protested so vigorously that the promoters had to give in and withdraw the clause.

The Bill passed all the remaining stages of its journey through Parliament and on 2nd August, 1877, the Lerwick Harbour Improvements Act received the Royal Assent. It sanctioned the construction of the works as planned and authorised the formation of a body of Trustees to take care of the developments and with powers to borrow up to £20,000 to enable the work to proceed. The Trustees would include three members appointed by the Corporation of Lerwick, three members appointed by the Commissioners of Supply, three elected by shipowners in Lerwick, and three elected by the business people in the town as payers of harbour rates.

The first meeting of Lerwick Harbour Trust was held in the meeting room of the Corporation of Lerwick on 20th November, 1877. Those present were Major Cameron of Garth, John Bruce, Esq., of Sumburgh, Lewis F. U. Garriock, Esq., of Scalloway, all important landowners and businessmen, and Messrs Joseph Leask, John Leisk, John Robertson (Sen.), John Robertson (Jun.), Arthur Laurenson, L. G. Stove, Gilbert Harrison (Jun.), Andrew Smith and William B. Harrison, all merchants in Lerwick. Major Cameron was unanimously elected Chairman and John Robertson (Sen.) Vice-Chairman. Messrs Sievewright & MacGregor were appointed clerks and it was agreed to hold meetings four times a year.

A year later by a disposition dated 31st July, 1878, the Commissioners of H.M. Woods and Forests conveyed to Lerwick Harbour Trust the Crown's interest and estate in the lands facing Lerwick harbour between the Gas Pier and Hay's Pier and bounded on the west by the roadway of Commercial Street, and on the east by the ordinary high water mark as it existed on 30th December, 1866. This was recorded in the General Register of Sasines applicable to Orkney and Zetland on 5th January, 1881.

Legislation was safely behind them but the Trustees had still to overcome the problem of finance for no matter how much faith they had in their scheme they could not convince the banks of its viability. Although they had powers to borrow £20,000, the right to levy half rates on goods landed within the rating limits would not raise sufficient money to pay even the interest charges on such a loan.

For five years nothing happened, then in 1882 the Trustees decided to make a final effort to raise the money locally. They advertised for tenders for the work and on 15th June accepted that of A. Morrison & Son of Edinburgh for £12,700. They next approached the Trustees of Shetland Fishermen's Widows Relief Fund who promised a loan of £5,000 if the Harbour Trustees would raise £10,000. The latter responded to the challenge. The Trustees themselves guaranteed the sum of £2,000 and 59 merchants and others guaranteed a total of £10,200. A deputation of Trustees proceeded to Glasgow and on the strength of the security guaranteed were able to negotiate a loan.

It must be pointed out that in the five years since the scheme was first proposed the whole economic atmosphere of Lerwick had improved with the growth of a thriving herring fishery. But this in no way detracts from the generous contribution made by Lerwick's business community in guaranteeing what was then a very large sum of money.

C

THE RISE OF THE HERRING INDUSTRY

The revival of the herring industry is one of the most exciting chapters in the history of Shetland. It began in June 1875 when Hay & Co. enticed ten boats from the North-East of Scotland to fish for a few weeks at Lerwick. In April, 1876, three Buckie boats of the same type arrived at Lerwick to fish with long lines for ling and cod, then stayed to fish for herring. The first vessel of this type to be purchased by owners in Lerwick was the "Defiance" which arrived in 1877, bought by Mr Robert B. Irvine, a baker by trade. Another early arrival was the "Vine" purchased by Mr Gifford Gray.

More boats arrived in the following years and by 1885 there were 350 of them in Shetland. Not all of them were purchased second hand since building was resumed on a large scale by Hay & Co. at Freefield, and by L. Goodlad at the Malakoff.

The boats were fitted out in March for the new Spring fishing, ling, cod and tusk being purchased for salting by John Robertson and Gilbert Harrison & Son at their yards at the North Ness. In 1881, on the death of its sole partner, the latter firm became known as Richmond Harrison & Co., with John Harrison the moving force. He is given the credit for opening a market in the South for halibut, a fish formerly discarded as unsaleable. He imported ice from Norway and chartered a small steamer to carry the fish South.

At that time there were two distinct periods in the herring fishery. In June and the first half of July fishing operations were carried out from west side ports but in the latter half of July and throughout August fishing became concentrated on the east side, especially at Lerwick.

Merchants came from Fraserburgh and other ports in the North of Scotland, one of the best known being James Mitchell who arrived in 1881 and acquired land at the North Ness. Lerwick's own merchants took advantage of the new trends in the industry and Richmond Harrison & Co. expanded their activities at the North Ness.

At Garthspool Mr Joseph Leask let ground for herring stations to Mr Harper and Mr Dowell of Wick and Mr McCombie of Peterhead. Mr Leask died in 1882 and he was succeeded by his nephews, John B. and Charles Leask, who carried on the business as A. J. Leask & Co. They extended their activities at Garthspool and built the block of tenements known as Garths-pool Place and also the Fishermen's Lodge.

Freefield was again a hive of activity with Hay & Co. building and repairing boats and curing herring. They had the benefit of skilled workmen and foremen, one of them, David Williamson, being sailmaker foreman for 42 years between 1860 and 1902. Also at Freefield John Brown had his engineering shop where in 1874 he installed a steam-driven hammer — the only one north of Aberdeen — which enabled him to tackle heavier jobs. When the fishing developed in the late 1870s he applied his ingenuity to developing labour saving devices and for many years Brown's Patent Line Hauler was the best on the market, being bought in large numbers by Swedish fishermen. Equally successful was his patent net hauler used by herring fishermen and known locally as the "iron man."

In the 1880s John Brown went into partnership with John Irvine, under the name of Irvine & Brown, as curers of herring and white fish. The partnership was dissolved when Mr Irvine started business as a shipbroker but Mr Brown carried on the business himself and opened branches at Hillswick, Mid Yell and Levenwick. He owned a fairly large fleet of fishing boats, all of them successful fishers.

Preparations for the late season began many weeks beforehand when smacks and schooners arrived with cargoes of salt and piles of barrels began to accumulate on the piers and jetties. Then the gutters and coopers arrived by steamer to take up residence in wooden huts at the North Ness, Freefield and Garthspool, being joined in their work by men and women from Lerwick, and neighbouring districts. Finally the boats began to arrive with herring, the Shetland boats, their west side fishing over, and a large fleet from the Isle of Man and Ireland. Most of the Scottish boats, however, after participating in the early fishing went to their home ports for the late fishing there.

For six or eight weeks Lerwick was a bustle of activity then suddenly it was all over for the season. The boats returned home to be hauled ashore on the beaches while Lerwick's own fleet was drawn up at Garthspool and Freefield. But no matter how short the season the growth of the herring industry was a boost to the entire town of Lerwick and led directly to the growth of the "new town" of the 1880's. And no less important was the effect on the harbour and on the Trustees for it was in this general mood of optimism that they were able to embark on the greatest period of development that Shetland had ever seen.

THE NEW HARBOUR WORKS

Work commenced on 12th March, 1883, and on 31st July the foundation stone was laid with full Masonic honours by Sheriff Principal Thoms. Not surprisingly the Trustees found it impossible to build the works exactly as shown in the plans. Estimates now exceeded the £20,000 which the Trustees were authorised to borrow and it was necessary to curtail the works slightly. Hay's Pier was built a little smaller than planned, the wharf on the North side of the pier — Albert Wharf it was called — was reduced from 300 ft to 80 ft, but three small wooden landing places were added farther north to accommodate the large number of small craft then in use. The wharf planned for the south side of Victoria Pier was reduced to a small platform and steps while the branch road planned at the north end of the works was omitted altogether.

At that time there was only a narrow road below Fort Charlotte which a few years earlier the Town Council had protected by a wooden railing on the seaward side. When the harbour works were completed the Trustees extended this railing along the "upper" road and erected a second railing along the new "lower" road just above the sea out as far as the Gas Pier where the two roads converged.

In places it was difficult to marry the new developments with the old on account of differences in level. At Victoria Wharf, for example, the Esplanade actually stood higher than the foundations of Mr Robertson's buildings so a protective wall had to be built to protect the public. The original idea of having a mole and bridge was abandoned before work commenced and Victoria Pier was built as a solid structure out from the Esplanade.

23rd June, 1886, was an important date for Lerwick with no fewer than three ceremonies to be carried out. First came the laying with full Masonic honours of the foundation stone of the Grand Hotel, then followed a similar ceremony at the Poor House and finally came the formal opening of the harbour works.

H.M.S. "Eagle" and a number of Grimsby smacks anchored in the harbour were dressed overall while the long mast head-pennants of the Dutch herring vessels added their own splash of colour to the scene. A large crowd watched as Sheriff Thoms and a party representing the various public bodies boarded the "Earl of Zetland" at Albert Wharf and were taken for an hour long cruise before returning and heading for Victoria Pier where the "Earl" had the honour of being the first vessel to berth alongside. When the mooring ropes were made fast Mr John Leisk invited Sheriff Thoms to step ashore and formally open the pier.

The opening ceremony completed, the chief citizens of the town formed a dignified procession and marched to the Town Hall by an indirect route which covered as many streets as possible. The procession included the town's Police Force, the Good Templars, the Oddfellows, members of Lodge Viking and Lodge Morton, the clergy, legal practitioners and magistrates, the Town Council and officials, the Harbour Trustees and harbour officials, the engineer and contractors responsible for the scheme, Sheriff Thoms and the Sheriff Substitute and finally the County Police. At the Town Hall the party were entertained by the Trustees to a cake and wine banquet in honour of the occasion.

With the completion of the works the whole seafront was altered. The Cockstool, Sinclair's Beach, Morrison's Pier, Tait's Pier, the North Pier and all the many piers in between were buried under a mass of rubble and concrete. No longer could boats be hauled ashore at the back of R. & C.'s and as for the lodberries, since they were now separated from the sea, their usefulness was at an end. And for some people — the boatmen who used to man the flitboats — the coming of the new pier meant the end of their livelihood. It brought progress but it also brought to an end a colourful chapter in the history of Lerwick.

With the completion of the works the Trustees were able to charge full dues on the shipping that used the quays under a scale of charges laid down by the Act of 1877, varying from 4d per ton on vessels under 15 tons to 10d a ton for those over 150 tons. But the Trustees had no authority to levy a charge on vessels that merely anchored in the harbour. This right had been refused on the grounds that the harbour was a natural one and that the works would do nothing to improve the actual anchorage.

In September, 1886, Capt. George Allison, a Dunrossness man, was appointed Harbour Master at a salary of £60 per annum plus uniform. The Trustees were fortunate to find such a man since they were in no position to offer a handsome salary but the arrangement suited both parties. Capt. Allison had retired from the sea in 1883 when he built the house known as Seaview at Sound. He was delighted to find employment where his nautical experience could be put to good use and it can be said truly that the financial reward was of secondary importance to him. He later moved to a house in town when he built Beverley Villa in King Harald Street. A week after Capt. Allison's appointment an assistant was found in John Tait of Lerwick.

A great deal of work had fallen on Messrs Sievewright & MacGregor in their capacity as Clerks to the Trust. They had successfully promoted the Bill in Parliament and had negotiated with consultants and contractors at every stage. They too realised that the Trustees were in no position to pay them on a scale which their time and labour warranted and indeed they kept no account of the time spent on Trust work leaving it to the Trustees to decide when and how much they should be paid. In 1887 it was agreed to pay the firm the sum of £250 as remuneration over the previous ten years.

The firm's association with Lerwick Harbour Trust continued, their partner Mr Alex MacGregor taking on Trust affairs as one of his own duties. In February, 1890, Mr Alex Bain, an employee of the company, was appointed Clerk in place of Mr MacGregor at a salary of £10 per year. There was no recognised meeting place for the Trustees who met in the solicitors' office or the Burgh Chambers as was found most convenient. A further change occurred in February, 1899, when Mr William Johnson was appointed Interim Clerk and later that year his appointment was made permanent.

The revenue of the Trust rose steadily from £389 in 1878 to £650 in 1885 and in 1886 when the new works were in full use the figure climbed over the thousand pounds mark to £1178. The shipping company contributed a great deal to this satisfactory state of affairs. It did not exercise its right to the 40 voyage clause since a special arrangement was made whereby a compound rate of £500 a year was paid, increasing to £580 when the small company that operated the "Earl of Zetland" was absorbed in the larger company.

Chapter Four

THE DIFFICULT YEARS

The Trustees continued to meet four times a year the most important meeting being the Annual General Meeting in November. In addition a Working Committee met as often as was required. The minutes of the various meetings give a marvellous insight into the running of a small port and add much of historical interest regarding the town of Lerwick. In 1887 the Trustees were concerned at the danger caused by the projecting bowsprits and mizzen booms of herring boats lying at anchor and a byelaw was introduced to compel the crews of these vessels to stow their spars while at anchor. In May, 1888, while the old houses in the Roost were being demolished, stones and rubble were taken to form an embankment on the south side of the Gas Pier where small boats could be hauled up. In October the same year the Trustees received an application from Lerwick Co-operative Coal Company for a site for a coal store. They were granted a site on reclaimed ground below Fort Charlotte.

But soon the Trustees had for more weighty matters to consider — the financial position of the Trust. In 1887 the Trustees obtained a loan of £20,000 from the Public Works Loan Board but on very unfavourable terms. Had the fishing industry continued to be as profitable as it had been in the early 1880s revenue would have been adequate to meet the annual repayment but there was a serious decline in the herring fishery after 1885 caused by a combination of factors. There was an unusual scarcity of herring on the grounds, while some years the grounds were infested with dogfish, and added to this were marketing problems on the Continent which forced many owners into liquidation. The Trust's income suffered and the only way they could meet the demands of the Public Works Loan Board was by taking an overdraft of £3,000 from the Union Bank, the sum to be gradually reduced each year.

The Trustees tried to effect economies wherever possible and asked the Union Bank to fix a low rate of interest on the overdraft. The Bank proposed to levy a charge of $4\frac{1}{2}\%$ on the overdraft but the Trustees countered with a request for one of 4%. The Trustees also asked the Harbour Master to try to get his assistant to accept a reduction in his salary which was then £40 a year. The cost of the banquet held at the opening of the works now caught up with them. Mr Sinclair of the Queen's Hotel submitted an account for £44 for wine but the Trustees argued that some of the wine was returned unopened and they admitted liability for only £31.

Matters came to head in July, 1890, when the Trust sent a cheque for £580, being the next instalment due as repayment to the Public Works Loan Board. The Union Bank refused to honour the cheque claiming that the Trust should first try to reduce their overdraft as they had promised and send the Treasury only the balance that remained.

At the next meeting of the Trust the Chairman laid before the members a memorandum which he had drawn up. It pointed out that in the current depressed state of trade in Lerwick it was impossible to continue to meet the half-yearly instalments out of revenue and at the same time maintain the works upon which the whole security of the loan depended. He suggested however that if an easier system of payment by terminable annuity could be arranged at 3% interest it would be possible for the Trustees to repay the loan fully with interest within the agreed period. He produced figures to prove that under the suggested system a deficit of £200 for the year ending 31st December, 1889, would have been converted into a surplus of £139 leaving £100 to be set aside for contingencies and £39 to lessen the overdraft that was such a bone of contention. It was agreed that copies of the memorandum should be sent to Lord Lothian and to Mr Lyell, M.P., for Orkney and Shetland.

The Board replied coldly but politely, pointing out that they had granted a loan of £20,000 on the security of a first charge on the undertaking and that the Bank must have been aware of this when they made their advance to the Trust. A reduction in the annual repayment to the Board would certainly improve the position of the bank as second creditors; but this would not afford a sufficient reason for the Board to recommend to the Treasury a reduction in the terms of the loan unless the Bank would guarantee and become responsible for the punctual payment of the reduced annual payment.

Further correspondence followed and on 30th October, 1890, the Board agreed that the balance of the loan should be repaid by way of an annuity as the Trust had suggested with an interest rate of 4%. The Clerk replied thanking the Board for the offered concession but regretting that even if the new arrangements were made retrospective to cover the instalment due on 28th July (but not then paid) there would not be a sufficient margin to ensure the punctual payment of future instalments. But, on the other hand, if the interest were reduced to 3% the Trust's income would be sufficient to warrant the Treasury in making this concession.

Fortunately for Lerwick Harbour Trust assistance came from the Western Highlands & Islands Commission, a body that visited Shetland in October, 1890, listened to the many grievances and did more than any previous body to help the islands. As a direct result of their visit lighthouses were built at Vaila, Hamnavoe, Muckle Roe, Hillswick and other places, an extra steamer was introduced sailing direct to Aberdeen and Lerwick Harbour Trust's financial problems were sympathetically dealt with.

In a letter of 27th May, 1891, they wrote to the Trust making the following recommendations.

1. The principal of the loan from the Public Works Loan Board should be reduced to £16,500 as from 1st July, 1891, (in effect a grant of £2,500).

2. Repayment of the loan should be effected by means of an annuity of £788 payable half yearly for 46 years.

3. Interest on the debt of £19,000 from 28th January, 1890, to 30th June, 1891, should be paid to the Board before the latter date — a sum of £1078.

4. The Bank overdraft should be extinguished by annual payments of three quarters of the Trust's surplus revenue after charges for debt and maintainance.

5. The remaining one quarter should be devoted to the formation of a Reserve Fund to meet any unforeseen expenses for repairs until such a fund should amount to £2,500.

At a meeting of the Trustees on 10th June, 1891, it was decided to draw up a formal agreement with the Bank accepting these proposals.

SINCLAIR'S BEACH

Again the meetings of the Trust were concerned with the minor day-to-day problems that arose — should the Trust pay for the gas consumed in the goods store let to the shipping company? Should the lights on the pier be extinguished? Should they, perhaps, be kept extinguished all night when the moon was full? There were minor crises such as occurred when the sailing vessel "Surveyor" was being ballasted at Leask's Jetty — the most northerly of the three wooden jetties in the face of the North Esplanade. The planks proved to be so rotten that the horse's legs went right through the decking of the jetty. The pier was closed to traffic pending its repair by its new owner Mr R. D. Ganson but a concession was made to the Co-operative Coal Company allowing them to unload cargoes of coal by wheel-barrow.

Then another serious problem arose for the Trust although when first discussed it seemed a trivial matter. It concerned the tiny patch of ground known as Sinclair's Beach lying between Commercial Street and the South Esplanade and bounded by the Seamen's Home and to the north by the large house once owned by Robert and William Sinclair. It had indeed once been part of the foreshore but was now isolated from the sea by the Esplanade. The Harbour Trust believed that it was part of the property conferred on them by the Act of 1877 and by the Disposition by the Commissioners of Woods and Forests giving them rights to the foreshore.

Sinclair's Beach had been a bone of contention for several decades. The first dispute arose in 1838 between the Commissioners of the Burgh of Lerwick and Mr Scott of Melby when the Commissioners wanted to set back the wall below the street opposite Mr Scott's house (now the Shetland Times Bookshop). Mr Scott protested to safeguard what he regarded as his property but the improvement was carried out nonetheless.

In 1846 this was earmarked as the site for the new Free Church but a more suitable site was found elsewhere. Later the Commissioners of Police proposed to erect a public lavatory here but the Roman Catholic Church, who then claimed the site, demanded full compensation if the scheme were to go through. In 1879 the house across the street was purchased by Mr Andrew

Smith, shipbroker, and with the house he purchased Sinclair's Beach.

The Trust were first made aware of a rival claim to the beach on 20th December, 1887, when a letter from Mr Smith's solicitors was read to the members. The Clerk pointed out that he had taken the opportunity of inspecting Mr Smith's titles to the ground and he read excerpts from them. After some discussion the Trustees concluded that Mr Smith had no valid title to this part of the foreshore.

In May, 1892, another letter from Mr Smith's solicitor was considered by the Trust. The ground had been leased by the Trust to Messrs Hay & Co., who were storing building material on it in spite of Mr Smith's continuing claim that it was his property. Mr Smith intended to seek a judicial decision on the subject but had decided to wait for the Trust's comments before taking such a step. The Clerk was instructed to write to the solicitors repudiating Mr Smith's claim to Sinclair's Beach. Next Mr Smith ordered the Trust to remove not only the building material but also the wooden shed erected by them above the Esplanade and used originally as a cement store while the works were being constructed. After taking legal advice the Trustees decided to defend any action which Mr Smith might bring against them.

The case of Smith versus Lerwick Harbour Trust dragged on for several years and on 3rd March, 1897, Mr Smith's solicitors in Aberdeen informed the Trust that the summons was now ready for service. They wished to know whether it should be served on the Clerk by messenger or whether an agent in Edinburgh would be empowered to accept service. The Trustees agreed to instruct Messrs. MacKenzie and Kermack in Edinburgh to accept service of the summons and to take the necessary steps to defend the action.

A year later it seemed that the case might be abandoned when the pursuer declared that he was willing to abandon his action if each party would pay for its own legal expenses. The Trustees after consideration of the proposal decided that having gone so far and having incurred so much expense they were not prepared to consider any settlement that did not include payment of their expenses.

The Trust could scent victory. In April they leased the ground at a rate of £2 per annum to Mr John G. Anderson for the storage of stones from the Ord quarry to be used in the building of Mr T. J. Anderson's new premises. Then on 16th August, 1898, the Clerk reported that the case was settled as the Trustees had suggested. Unfortunately this was merely the end of the preliminary round and the battle would be rejoined within a few years.

THE GALE OF 1900

During the seven lean years that followed 1887 the Trust's revenue dropped to an average of around £1100 a year, but the fishing industry revived and the Trust's income began to rise again. In 1899 it jumped to a record £2145 and the Trust seemed set for an era of unprecedented prosperity then like a sting in the tail of the 19th century came the gale of Friday, 16th February, 1900, a storm such as no person then alive had ever seen or would ever see again.

The weather had been unsettled all week and by Thursday it was blowing a gale from the south. The wind increased in strength as night fell and by morning it was blowing a hurricane from the south-east while the spindrift flew through Lerwick harbour like snow.

The seafront bore the full brunt of the storm and at Gillie's Pier, Stout's Pier, Bain's Beach and other openings the sea was making a clean sweep across the street. The South Esplanade suffered most as heavy seas sweeping in from the south met the backwash from Victoria Pier to come crashing in below the coal store at Sinclair's Beach. By 11 am, the coal store had been undermined and a wide breach had been torn in the Esplanade underneath its concrete parapet. The hole rapidly widened until there was a length of 50 ft of wall standing unsupported except at either end. The next heavy sea made this collapse and soon the Esplanade was reduced to a beach along half its length. In the meantime the coal shed was reduced to rubble and matchwood.

Actually Shetland escaped lightly considering the severity of the storm. Throughout the islands buildings and walls were damaged. Scores of haddock boats were smashed on the beaches and smacks were driven ashore from their moorings. A Bressay man was drowned as he sought to secure his boat; a Norwegian barque was wrecked at Nesting with the loss of all hands, and another was wrecked at Fetlar with the loss of two men. At

Sumburgh Head a steam trawler was wrecked — one of a dozen or more that disappeared that night with all hands.

Lerwick suffered no loss of life but a great deal of damage was done. All the way from Slett's Park to the north boundary of Seafield the stone wall had been demolished and at the Ayre of Clickimin the water pipe had been severed while only traces of the road remained. Most serious of all was the damage to the Esplanade which it was feared would take a considerable sum to repair. As for the old coal shed most people regarded its removal as a decided improvement and an opportunity to give the whole area a face lift.

It was bitter blow to the Trust to realise that they might have to find £1000 for repairs. At a special Committee meeting on Tuesday, 29th March, the report of their new consultant engineer, Mr Barron, was considered. The damage to the South Esplanade began 140 ft south of Victoria Pier and continued southwards for 130 ft. Over this distance the parapet had been demolished and about 1000 cu yds of material from the hearting and roadway had been washed into the sea. The concrete protecting blocks at the base of the sloping wall were, however, with one exception intact.

Mr Barron recommended that the wall and parapet should be built as before but that a larger class of stone should be used both for the face and for the fill while the face should be grounded with concrete. The parapet had been demolished in sections, each piece weighing about 4 tons and they were suitable for re-use if a crane could be acquired for their recovery. It was agreed to proceed with repairs as recommended by Mr Barron and immediately steps were taken to employ a suitable foreman and to secure a crane.

Repairs cost £483 — far less than orginally anticipated yet still a serious drain on the Trust's resources. But it was a repair bill they were able to meet for 1900 was a good year for the Trust with a surplus of over £874.

SINCLAIR'S BEACH AGAIN

At a meeting of 26th December, 1900, the Trustees were informed that the case of Smith versus Lerwick Harbour Trust was to be re-opened to get final judgement. The new summons served on the Trust was almost identical to that which had been served in 1897 and the principal characters in the case were

the same. MacKenzie and Kermack were re-employed to defend
the action while the local agents of the Trust were Messrs.
Sievewright and MacGregor.

The case went to proof and in July when the Lord Ordinary
gave his decision it was depressing news for the Trust. In his
opinion the pursuer's title went back to 1819, and the disposition
of that date included the phrase "together also with the property
below the street belonging to my said house above described,
from the street down to the lowest low water mark". In the
opinion of Lord Kincairney there was no doubt that this was
a disposition of the shore *ex adverso* of the pursuer's house as
was usual under the ancient udal law which had never been
repealed in Shetland. He went on that udal law with its incidents
prevails over the whole of Shetland except where it is displaced
by arrangement with the Crown. The pursuer's holding was udal
and his recorded title which had not been feudalised was held
to prevail over that of Lerwick Harbour Trust who held their
property under a Crown grant. So Lord Kincairney upheld Mr
Smith's claim to the beach and found him entitled to expenses
against the defenders.

The Trust would have been well advised to have admitted
defeat at this stage but their Counsel declared that they could not
agree with the reasoning of the Lord Ordinary and advised the
Trust to lodge a Reclaiming Note. Sensing here a glimmer of
hope the Trustees agreed unanimously to follow the advice of
Counsel.

The case was finally settled in March, 1903, when the
First Division of the Court of Session upheld the decision of
Lord Kincairney and found in favour of Andrew Smith. Even
now the Trust's legal advisers were reluctant to admit defeat and
the Board of Trade advised the Trustees to appeal to the House
of Lords. But on 11th July, 1903, the Trustees instructed their
legal agents that as far as they were concerned the case was
closed and they requested that an account for all expenses
should be submitted to them with the minimum of delay.

Having won his case Andrew Smith did not let go so easily.
A list of accumulated expenses came in totalling £1455 and in
the words of the Chairman, John Leisk, the Trust had no option
but "pay and look pleasant". Then Mr Smith submitted a claim
for the income received by the Trust for the lease of Sinclair's
Beach including the site of the old coal store since he became

proprietor in 1879. The Trust's solicitors replied that as *bona fide* possessors of the ground until the termination of the recent case they were protected against such a claim. Furthermore the solicitors asserted that the Trustees would have a claim of recompense in respect of improvements made amounting to considerably more than any claim Mr Smith might have. But Mr Smith's solicitors pointed out that the Trust had not been *bona fide* possessors and again threatened legal action to enforce Mr Smith's new claim.

The Trust were compelled to compromise and eventually agreed to pay £50 in settlement. They were thankful to see the end of the now famous Sinclair's Beach case, especially as this was only one of the problems which they were having to tackle at this difficult time. It was a most unfortunate case from start to finish and a costly one for the Trust. In supporting their claim to a piece of ground that brought an income of £2 per annum they had to pay the sum of over £1,500 in expenses — a fortune in those days.

THE 40-VOYAGE CLAUSE

Generally speaking relations between the Trust and the North of Scotland and Orkney and Shetland Steam Navigation Company were excellent. Each was at times stubborn in its dealings with the other but willing to compromise when the other's strength was apparent.

No-one was ever in doubt as to the contribution made by the company towards the improvement of life in Shetland but inevitably, owing to the absence of competition, there were frequent complaints from the public over what they considered high freight and transport charges. In 1902 a new shipping company, The Shetland Islands Steam Trading Company, was formed by several prominent businessmen. Its secretary was John W. Robertson, a young man whose ambitious schemes over the next 50 years would play such an important part in the deliberations of the Trust and in the economic life of the islands. The aim of the company was to run a cargo-passenger vessel in competition with the vessels of the "North of Scotland" Company.

The latter was in a quandary. Its first action was to lower its rates to increase its competitiveness but these new rates would inevitably be levied on a smaller share of the islands' trade resulting in a greatly reduced income. The company would obviously have to effect economies without lowering the standards of the service provided and one obvious source of economy was the loop-hole in the Harbour Act of 1877 — the 40 voyage clause.

On 24th December, 1902, the company's manager wrote to the Trust enclosing a cheque for £145 being the composition dues for the last quarter of the year but informing the Trust that in future his company would exercise its right to pay dues in accordance with the Act of 1877. For vessels over 150 tons the rate would be 10d per ton per voyage while for those under 150 tons the rate would be 8d per ton and these rates would apply only to the first 40 calls at Victoria Pier each year.

On 13th January, 1903, the Trustees met to consider the position. The situation had changed radically since 1877 since the company had far more ships operating and with the frequency of the "Earl of Zetland's" trips the 40 voyages would be completed by the end of February. For the rest of the year the company's vessels would use the port free of charge resulting in a loss of revenue to the Trust of at least £300. It was pointed out that the company was already getting a very fair deal. In 1902 the accumulated tonnage of the company's ships using the harbour works was 85,000 tons which for a payment of £850 worked out at under 2d a ton. At the same time the high tonnage dues levied on other callers had the effect of driving away potential trade. The new company could also invoke the 40 voyage clause but in the words of John Leisk they could go one better. They could buy an old herring boat for £6 to £10 and run her between Lerwick and Dales Voe and she would very soon run up the 40 voyages. The situation was intolerable and the committee agreed to apply to Parliament at the earliest possible moment to have the 1877 Act amended by striking out the 40 voyage clause and also having a reduction in the high tonnage rates payable by less regular users of the port.

In the course of correspondence with the "North of Scotland" shipping company it became clear that there was another motive in terminating the long standing arrangement regarding composition dues. The manager pointed out that if the threatened opposition should not come into operation the company would be ready to reconsider the whole question. The Clerk to the Trust was directed to reply expressing surprise at this attitude and pointing out that the Trustees were not in any way responsible and had no control over the actions of the new company then in the course of formation.

Work proceeded under the Private Legislation Procedure (Scotland) Act 1897. The Trust's legal advisers employed a suitable Parliamentary Agent and a Provisional Order was drafted along the lines suggested by the Trust. At their meeting of 13th March, 1903, the draft was approved, the main points being the repeal of Section 42 of the 1887 Act and its replacement by new maximum charges of 4d per ton on all vessels over 15 tons. Lower rates would apply to small vessels and yachts while a flat rate of 6d for each trip would be levied on open boats calling to load or land livestock and salt fish.

In May the Trustees were informed that the Provisional Order would be opposed, a petition having been lodged by the "North of Scotland" company objecting to the new charge of 4d per ton which they feared would be applied on their vessels too, resulting in a doubling of their dues.

In the meantime the Shetland Islands Steam Trading Company had become organised and their secretary informed the Trust that their steamer "Mona" would soon be calling weekly at Victoria Pier and he hoped that store accommodation would be available in time. The Trust replied that under the existing arrangement with the "North of Scotland" company one quarter of the steamer's store was reserved for use by other traders such as the new company.

It was obvious that more storage space would be required on Victoria Pier and the Trust had intended to build a second store but when they heard that the Provisional Order was to be opposed with all the expense that entailed, they decided to abandon their plans for a new building. Instead it was proposed to build a 15 ft extension on the lower or eastern end of the old store and although the point of the pier was already congested the Trustees reluctantly agreed to the suggestion.

The position was becoming complicated with the Trust, already at war with one company, being drawn into the rivalry between the two of them. Fortunately common sense prevailed in the end. On 11th June 1903 a meeting was called at the instigation of the manager of the "North of Scotland" company between representatives of his company and of the Trust. The former explained how the new charges would have a disastrous

D

effect on their company but the Trustees stressed that they had
no intention of charging the company the full tonnage rates
and were prepared to make a concession for regular traders
under clause 43 of the Harbour Act. Furthermore, if the
company would withdraw their objections the Trust would
undertake, so long as they were able to meet their annual
liabilities out of revenue, to charge regular traders no more
than 2d per ton per trip.

The trouble between the two rival shipping companies
continued to simmer. The new company applied to the "North
of Scotland" company for use of the part of the steamer's store
reserved for other traders. The larger company was reluctant
to agree to this but the Trustees insisted that the store should
be made available to other users whenever it was required even
in the middle of the night.

On Tuesday 23rd June 1903 the s.s. "Mona" arrived at Victoria Pier just as the "North of Scotland" company's "St. Giles"
was about to sail. The event that followed had all the elements
of a comedy although probably no-one regarded them so at the
time. A large crowd had gathered to welcome the "Mona" and
they practically ignored the now old-fashioned "St. Giles" as
the new vessel altered course to take the berth on the north side
of Victoria Pier. Perhaps her skipper was too eager to impress,
his nervousness heightened by the presence of a rival on the
other side of the pier. She came in wide of the pier being blown
off by a strong southerly wind so that the ropes all fell short
of the pier and she had to reverse out into the harbour again.

Amused by the pathetic display put up by his rival the
captain of the "St. Giles" was determined to demonstrate to
the crowd an example of real seamanship. He gave three blasts
to warn his discomfited rival, now manoeuvring for a second
attempt, to keep out of his way. Then he moved quickly astern
— too quickly, for one of the doors of the gangway caught in
a fender on the side of the pier. The door was ripped off and
the fender badly damaged resulting later in a repair bill for £13.

The "Mona" was successful on her second attempt to come
alongside. Rival porters got out the rival gangway, the officials
of the new company went aboard their vessel which was soon
invaded by sightseers eager to inspect the ship that was to bring,
or so they hoped, such a saving in fares and freight charges.

Happily for the Trust the dispute in which they were involved came to an end. On 30th June two letters from the "North of Scotland" company were read to the Trustees. The first notified the Trust that the company had instructed their law agents to withdraw their objections to the Provisional Order. The second was even more conciliatory since it offered the Shetland Islands Steam Trading Company full use of the reserved portion of the store at all times if the new company would agree to pay the other's expenses for a trustworthy man to keep the store open after ordinary working hours.

The store extension was erected by Mr Morrison, Contractor, at a cost of £103. When it was completed the partition which had formed the lower end of the old store was moved westwards to separate the portion occupied by the "North of Scotland" company from the enlarged area on the eastern end now reserved for other users. The two lower doors of the old store were moved to the new end wall to provide access to the smaller section of the store while two new doors for the benefit of the "North of Scotland" company were taken out on the side of the store.

The larger section was then offered to the "North of Scotland" company at an annual rent of £42 while the seaward portion was offered to the new company at a rent of £18 per year. The companies accepted these terms and the war of words gave way to an acceptance to each other's right to exist and a price war in which rates were pruned to a less than economic level. Not surprisingly it was the smaller company that was forced out of business but not until 1907.

The Lerwick Harbour Amendment Act became law in November 1903. The Trustees, maturer and wiser after the ordeal of the previous 16 years, settled down to a period of even greater expansion and prosperity due to the unprecedented development of the herring industry.

Chapter Five

CHANGES IN THE FISHING INDUSTRY

Although the slump in the herring fishery during the late 1880s was no more than a temporary setback it had a serious effect on Shetland's economy. Many of the boats that had started the boom only a few years earlier were sold or hauled ashore never to fish again. Many of the curers were forced into bankruptcy and Lerwick lost in this way such important firms as A. J. Leask & Co. and A. H. Harrison & Co. Others managed to weather the storm, a good example being Mr James Mitchell who actually expanded his station by acquiring those vacated by Mr Harrison and by Mr Reid to make a magnificent station occupying most of the North Ness. When the recovery finally came Mr Mitchell was in a strong position to benefit from it.

One of the factors blamed for the curers' problems was the old system of selling by contract. The price was agreed before the season started and the curer was bound to accept a certain quantity of herring at this price. Unfortunately when the fleet struck shoals of poor herring the curer was bound to purchase them at the same price paid for those of normal quality. So in certain years fish were put in cure that were not worth having salt put on them. The result was that in most herring ports of the North and North-East of Scotland the contract price was replaced by the auction system of sales whereby the herring found their true market value each day.

In Shetland however the fishermen resisted the change fearing that owing to the lack of competition prices would fall to ridiculously low levels. So the first attempt to introduce the auction system at Lerwick, in July 1891, was unsuccessful.

In 1893 good landings were made at Lerwick in June showing how the former rigid division between the early and late seasons was gradually breaking down. These catches, being outside the normal contract period for Lerwick, were sold by auction and fetched up to 21/- (£1.05) a cran proving to the fishermen that it was possible to benefit financially from the

change. The late fishing saw a return to the old system with a
contract price of around 12/- (60p) per cran for the first 150 crans.

1894 saw the auction system coming into its own at Lerwick
with more than half of the boats adopting the new system.
Instead of proceeding to the station of the curer to whom each
boat was engaged the vessels made for Garthspool where the
auctioneers were waiting. When the bell was rung to announce
the sale, auctioneer and buyers went on board the boat and its
catch was sold as it lay in the hold to the highest bidder. Only
then would the boat proceed to the station of the curer who
had purchased the shot.

For a few weeks in July the system worked well with prices
up to 13/6 (67½p) a cran. Then inevitably at the beginning of
August there was a glut of herring on the East Coast and curers
became worried in case the continental market would collapse.
When the price fell to under 10/- (50p) a cran the fishermen
became alarmed. They declared that they would not fish for
less than 10/- a cran and that in any case the auction system
was not operating fairly since so many boats were bypassing
the auction quay and going straight to the curers who had
agreed to pay the current rate each day. Again the fishermen
sought a return to the contract system with a guaranteed price
of 10/- a cran for the first 100 crans during the next fortnight.
But the curers refused to consider this in spite of the fishermen's
threat to stay ashore.

Within a few years the market improved considerably and
the herring fishery started the second phase of its development
with the auction system firmly established at Lerwick although
the contract system still remained in force at most of the "early"
ports.

THE GROWTH OF THE FRESH FISH TRADE

Until the late 19th century Shetland's fishing industry was
founded soundly on the salt fish trade. This was the only way
to overcome the islands' remoteness from southern markets.
In the 1870s however there came a growing demand for fresh
fish due to the growth of fishing centres such as Grimsby, Hull,
North Shields and Aberdeen linked by a new rail network to
the main centres of population.

Shetland was debarred from participation in this trade by
the inadequacies of the steamer service which provided two

sailings each week in summer and only one a week in winter. But in 1881 the "North of Scotland" company increased its sailings to three times a week in summer and twice a week in winter, the extra run serving the west side of Shetland. Among other benefits this enabled Shetland to participate in the fresh fish trade, especially in winter.

At that time, before the coming of the steam trawler, the waters around Shetland were rich with shoals of haddock and this species became the basis of a considerable industry. Lerwick was one of its major centres although in this instance Scalloway for long retained the lead.

In Lerwick the firm of Richmond Harrison & Co., were heavily involved both in freshing and smoking. The firm was founded in 1881 as successor to G. Harrison & Son and in 1886 it was taken over by A. H. Harrison & Co. The fish were taken on "small" lines baited ashore by the women of the family, then shot on the haddock sands around Bressay and Noss. The haddock boats were small vessels of Shetland model design and many of them were built at Lerwick by Hay & Co., and by Laurence Goodlad in his yard at the Malakoff.

The industry assumed major proportions reaching a peak in 1888 when the 360 boats engaged at Shetland landed a total of 28,000 cwts. But then a decline set in owing to the many problems which dogged this industry too. Most obvious was the problems of low prices which seldom exceed 6/6 (32½p) a cwt. To be fair to the buyers they also had many problems to face. They were competing in the markets of Aberdeen and Leith with landings from a large fleet of local line boats and a growing fleet of steam trawlers. Consignments of fish from Shetland were generally oldest on the market and when supplies were heavy were the first to be condemned to the manure factory.

The most serious single problem was still the inadequacy of the steamer service. The people of Shetland were not satisfied with two sailings a week in winter and following a public meeting in Lerwick Town Hall in October 1887 the company was requested to continue the third weekly sailing throughout the year with a steamer leaving Lerwick each Saturday night.

The company turned down this request but tried to help the fishermen and on several occasions the little "Earl of Zetland" made a special trip to Aberdeen with a cargo of fish leaving on Saturday morning and returning to Lerwick late on Monday or early Tuesday morning.

No opportunity was missed of bringing this problem to the notice of influential groups and individuals. In October 1890 the problem was explained in detail to members of the Western Highlands & Islands Commission. Largely through their efforts Shetland was granted an extra steamer in 1891 bringing the service to four sailings a week in summer and three in winter including for the first time a direct link with Aberdeen — a route that would remain the corner stone of Shetland's fresh fish trade.

About this time there arose another problem for Shetland's fishermen with the arrival of the steam trawler. Generally owned by syndicates in Aberdeen, Peterhead, Dundee and North Shields they extended their activities to waters around Shetland in the 1890s. Not content with trawling offshore where they competed with the ling and cod fishers they even fished within the three-mile limit which then as now was theoretically closed to trawling.

The effects of illegal trawling were already well known since all along the Scottish coast little communities that once based their existence on line fishing saw their livelihood destroyed as the trawlers swept the grounds. Shetland, because of its remoteness was merely the last to suffer.

In January 1898 there occured an event of great importance for Lerwick, although it was not regarded at that time, when the BF registered herring boat "Violet" arrived to operate from Lerwick. The crew had brought their haddock boat with them and immediately they started to prosecute the winter fishing. A few weeks later a man and two lads arrived to try their luck on Shetland boats and later the same year at least one more "Scotch" crew were based at Lerwick. A year later six "Scotch" boats were based at Lerwick with between 30 and 40 fishermen and most of them had brought their families with them intending to settle permanently.

This was the start of the "Scotch" colony at Lerwick for their numbers grew steadily within the next few years. Few of them were well off financially and most of them settled in the poorest part of Lerwick at Pig Street and Fleet Street and the North Road area — parts of Lerwick long a source of worry to the local authorities. But they were dedicated and successful

fishermen and their contribution to the port and town of
Lerwick cannot be too highly emphasised.

THE DECLINE IN THE SALT FISH TRADE

The spring fishery for ling and cod pioneered by the big
boats of the 1870s declined steadily throughout the remainder
of the 19th century. The trawlers were largely to blame, spoiling
the grounds for lining and with their increased landings at their
home ports helping to lessen the demand for Shetland's salted
product. 1897 saw a great decrease in the catch at Lerwick while
the price there was so low that Scottish boats ran home with their
catches to get three times the price they would have got under
contract at Lerwick. In the following year came another departure
from tradition when Scottish vessels, finding the weather too
stormy to "trip" south, landed their catches at Lerwick where
they were sold by auction.

So as the herring fishery came to dominate the economic
life of Lerwick the spring fishing declined until it was hardly
worth noting. The haaf fishing too declined since the sixerns
could not cope with the changes of the period. Best known of
Lerwick's last fleet of sixerns was the "Ant" skippered by L.
Isbister although it was as a herring fisher that she hit the
headlines. One day in August 1891 she shot her nets off Bressay
Lighthouse and returned "just lipperin" with 38 crans of herring
— one of the biggest shots ever landed by a sixern. In June
1893 she was around at Scalloway where she landed several good
shots of up to 16 crans. At the end of her fishing career the
"Ant" was not scrapped but put into service as a mail boat
operating between Whalsay and Skerries.

The smacks fared rather better than did the sixerns. There
was a revival in their sector of the industry in 1891 and in 1892
Andrew Smith of Lerwick purchased the ex-Grimsby smacks
"King Arthur" and "Boreas". The former, a ketch-rigged welled
smack of 83 reg. tons was built at Scarborough in 1883. She
was put under the command of Peter Hawick while the 73 ton
"Boreas", built at Grimsby in 1876, was put under the command
of William Herculeson. In 1894 19 vessels sailed from Shetland,
eight of them belonging to the port of Lerwick. They were the
"Prince of Wales", "Sapphire", "Contest", "Lily of the Valley",
"Boreas", "King Arthur", "Summer" and "Danish Rose". The

season was unusually successful and in 1896 Andrew Robertson purchased the Grimsby vessel "Cuxwold".

Thereafter the fleet declined. In the spring of 1899 the "Cuxwold", "Boreas" and "Contest" were all sold for coasting. The "Contest" did not long survive in her new career for in October 1899 she was wrecked near Yarmouth while loaded with slates and building stones.

1900 saw the "Lily of the Valley" employed in the coasting trade and by 1901 Lerwick's fleet of cod fishers had been reduced to three — the "Research", "King Arthur" and "Buttercup", a late arrival purchased by Hay & Co. In 1903 only the "Buttercup" sailed for Faroe joined there by the "William Martin" from Scalloway. For the next four years this pair kept alive a 90 year old tradition but they too had to admit defeat. In 1908 the "Buttercup" was fitted out as a herring fisher under the command of Laurence Williamson of Scalloway and for a few years she tried to operate like a Dutch buss curing her catch on board but the system proved uneconomical. The "Buttercup" was laid up but it was not until September 1919 that she was sold to Faroe thus severing one of Shetland's last links with the Faroe cod fishing.

THE GROWTH OF THE HERRING FISHERY

Perhaps the greatest reason for the decline of the haaf fishing, the Faroe fishing and the spring fishing for ling and cod was the growth of the herring industry. There were poor periods and even disastrous seasons but steadily and relentlessly the summer fishing came to dominate the economic life of Shetland in general and of Lerwick in particular.

The industry revived in the late 1890's as more and more improved sailing drifters complete with steam capstan were added to the Shetland fleet and more herring merchants came north to establish curing yards. The fishery was still divided into two distinct seasons of which the early season remained the more important as regards both number of vessels and total catch. The fleet fished at the West Side during June and part of July while from mid-July to early September Lerwick came into its own as the main port for the late fishing.

The auction system was now firmly established at Lerwick and although the average price realised was little better than that obtained under contract it was the high prices occasionally recorded that fired the imagination. On 29th August, 1899, the price reached a staggering 42/6 a cran — at that time a record for Shetland. It is not surprising that when the contract period was over in mid-July crews were unwilling to re-engage even when prospects were promising. Instead they were lured to Lerwick to take their chance "at the bell". Indeed the introduction of the auction system at Lerwick was an important factor in a process that would continue for the next few years — the centralisation of the herring industry at Lerwick.

1900 was a memorable year for Lerwick. Before the start of the season a beautiful new vessel was launched from Hay & Co's yard at Freefield. She was 67 ft long overall with a keel of 60½ ft. and a beam of 20 ft. Built of larch and pitch pine on oak she was fitted with a steam capstan "and all the latest labour-saving devices". She was named "Swan", the naming ceremony being performed by Miss Ottie Isbister, daughter of her skipper, Mr Thomas Isbister. The "Swan" was the largest herring boat to be built at Lerwick and the last to be built under the guidance of Mr David Leask, for many years foreman carpenter at Freefield.

The season started unusually early at the end of June. Then in July local boats were joined by 200 Scottish vessels coming down from Baltasound. They intended to stay a week or two but results were so good that they stayed the whole season — the first time that east coast boats had done so. It was a poor season at Fraserburgh and other east coast ports and mid way through the season many curers moved their entire work force and curing stock to Lerwick where the vacant spaces at Garthspool were quickly transformed into curing yards. Throughout the season further cargoes of stock arrived and the Esplanade was at times blocked with piles of empty barrels.

The 1900 season saw even more innovations. One was the export of large quantities of "roused" herring — herring ungutted but partially preserved with salt — to the herring hungry yards of Helmsdale, Fraserburgh, Aberdeen and other ports, over 26,000 crans being disposed of in this way. Another innovation was the arrival of foreign steamers to cure herring on board. Still another departure from tradition was the arrival of the Swedish steamer "Gadus" to can herring. She stayed for two months and when she finished operations she had processed 900 crans amounting to 70,000 tins of herring.

Prices were generally high on account of the scarcity elsewhere and several individual shots realised over £200. On 21st August however Lerwick was swamped with herring when 367 boats landed 19,084 crans to give an average of 52 crans. A large amount was sold for manure at 2/- (10p) a cran and hundreds of crans remaining unsold were dumped into the harbour. The "Swan" had to take her shot "around the heads" to Scalloway to fill a small outlet there.

The greatest number of vessels to operate from Lerwick was 370 and this figure included a few steam drifters — first of a class that would soon revolutionise the industry and bring to an end the long era of the sailboat with mixed results for Shetland. But not even this tiny cloud of doubt could dim the brightness of the 1900 season at Lerwick, for when operations ceased the books of the Fishery Officer showed a total of 132,173 crans out of Shetland's total of 320,000 crans. Lerwick was top herring port for Scotland that year, ahead of Fraserburgh and Peterhead and its nearer rival, Baltasound, which could only produce 80,272 crans.

1900 was the year that put Lerwick on its feet. It marked the start of a period of development in which Lerwick changed from being just a relatively small fishing port to become the greatest herring port in Scotland. Vessels came from Ireland, the Isle of Man, Campbeltown, Stornoway and all the many east coast ports of Scotland, while steam drifters came from Yarmouth and Lowestoft. In addition boats from Norway, Denmark, Sweden and Germany called for stores and shelter and in the early part of the season Dutch boms and luggers arrived in their hundreds.

The shore workers were as cosmopolitan. Highlanders, Lowlanders and Shetlanders staffed the curing yards on both sides of Lerwick harbour and Germans, Swedes and Norwegians were busy on their own vessels. At weekends Lerwick's streets were thronged with fish workers and fishermen. Shops and bars did a roaring trade yet surprisingly the town's small police force had little trouble in enforcing law and order.

Most colourful of the visitors were the Dutch. It was said that they caused most of the congestion on Commercial Street, since one Dutchman took up as much room as did two ordinary people. Hands deep in their pockets or clutching tins of peppermint and the large red handkerchiefs in which they carried small purchases, they sauntered leisurely along Commercial Street and the Esplanade as if the place belonged to them. And in a way it did for the Dutch were coming here centuries before the Shetlanders lost their heads over the herring shoals.

There was some uncertainty on the part of the Dutch in 1900 when the Boer war was at its height. At that time no Britons were more patriotic than were the Shetlanders while the Dutch naturally supported their own kinsmen in distant South Africa. But the Dutch need not have worried for there was a tacit understanding that nothing would ever upset the centuries old Lerwick-Dutch friendship. 623 Dutch vessels fitted out that year and the greatest number to call at Lerwick at one time was 200.

The Dutchmen must have been aware of the change in the life-style of the people of Lerwick. A degree of affluence had brought changes in tastes and even the famous Dutch tobacco was less popular than the commodity which could be acquired locally. The appearance of the town, too, was changing and was to change even more as Lerwick Harbour Trust embarked on the second phase in the development of the harbour — again on account of the changes brought by the herring industry.

Chapter Six

ALEXANDRA WHARF

Sales by auction started at Garthspool but this activity soon shifted to Freefield Docks where there was more room for the growing fleet of sailers. Even here accommodation became inadequate and congestion was acute as those vessels that arrived first were hemmed in by late arrivals. There were occasions when vessels had to wait for hours for a chance to proceed to the curing stations and this resulted in deterioration of the catch and a delay in getting to sea again.

On Thursday 18th January 1900, a special committee meeting of Lerwick Harbour Trust was called to consider a memorial from a large number of fishcurers and fishsalesmen. They pointed out that the Trust could provide accommodation for the industry by erecting a suitable staging or jetty as the sole fish market for the port of Lerwick. Assuming that an average of 300 boats were to fish annually at Lerwick a charge of 5/- (25p) levied on each of them would realise £75 a year. Furthermore if a proper market building were provided the salesmen would be prepared to take office accommodation paying such rent as would recoup the outlay for its erection or on terms similar to those prevailing in the principal fishing ports of the East Coast of Scotland.

The matter was discussed fully by the Trustees who were divided in their opinions. Some thought it would be an advantage, others were of the opinion that there was plenty of room at Freefield. However it was resolved to obtain a plan and estimate from John M. Aitken, architect and contractor. But first a committee consisting of Messrs. Leisk, Stove and Harrison was given the remit to meet Mr Aitken and to inquire as to the cost of preparing the plan. If his fee seemed reasonable they were to instruct him to proceed.

The plan was ready for discussion at a meeting of 20th February but it could not have landed at a less opportune moment for the main question to be discussed was the damage

to the South Esplanade caused by the great storm the previous
week. The Trustees listened as details of the damage unfolded
and it was clear that a considerable sum of money would be
required in repairs.

At the very end of the meeting Mr Aitken's plans for a
new wharf were produced. They showed a wharf with a frontage
of 300 ft to be built at an estimated cost of £1200. The Trustees
were in no mood to contemplate added expense — indeed one
member refused to look at it. But the Chairman effectively
deferred consideration of the question by saying it would be
useful to have it a as guide for the future.

At Freefield, Hay & Co. tried to provide the facilities
required by the herring trade. First they set aside an area for
the sale of herring by sample which ended the tedious system
of clambering from boat to boat to bid on the catch, then in
1901 they built at Freefield a wooden fish market with stances
for 12 salesmen. It was opened on Monday, 20th July, being
commemorated by a gathering of salesmen, merchants and
others connected with the industry. Sales commenced the
following morning.

But it was obvious that this building was too small and in
any case it did nothing to remedy the congestion at the quay.
At a meeting of the Trustees on 19th November, 1901, there
was again a petition from the trade reminding them of the
memorial which was still in their possesson and pointing out
that developments in the herring industry had made the question
of a fish market and quay more urgent than ever. It was also
in the interests of the town of Lerwick and the whole trading
community that the Harbour Trust should derive as much
income as possible from the trade now coming to the harbour.
The petition was signed by no fewer than 76 merchants, curers
and others.

In the meantime the damage to the Esplanade had been
repaired more quickly and more cheaply than had seemed
possible that dark March day in 1900. This confidence of the
Trustees had returned with the growth of the herring industry
and this time the petition was well received. It was decided
to invite Mr Barron of Aberdeen, an engineer with wide
experience in marine works, to come to Lerwick to discuss the
matter with the Trustees. It was also agreed to pay Mr Aitken
his fee of four guineas for having produced the initial plan.

Opposition to the scheme came from an unexpected quarter — the fishermen of Mid Yell who regarded the site chosen as dangerous and far less convenient than Hay's Dock. If the new quay were erected as a market they argued, boats coming from northern grounds would pass all the stations on their way in and might have to fight their way back again against wind and tide. Some fishermen even threatened to seek engagements with the curers rather than land under these conditions and the Mid Yell fishermen were joined in their protests by a large group of men from Whalsay.

Undaunted the Trustees went ahead with their plans, and at a meeting of 4th February, 1902, Mr Barron's proposals were discussed. There were two possibilities — a jetty 150 ft long and 30 ft wide running out from the Gas Pier which would cost around £1,400 or a quay with a 300 ft long face built between the Gas Pier and the Esplanade at a cost of around £2,500. Mr Barron further recommended that an auction mart and offices should be provided and he had earmarked a site for this purpose near the Gas Pier. He had submitted sketch plans of various types of building ranging from one with 16 offices to cost £1,400 down to a simple auction mart without offices to cost a mere £300.

At the quarterly meeting of 18th February, 1902, the project was again considered and it was decided that a wharf was more desirable than a jetty but they chose the cheapest of five types of market building — a plain wooden structure with a slate roof which they visualised being placed about the middle of the quay. The question of office accommodation was left to a future date.

The Public Works Loan Board was next approached for permission to use the Reserve Fund then standing at over £1,800. But the Board refused to depart from the arrangement agreed previously that one quarter of the annual surplus should be allowed to accumulate until the sum of £2,500 was reached. However, since the debt to the Union Bank had been discharged in 1899 the Board had no objection to a sum of £895 paid into the Reserve Fund over and above the annual quarter being used for this purpose.

Little progress was made in 1903. In January it was agreed to seek government aid and in March Mr Barron was requested to produce a specific scheme for this purpose. The project was enlarged considerably and the estimated cost rose to £13,500.

In September there was a change in the position of Clerk to the Trust when Mr William Johnson resigned and Mr Arthur Sandison who had been associated with the Trust in its infancy through his employment with Messrs Sievewright and McGregor was appointed clerk at a reduced salary of £25 per annum. Mr Sandison had served as part time Town Clerk since 1874 but in 1890 when this job demanded a full time official he had resigned from his post with the solicitors. In addition to being Town Clerk and Clerk to the Harbour Trust Mr Sandison was also Clerk to the Feuars and Heritors of Lerwick. After his appointment the various meetings of the Trustees were held in Mr Sandison's office in the Town Hall.

Throughout the remaining months of 1903 these meetings were occupied almost entirely by the case of "Smith versus Lerwick Harbour Trust" and the problems raised by the rival shipping companies, but in 1904 events moved more quickly. In January the Board of Trade gave its permission for the fish market scheme to proceed but a new threat came from "several proprietors, traders and residenters in that part of Lerwick lying to the south of Victoria Pier", who suggested that before expanding the harbour works northwards the Trust should first complete the works they had been authorised to construct under the Act of 1877. The objectors claimed that the South Esplanade was a poor substitute for the numerous piers, steps and jetties which they had found so convenient for their private use and had expected rather more to be built in 1886 than the small landing place south of Victoria Pier and the steps built in lieu of Hay's Pier.

This time the Trustees successfully brushed aside the objections, proved that the works as modified and sanctioned by the Board of Trade were completed in full satisfaction of the requirements of the Act and that the additional works now contemplated were made necessary by changes in the fishing industry. They applied to the Treasury for a grant towards the cost of the scheme being supported in their application by Zetland County Council while Mr Cathcart Wason, the islands' MP, took a deep interest in the scheme.

On 5th August, 1904, the Trustees read with satisfaction a letter from the Treasury: "In view of the importance of Lerwick as a fishing centre . . . My Lords will be prepared to

1. *The foreshore of Lerwick in the 1870s with Morrison's Pier in the foreground.*

2. *Charlotte Place and the North Lodberry c. 1880 looking south from the cliffs below Fort Charlotte.*

3. The North Ness c. 1880 showing sailboats at the herring stations.

4. Another view of the North Ness c. 1880 with a barque discharging timber at Stove's Pier.

5. *The opening of the harbour works in 1886 with the ss Earl of Zetland alongside Victoria Pier.*

6. *Victoria Pier and goods shed with the paddle steamer St. Magnus alongside. In the foreground is the Diana fountain erected in 1890.*

7. *The herring market at Freefield in 1901. Steam drifters are still out-numbered by sailboats.*

8. *Steam drifters berthed at Albert Wharf in 1905. The house on the left is Victoria Buildings and the vacant space to the south was soon to be occupied by Ellesmere Buildings.*

ask Parliament at the proper time for a grant not exceeding £4,500 or a third of the total cost of the works whichever is less." The grant would be payable only when two thirds of the works should be completed and to enable the work to proceed the Union Bank agreed to provide interim assistance by way of a loan up to £9,000. It was assumed that the Public Works Loan Board would again provide assistance so enabling the Bank's loan to be repaid.

Working plans and specifications were drawn up and tenders invited for the construction of the wharf. Eleven firms submitted tenders and at a meeting of 14th October, 1904, Mr John M. Aitken's tender amounting to £9,444 was accepted. It was also decided to employ "a suitable steady man" as clerk of works at a salary not exceeding three guineas (£3.15) a week.

In November Mr Aitken began to erect his staging and purchased a steam engine to drive his crane. The old smack "Lily of the Valley" was converted into a dredger and began work on the line of the new sea wall. Machinery and material were assembled on the North Esplanade which the Trust agreed should be closed temporarily from the coal store northwards. It was fortunate that the Town Council had just completed a scheme of road widening on the "upper" road below Fort Charlotte so the closure of the "lower" road caused little inconvenience to the public. A "suitable steady man" was found in the person of James Davidson who was engaged at £3 a week. Finally quarries were opened at the South Ness from where stone was transported by cart.

At first the Trustees were alarmed at the slow rate of progress. It was pointed out that Mr Aitken was employing under 30 men but he contended that more men could not be usefully employed. Mr Barron suggested that he ought to work double shifts during the summer months and reminded him of a penalty clause in the contract which would be invoked if less than 300 ft of quay were completed by 1st August, 1905. In fact only 200 lineal feet of quay wall was completed within the stipulated time but Mr Aitken pointed out that he was having to work in far deeper water than was shown on the plans.

In September the first vessel to use the quay, the three masted schooner "Salvador", discharged a cargo of timber for

E

Messrs. Mouat & Co., the proprietors of the saw mill founded by the Stove brothers. The work speeded up considerably when a stone crusher was installed on site while a new crane dredging material at the south end of the works was said to be making better progress than all the carts bringing material to the north end of the quay. The Town Council helped to some extent when they were given permission to dump town refuse and offal from the slaughterhouse as fill for the new works — a practice that caused numerous complaints on account of the resulting stench.

By October the Trustees were satisfied with progress and at the Annual General Meeting of November, 1905, work was so far advanced that the Trustees could consider the possibility of erecting a temporary fish market on the south end of the quay to serve for the coming season. They realised that if the new quay were to derive any income in 1906 the fish market was essential. Besides they were now in a position to compete with Freefield as regards quay space. It was also decided at the A.G.M. to hold meetings of the Trustees monthly instead of quarterly while meetings of the Works Committee would continue to be held as often as required. This change indicates the increasing importance of Lerwick Harbour Trust as well as the increasing amount of business to be transacted.

It was also time to give some thought to what was required in the way of a permanent fish market. On 24th August, 1905, a meeting was held with a group of 15 salesmen all of whom expressed their willingness to rent offices in the building. One of their number, Mr Mitchell, then produced a plan of the type of building he and his colleagues had in mind. This showed a central mart with a two-storeyed wing on either side with offices on the first floor and stores underneath. The meeting approved of the plan in principle although at the next meeting it was decided to have offices on the ground floor of each wing too. The plan with the Trustees' comments was sent to Mr Barron as the basis for working plans and specifications. A site for the building was tentatively fixed on the new wharf opposite the foot of Harbour Street.

On 20th March, 1906, rates were fixed for fishing vessels using the new works. Sailing drifters of the old fashioned type would pay a compound fee of 10/- (50p) for the season or alternatively 1/- (5p) per arrival. For those with steam capstans the rates would be £1 and 1/6 (7½p) respectively while the modern steam drifters would pay £2 and 5/- (25p) respectively. Boats engaged in the winter haddock fishery between October and May would pay 10/- (50p) if under 50 ft long and £1 if over 50 ft long. No charge was to be levied on fish landed at the works except in the case of herring roused for immediate shipment which would be charged at the rate of 3d a cran. In May it was decided to give the new wharf a "Royal" name as had been done in the case of Victoria Pier and Albert Wharf. It was named Alexandra Wharf in honour of the Queen.

The temporary market was a great success. It was a plain wooden shed supplied with toilet facilities and designed for use by 19 salesmen who paid a flat rate of £1 for use of the market and 10/- (50p) ground leave for their portable "box" offices which stood around the building. A temporary telephone office had been planned to provide communications with outlying stations but the scheme fell through following the collapse of negotiations with the National Telephone Company.

It opened for business on Tuesday, 5th June, 1906, without speech or ceremony. The first shot of 20 crans being sold by Captain James Johnson, auctioneer, to Messrs Williamson, kipperers, for £1 a cran. The day proved an auspicious start for the market with 105 arrivals averaging 27 crans.

In August the £9,000 credit from the Union Bank was exhausted and further instalments were due to the contractor before the loan promised by the Public Works Loan Board could be obtained. It was decided to apply to the Union Bank for a further advance £1,000 to be repaid along with the existing overdraft out of the loan promised by the P.W.L.B. But the Trustees need not have worried for the local branch manager had foreseen this difficulty and had already applied to his Head Office for permission to increase his client's overdraft and permission was readily given. How different the case of 1890 when the actions of the Union Bank sparked off a major crisis for the Trust.

On 3rd September, 1906, after a further meeting with a deputation from the herring trade, it was decided to proceed with the building of a permanent fish market — a central eight-sided mart with eight offices overhead and two wings each of two storeys with 14 offices on the ground floor. The upper floor of each wing also had 14 offices disposed seven on either side of a 4 ft wide corridor lit from the roof. There was thus a total of 64 offices of which the eight nearest the mart on the ground floor had the added luxury of a fireplace.

In December the tender of Mr George Lyall, Aberdeen, to build it for £3,104 was accepted and work started almost immediately. Rapid progress was made and on 1st July, 1907, the fish market was formally opened with a cake and wine banquet given by Lerwick Harbour Trust. It was an elaborate building of red brick with white tiled facings at corners, doors and windows and in the middle was the octagonal sale ring with its cupola that would for so long be a prominent feature of Lerwick's seafront. Sales began a week later, the first arrival being the steam drifter "Fern" of Banff. Her 10 cran shot was sold for 27/6 (£1.37½) a cran to Messrs Still and Goodall for kippering.

On 23rd July Mr William Allan was appointed caretaker and the list of his duties was formidable. He had to open the mart at 8.30 am and close it at midnight every day of the week except Sunday. On Monday he had to wash out the floors of the mart while on Tuesday and Wednesday he had to wash the floors of the passages and stairs. He had to clean the lavatories daily and make sure they were supplied with clean soap and towels. He had to prevent "idlers" loitering on the mart but could allow visitors to watch the sales from the gallery on the ground floor. He had to clean the windows and supervise the water, sewerage and gas systems and generally supervise the whole building. For this he was paid £1 a week for half the year while from 11th November to 15th May he was retained as caretaker at 18/- (90p) a week.

The wharf took longer to complete, the work dragging on long after the contract period had expired. It received a setback on 2nd January, 1907, when yet another severe storm struck the islands. Again the wind was from the south-east and the waves tore out a large hole at the junction of the new wharf and the North Esplanade. The surface of the wharf was severely eroded and serious damage to the quay wall itself was caused by the Aberdeen trawler "Caspiana". She had been berthed alongside when the storm broke and found it impossible to get clear of the wharf. She was battered so severely that she keeled over and sank. As she rolled her gallows repeatedly struck the quay and eventually gouged a great hole in the quay wall.

In July, 1907, defects were apparent at other parts of the

wharf and Mr Aitken was instructed to rectify them. In January, 1908, the south-east corner of the wharf was found to be defective and Mr Davidson was recalled from Aberdeen to make an inspection. He found the foundations undermined and again Mr Aitken was ordered to repair the damage which he did but submitted a claim for £209. The Trustees refused to pay it and the matter was referred to Mr Barron for arbitration. The engineer visited Lerwick in October and succeeded in having a final agreement worked out between the Trustees and Mr Aitken.

Alexandra Wharf was not built strictly according to plan. Mr Barron's original plans showed two "knuckles" in the sea-wall, one a third of the way from the north end, the other a third of the way from the south end. The purpose was to break the force of the sea running along the face of the wharf but when the more southerly of the two had been built it was found that the sea became extremely confused in this area during severe weather and so the other "knuckle" was omitted. The total cost of the wharf was £10,553 — over £1,000 more than the estimate.

The fish market, that handsome building of red and white brick was a disappointment from the start. It soon began to settle owning to the softness of its foundations — an infilling of town refuse and slaughterhouse offal is not conducive to stability. In 1911 extra office accommodation was provided in an extension to the north wing. It was a difficult job owing to differential settling and the south wall of the extension was left unlined to lessen the risk of fire should the building collapse. A few months later a similar extension was added to the south wing to provide still more offices.

In spite of so many imperfections Alexandra Wharf played an important role in the growth of Lerwick throughout the entire herring boom and for this reason John M. Aitken's contribution is undeniable. It was one of the least satisfactory of his works but as builder of Lerwick Town Hall, the Grand Hotel, the beacon on the Voder, the lighthouses at Sule Skerry, Noup Head, Tumpan Head and dozens more buildings and marine works his personal reputation also is assured.

From the Trust's point of view Alexandra Wharf and the Fish Market enabled them for the first time to benefit directly from the herring boom since they were now able to levy a charge

of 1d per cran on herring landed. Before 1906 they had certainly
benefited from increased general activity but all the buying and
selling was carried on outwith the area of the Trust's jurisdiction.
In 1904 the gross revenue of the port was £2,362 but by 1908
this had risen to £4,361 giving a clear indication of the part
played by the wharf.

And once again a new harbour development meant a
change in a long established pattern. Until 1905 small boats
and yachts used to moor below Fort Charlotte but with the
construction of Alexandra Wharf they were pushed to the
area south of Victoria Pier and another picturesque feature of
old Lerwick was lost forever in the name of progress.

Chapter Seven

CHANGES ALONG THE SEAFRONT

The growth of the herring industry was a boost to the entire town giving an incentive to every sector of the community and resulting directly or indirectly in a spate of development all along the seafront.

In 1910 a handsome new Post Office was erected on the open ground between Commercial Street and the Esplanade on ground belonging to Mr Andrew Smith and Miss Umphray and covering Sinclair's Beach which had once been such a bone of contention. The new building covered what remained of Sinclair's Pier and the steps leading down to it but Lerwick Harbour Trust insisted that space be left at the south end for a new flight of steps between Commercial Street and the Esplanade.

But prior to that many other important changes had taken place farther north. In 1906 Mr George Leslie of Laxfirth bought the premises known as Victoria Wharf formerly owned by John Robertson and had the block rebuilt as Ellesmere Buildings. The ground at the east end of the building was made up to the level of the Esplanade and in the process the sunken passage and old railings that marked the boundary with Trust property disappeared, being replaced by a pavement.

The building immediately to the north of this, Victoria Buildings, had been rebuilt in 1905 by its owner, Mr James H. Allan, and the road along its northern side was improved with pavements on both sides following an agreement between Lerwick Harbour Trust and the Roads and Streets Committee of the Town Council as to the line of demarcation between their properties. Another agreement with the Town Council dated 3rd December, 1909, settled the line of demarcation between Trust and Town Council property at the Market Cross.

The ground across the roadway from Victoria Buildings belonged to Lerwick Harbour Trust and here in 1906 Messrs Jamieson Brothers began work on a new harbour office with a flat on the first floor intended for the Assistant Harbour Master. Part of this site was occupied by a shed owned by the Town Council which served as an office for the Police and Sanitary departments. The Trust agreed to remove this shed to another site and to incorporate in their new building a Police Office and a room for the inspection of meat.

In 1908 there was built in the space north of the new Harbour Office a much needed public convenience. The Trust contributed £75 towards the cost of the gentlemen's section but the cost of the ladies' section which went under the more delicate name of "waiting room" was borne by the Trust themselves.

In the meantime the "North of Scotland" Shipping Company had vacated their premises on Commercial Street when in 1899 they built the attractive premises on the Esplanade which they still occupy. Another old property to be rebuilt was the North Lodberry which, when the Trust was set up, stood in the sea. On its northern side Mr Ross Smith had enclosed a small piece of foreshore and built a photographic studio with a cellar below. The building burned down and when it was rebuilt as a bakeshop for Messrs Mangan and Irvine, Lerwick Town Council insisted that a flight of steps should be constructed to link Commercial Street with the Esplanade. Eventually Ganson Brothers acquired the North Lodberry and in 1895 they had it rebuilt.

A great deal of discussion between Messrs Ganson Brothers and Lerwick Harbour Trust centred on the steps to the north of the building. Gansons wished to rebuild the steps and extend the platform so as to give access to their premises. While doing this they were given permission to incorporate a store below the steps but the wording of the agreement was vague and many years later was again the subject of considerable discussion.

Throughout 1904 Lerwick Town Council and the County Road Board were busy carrying out improvements to the road below Fort Charlotte. The roadway was widened, partly by excavating the cliff itself. An agreement was reached with Lerwick Harbour Trust whereby the old wooden railing above the North Esplanade was removed and replaced with a high stone retaining wall and a wide pavement — half the cost of the wall being borne by the Trust. Near the north end of the wall an opening led to steep wooden steps between Commercial

Road and the Esplanade and farther south an opening in the wall provided access for an ash depot below the wall.

The building of the retaining wall meant that the Trust had to shift their ballast yard to a new site north of the Co-operative Coal Company's store. And the old Police Office — a wooden hut with roof of corrugated iron — was raised from its foundation by hydraulic jacks and transported bodily to a new site north of the ballast yard. In June, 1906, it assumed a new role when it was let to Messrs Malcolmson & Co. as refreshment rooms. The following year it was let to Mrs R. Jamieson on a three year lease as a restaurant but its connection with raw meat had not ended for in 1910 it was discovered that she was using part of it as a butcher's shop — a practice that the Trust suppressed immediately.

The refreshment room was much patronised by fishermen and others in the trade and also by farmers who drove in their sheep, cattle and ponies for shipment. For this reason a watering trough was provided outside the refreshment rooms for the benefit of livestock.

Considerable improvements were made to the quays and road surfaces in the harbour area. On 2nd December, 1904, the Trustees met to consider a letter from the Home Office regarding the safety of Victoria Pier. It had acquired a certain notoriety on account of the frequency of accidents. Early in February, 1905, another man fell into the sea and the situation became even more urgent. Gradually Victoria Pier and Albert Wharf became protected by iron posts and chains and with ladders on each face. The chains were put in place at night when the gas lamps were lit.

The surface of the quays was much improved by laying granite setts on parts of the Esplanade and at the head of Victoria Pier where wheeled traffic was heaviest. This was the start of a process that was to continue until practically the entire property of the Trust was covered in this way. In September, 1905, a further 150 tons of setts were purchased from John Fyfe of Aberdeen at 15/6 (77½p) a ton F.O.B. Aberdeen. The "North of Scotland" Shipping Company offered to transport them to Lerwick for 8/- (40p) a ton but a counter offer came from the Shetland Islands Steam Trading Company to transport them to Lerwick for 6/6 (32½p) a ton.

The new company was still in existence although struggling

on account of the low rates which it was able to charge. In
1903 the s.s. "Trojan" was chartered in place of the "Mona"
to carry cargo and livestock then in January, 1904, the company
purchased the 430 ton s.s. "Minnie Hinde" which for some
years had plied between Belfast and Whitehaven. She was renamed "Norseman" and when she arrived at Lerwick she was
greeted by a large crowd and a salute of rockets and cannon
fire. The Trust gave the company permission to use the north
side of Victoria Pier for their operations since the "Norseman's"
winches worked on the port side.

Both companies were complaining that they had insufficient
storage space and this was remedied in 1906 when the first part
of Alexandra Wharf was completed. The Trust had a new store
built at the south end of the wharf for the exclusive use of
the Shetland Islands Steam Trading Company. However they
did not use it for long since the company was forced into
liquidation and the "Norseman" was sold. The store was leased
to Mr John W. Robertson for use in his coaling business but
for many years it was known in Lerwick as the Norseman's
store.

As work on the wharf proceeded more space became available
and the Trustees were inundated with requests for stores and
workshops. In 1907 a store was built at the north end of the
wharf for the Smith Dock Trust Company, one of the firms
that had introduced the steam drifter to Shetland. It was a
plain wooden building of two storeys, the upper of which was
surrounded by a verandah for the drying of herring nets. In
the following year, in the space behind, two smaller stores were
built, one for Messrs Peacock & Co., and the other for the
Lowestoft Steam Herring Drifters Co. Ltd.

Back in the area of the North Esplanade the space below
the retaining wall was gradually becoming fully utilised. The
coal company, seeking additional space, were granted the use
of Mr Aitken's now disused cement store and in 1908 they
were given permission to sheath it with corrugated iron. The
temporary fish market after being used for a time as a net
store was removed to a site north of the Norseman's store
and it became the office of the fishery officers. In 1908 John
Robertson, the diver, was needing room for his diving gear
and a hut was erected for this purpose north of the refreshment
room.

The entire North Harbour area underwent great changes as the herring boom continued, while the area of Garthspool and Skibbadock was transformed beyond recognition. Where there had once been a skerry linked to the shore by a causeway Andrew Smith carried out a process of reclamation and by May, 1903, the whole of the area inside the causeway had been filled in. In this way an extra acre of ground was provided for herring stations.

Along the North Road wooden houses for fishermen gradually extended towards the Standing Stones while along the shore the curing stations continued their northwards advance. Upon receiving an application the Board of Trade invariably consulted the Trustees and usually the latter commented favourably on the application. In 1906, however, they objected to herring stations being erected between the Green Head and the Point of Scotland on the grounds that they would impede navigation. The Board of Trade granted permission nonetheless.

The Trustees also objected to John M. Aitken's plans to build a curing station at Scarfa Taing between Stout's Pier and MacBeath's Lodberry, being joined in their protests by 125 "proprietors and residents in the south end of the town". The Trustees objected on the grounds that removal of the sunken rocks as proposed by Mr Aitken would destroy what was then a natural breakwater protecting the Trust's property. An enquiry was held by the Board of Trade and all the objections were over-ruled.

The impulse of the herring boom was so great that in 1908 there were actually plans to build herring stations at Twageos on ground owned by the Sumburgh Estate. Again there were numerous objections from people in Lerwick including those who used the beach for bathing. The Bressay people were up in arms because they claimed that a concentration of curing activity at this spot would make it unsafe to cross the harbour in a small boat. In May, 1909, the Board of Trade informed the Trustees that they had acceded to the objections and refused the application.

Another scheme that did not materialise was that for a hauling slipway at the north end of Alexandra Wharf between the wharf and the Gas Pier. The need for a slipway had been apparent for many years and was discussed in the columns of "The Shetland Times" in the 1870's. In the 1880's a site was advertised for this purpose at the North Ness, west of Mitchell's Station, but nothing came of the suggestion and the area was leased to Mr Reid as a herring station. The Trustees had raised the question in November, 1904, and sought Mr Barron's advice. He estimated that with hauling equipment a slipway would cost £1,100 and suggested that a suitable site lay next to Gunther's Station at the North Ness. But the right of way to the North Ness was a problem and ruled out immediate development of this site.

In July, 1905, a deputation of boat owners representing fleets numbering 140 vessels met the Trustees to stress the need for providing repair facilities for steam drifters. The respective merits of slipways and pontoon docks were discussed and the Trustees decided that a pontoon dock should be incorporated in the new works.

Mr Barron set to work and submitted a plan showing a pontoon dock with a lifting power of 425 tons which in his opinion could be sited at the north end of Alexandra Wharf at a cost of £10,000. The Trustees expressed their surprise and disappointment that the cost was so high. The scheme was obviously beyond their means and was abandoned, although the suggestion was raised again a few years later.

In spite of this disappointment the Trustees had reason to be satisfied with what they had achieved. They had successfully carried out a major scheme that was to enable Lerwick to adapt to the changes of the next few years. The status of the Trust had also changed radically. As early as November, 1905, the editor of the "Shetland News" had commented: "at one time Lerwick Harbour Trust occupied a position of quite secondary importance amongst the public bodies of the town. Meetings were held quarterly and so little interest was taken in the work that even at the quarterly meetings it was often difficult to get a quorum. Matters are now beginning to wear a different complexion . . . . There is no doubt that for the next few years the harbour and harbour affairs will be matters of supreme importance to the town."

The completion of Alexandra Wharf and the Fish Market marked the end of the second chapter in the development of the sea front under the guidance of Lerwick Harbour Trust. There had been changes in the membership of the Trust since its inauguration. One man who did not live to see the completion of the work was John Robertson — "Young John o' da Trance" as he was called — to distinguish him from his uncle, Bailie John Robertson. The younger John, a general merchant and fishcurer, was a leading light in practically every public movement in Lerwick in the latter half of the 19th century. He was a member of several boards in Lerwick, a Justice of the Peace, and was at one time Vice-Convener for the County. He served as a Trustee of Lerwick Harbour from 1877 to 1904.

In January, 1908, Captain Allison announced his decision to retire from the post of Harbour Master. From 20 applicants Captain Gilbert Gray, a Bressay man then living in Grangemouth, was chosen as successor. He started work on 1st May. On 1st June Captain Allison was invited to attend a meeting of the Trust where he was presented with a gold watch. It was an expensive watch, having cost just under £24 — a large sum for a watch in those days. It was inscribed as follows: "Presented by the Lerwick Harbour Trust to Captain George Allison as a mark of appreciation of 22 years faithful service as Harbour Master. 1st June, 1908". Fortunately the Trust did not lose his services altogether for within a few months he was again present at meetings — this time as a member of the Trust.

Chapter Eight

THE DOMINANCE OF THE STEAM DRIFTER

Shetland's herring boom reached its peak in 1905 with a catch of 645,000 crans worth almost £600,000, while at the height of the early season there were 1,815 boats operating from ports all over Shetland. But these figures are misleading since only a small share of the total earnings remained in Shetland. A large proportion of the sailing fleet came from ports in the North and North-East of Scotland, from Ireland and the Isle of Man and more significantly a large part of the catch was taken by English and Scottish steam drifters.

In the next few years the steam drifters came to dominate the industry. They came in ever increasing numbers, owned by syndicates such as Westmacott Ltd. of Yarmouth and the British Steam Fishing Company of Hull. One of the largest fleets was that of the Smith Dock Trust Co. of Yarmouth, whose vessels were named rather unimaginatively "One", "Two", "Three", etc. There was even a "Thirteen". From Shetland's point of view the most important of these companies was the Lowestoft Steam Herring Drifters Co. Ltd., which was later to play such an important role as fish salesmen. The company's early drifters were the fleet named after various Lords.

The steam drifters used Baltasound, Scalloway and Sandwick to a certain extent but the trend towards centralisation of the industry had begun and Lerwick gained in importance at the expense of these ports too.

In 1906 the herring were slow to appear at Scalloway and Baltasound and for the first time Lerwick was in full swing before them. The once late fishing centre had become an early centre as well, to explode another old myth that only at the western and northern ports were marketable herring available in June. Everything was working in favour of Lerwick and the other ports could only stand by helplessly and watch. So while Shetland in general suffered a decline in the herring industry after 1905, Lerwick continued to expand as a herring port and soon came to account for almost the entire Shetland catch.

A change in the movement of the herring shoals certainly contributed to the growth of Lerwick but the contribution made by Lerwick Harbour Trust cannot be overlooked. With Alexandra Wharf and the Fish Market, Lerwick was able to adapt to the many changes of the period, becoming established as the main herring port in Scotland.

The change in Lerwick harbour was profound. At the turn of the century Lerwick was dominated each summer by the tall masts and brown sails of herring smacks and luggers but in the next few years there was a change to rows of soot-blackened funnels belching out clouds of grey smoke that coalesced to hang in a pall over the town whenever the wind was blowing off the harbour. Coal and dust were an inseparable part of the summer scene, like the boats and herring gulls and the herring themselves. Thousands of tons of coal were consumed each season; clouds of dust rose in the wind during coaling operations, settling on the housewives' washing, sifting in through doors and windows and contaminating stationery in the offices along the front.

The large companies organised the coaling of their own vessels but nevertheless the demand for coal provided a boost to local firms such as Hay & Co. who also owned the coal hulk "Havana", and Lerwick Co-operative Coal Company which entered the steam coal trade in 1907. The Shetland Islands Steam Trading Company also took advantage of this trade, supplying coal from their coal hulk "Richelieu" moored off Gardie. The company's facilities were later taken over by John W. Robertson who in 1912 also acquired the hulk "J. S. Sterry".

The coal hulks played an important part in the operations of the port. They were mainly old sailing vessels saved from the breaker's yard because of the contribution they could still make to the age of steam. In the early part of the summer they were filled with coal and towed to Lerwick where they were anchored out of the fairway at the direction of the Harbour Master. The Trust, however, had no power to levy any charge on their operations. They were manned by a small team of workers to refuel drifters as they came alongside and as the supply of coal diminished fresh cargoes for the hulks were brought north by steamer. The hulks allowed local firms to extend their activities but they also allowed competitors from the south such as Bessey and Palmer and G. H. Hansell & Co. to obtain a foothold at Lerwick. In 1907 the fleet consumed 44,000 tons of coal and 125 cargoes of steam coal arrived during the season including the cargoes brought north by the nine coal hulks.

To many people in Shetland it seemed that the world had gone mad with the age of sail being replaced by an age of noise and dirt and speed. Lerwick harbour used to be a pleasant place where boys could spend an afternoon in a rowing boat watching the sailing fleet tacking out of the harbour or visiting the anchored busses to coax a few cigars from the genial Dutchmen. Now it was a dangerous place full of dirty black steam drifters racing shorewards to secure the best prices for their catches, their whistles shrieking to appraise the town in general of the success of their night's fishing. One blast for every ten crans was the system understood by everyone in Lerwick. They could hardly slow down to let a rowing boat get out of the way far less indulge in such a civilised pastime as discussing the sale of tobacco or gin. But even the Dutch fleet was changing at this time, the number of bomschuits dropping alarmingly as they were replaced by steam luggers.

The first accident at Lerwick involving a steam drifter occurred in July, 1903, when the YH registered drifter "Twenty-one" struck the sailboat "Brother's Gem" of Dunrossness and almost tore her stem out. After the collision the boats separated and the steamer next struck the "Shamrock" of Peel as she lay at anchor and cut her to the waterline. Although the Peel boat sank quickly her crew were rescued and there were no casualties on the "Brother's Gem" which was towed to Free-field for repairs.

For the people of Bressay a trip to Lerwick became an ordeal fraught with anxiety and danger and they did more than any others to urge Lerwick Harbour Trust to take positive action. The Trustees responded to these appeals and within the next few years rules were introduced to regulate the speed of steam drifters within the harbour while the provision of several beacons made a great contribution towards overall safety.

The Commissioners of Northern Lighthouses were well aware of the problems caused by insufficient lights. Bressay Lighthouse

9. *A Dutch bomschuit from Scheveningen.*

10. *German warships anchored off the Knab, 27th July 1904.*

11. *Construction work begins at Alexandra Wharf in 1905.*

12. *Alexandra Wharf in 1906 showing the temporary herring market and the portable offices of the salesmen.*

13. *A unique wartime photograph showing a submarine and other naval craft in the harbour and a motor drifter alongside Albert Wharf.*

14. *Alexandra Wharf and herring market between the wars.*

15. *A curing station at Lerwick between the wars, the farlins heaped with herring.*

16. *A mass of steam drifters at Alexandra Wharf — a typical summer scene at Lerwick between the wars.*

had been commissioned in 1858 and the Commissioners had placed two unlighted can buoys to mark shoals within the sound itself. The "south" buoy had been positioned in 1848 while the "north" buoy had been placed in position in 1886. A further improvement was made in 1904 when a beacon was placed at Rova Head and about the same time the Harbour Trustees had a light placed at the North Ness. In 1912 the latter was converted from gas to electricity, being connected to Messrs Mitchell's private plant at a cost to the Trust of £10 a year. When the generators were not working power was provided by storage batteries. In 1907 the Commissioners of Northern Light-houses built a concrete beacon on Loofa Baa but it was not until 1913 that it was marked by a light. Few lights anywhere in Britain have given better service than this one. Forty years later a new light was purchased for Loofa Baa and installed by Harbour Trust staff. The original lantern was sent to the makers for repairs then retained by the Trust as a spare. In 1908 a guiding light lit by gas was erected by the Lighthouse Board at the South Ness. A fog signal for Bressay Lighthouse was first proposed in 1891 and this was finally erected in 1908 by John M. Aitken.

In June, 1904, by-laws were introduced to limit the speed of steam drifters to four knots and the following year Mr W. A. A. Tulloch, one of the Trustees, having been to Holland on business had the harbour by-laws translated into Dutch and circulated among the Dutch and German fishing fleets. But it was one thing to introduce by-laws, quite another to enforce them. In 1905 it became clear that the new regulations were being ignored and the Trustees set about securing prosecutions in an attempt to enforce them.

To obtain proof of the speed of vessels two imaginary parallel lines were drawn, one from Gillie's Pier to Maryfield in Bressay, the other between the point of Victoria Pier and Gardie House, the lines being 300 yards apart. Armed with stop watches, Captain Allison and his friend, Captain Robert Sinclair, began timing the passage of drifters over the measured distance. As a result of their efforts the skipper of the Yarmouth drifter "Seventeen" found himself in court in June, 1905, charged with contravening the by-laws. He was fined £2 which was a modified fine for a first offence. In accordance with the custom in such cases half the fine was given to the Kirk Session for behoof of

F

the poor of the parish, the other half being retained towards expenses.

Several more prosecutions followed and in January, 1906, when the expenses had been deducted there remained the balance of £2 11/- (£2.55) in the hands of the Trustees. It was decided to divide this between the Harbour Master and his assistant "for their trouble".

Another accident occurred in June, 1906, when the Yarmouth drifter "Sixteen" ran down the Quarff boat "Active" near Maryfield in Bressay. The Quarff boat sank within minutes but her crew managed to scramble on board the other vessel. More prosecutions followed to enforce the by-laws and on 10th July, 1906, 12 skippers appeared in court being fined a total of £42.

The harbour staff was inadequate to cope with the hundreds of steam drifters that now fished from Lerwick each summer. In April, 1906, Mr Simon Smith was appointed berthing master and the following summer two berthing masters and a clerk to the Harbour Master were found necessary to carry on the work.

To add to the confusion in Lerwick Harbour, one day in June, 1906, 400 Dutch boms, luggers and steamers anchored in the harbour — the greatest concentration to occur this century. All day they came in a steady stream and just as their forefathers had done for hundreds of years they dropped anchor wherever it was convenient for them, consulting neither berthing master nor Harbour Master. The effect was chaotic and there followed the entirely unprecedented scene of an irate Harbour Master putting out in his boat armed with a large axe which he threatened to use against the hawsers of recalcitrant vessels. This was the only way he could clear a track for the passage of British vessels.

At the Annual General Meeting of 1906 about £35 collected in fines from steam drifters lay waiting to be allocated. It was decided to give £17 to the poor of the parish, £10 to Lerwick Sick Aid Society, £5 to the Gilbert Bain Hospital, while the balance was awarded to the Harbour Master "for his trouble". Again in 1907 the poor of the parish received a windfall of over £11 but the clerk to the Parish Council, Mr Innes, was not satisfied with the share awarded to him. He pointed out

that under the Act of Parliament which regulated the disposal
of penalties, the Inspector of the Poor was entitled to receive
half the fines collected. Sheriff Brown upheld this opinion and
the Trustees were forced to comply.

The rate of prosecutions came to a peak in 1909 when
almost every month saw a fresh batch of convictions. The English
fishermen, especially, were most indignant at the way they were
being treated. They pointed out how unfair it was that cargo
vessels could proceed at top speed, yet the smaller drifters were
limited to a speed of four knots and in many of the cases
dealt with their speed was only marginally over the limit. The
Englishmen reminded the Trustees of the benefits they brought
to the town and to local shopkeepers and hinted that they might
retaliate by boycotting local merchants and having their stores
sent north from England. No one took this threat seriously
but the following year the Smith Dock Trust Company opened
a grocer's shop on the Esplanade in competition with local
merchants.

There was a tacit agreement among the Trustees that they
would not bring any prosecutions the following year. But still
drifters continued to race through the harbour at speeds of eight
or nine knots. H.M.S. "Ringdove" visited Lerwick in 1910 on
fishery protection duty and her commander was appalled at the
careless manner in which these vessels were being navigated.
He set about securing his own prosecutions for infringement of
the by-laws, and at the end of August four skippers appeared
in court, being fined a total of £8 10/- (£8.50). Sheriff Brown
decreed that since the Trustees were not involved in any expense
on this occasion three-quarters of the sum should be handed
over to the Inspector of the Poor.

The "Ringdove" was back the following year to combine
the work of fishery protection with enforcement of the harbour
by-laws and her presence infuriated the Trustees and the public
in general. Apart from being a meddler and a nuisance in the
harbour at an exceptionally busy time of the year it was intolerable that a naval ship and crew should have such an easy
posting. Resentment culminated in remarks made at the August
meeting of the Trust when the "Ringdove" was compared un-
favourably with the Dutch, French and German protection
vessels that accompanied their fleets at sea, rendering help whenever it was required. Commander Blackwood of the "Ringdove"

took offence at this criticism and wrote the Trustees a strongly worded letter.

A special meeting was convened to consider a reply. It was pointed out that in a place like Baltasound where there was no harbour authority a gunboat would be an advantage to regulate traffic when the harbour was crowded. But Lerwick Harbour Trust had statutory powers to regulate the speed of vessels and to control the anchorage within the conservancy limits of the harbour. If, on the other hand, a smart fast-steaming vessel were to patrol Shetland waters to prevent trawlers poaching it would be an advantage to the islands. Furthermore, if such a vessel were to be provided with fishing gear for experimental purposes and wireless telegraphic apparatus to report the position of herring shoals she would be of immense benefit to the whole fishing industry. Commander Blackwood took the hint and in 1912 the old "Ringdove" concentrated her efforts on Baltasound.

It is unfair to the owners and crews of steam drifters to give the impression that they alone were the cause of all the collisions in Lerwick harbour. From the beginning of the herring boom with so many sailing boats operating from Lerwick accidents were unavoidable and scarcely a week passed without a stranding or a collision. It was a sailing boat that caused the most serious accident of the period, in September, 1910, when a small boat crossing from Bressay was run down by the sailing drifter "Children's Trust". The owner of the small boat saved himself by grasping hold of the large vessel's bob-stay and holding on until he was pulled on board. Two others were saved by the crew of Hay & Company's smack "Buttercup," then employed at the herring fishing. Unfortunately three of the small boat's occupants, an elderly crofter and two young women, were drowned.

It was ironic that this tragedy occurred at the very end of the season when the harbour was relatively quiet. It was also near the end of the sailboat era for in 1910 there were only 169 sailboats based at Lerwick, 112 of them being Shetland owned.

In the same year there were 734 steam drifters at the port and Lerwick's total catch was 380,338 crans out of Shetland's total of 449,855 crans. These figures indicate how completely Lerwick had come to dominate the herring industry.

THE EFFECT ON LERWICK

Although the herring fishery lasted for only four or five months each year the impact on Lerwick was considerable. For many years the population trebled every summer as 5,000 fishermen and 4,000 fish workers took up residence. For the merchants, especially the grocers and butchers, the herring boom brought greater prosperity. There was a great deal of competition in securing the custom of new arrivals and message boys kept a day-long vigil at the harbour. The English drifters were a greater source of income than were the Scottish since the latter usually managed a trip home once a month to visit their families and restock their provision lockers, whereas the Englishmen had to stay here for the duration of the season.

As can be imagined the summer influx of fishermen and fish workers put a severe strain on Lerwick's social services which could hardly be described as elaborate even at the quieter time of the year. The churches certainly did all they could to cater for the spiritual needs of the temporary residents and many denominations not represented in Lerwick sent a pastor to keep an eye on members of his flock.

None were so well organised as the Dutch who operated from Lerwick during June and July. For many years Albert Hall at Garthspool was hired as a social centre for Dutch fishermen and in 1896 for the first time a resident pastor, Dominie Van der Valk, was based at Lerwick. During the week he attended to fishermen's personal problems and each Sunday he conducted services in the Parish Church. After some years there began an association between the Dutch mission and St. Clement's Church and in July, 1911, a beautiful stained glass window was unveiled there — a gift from the Reformed Church of Holland.

Perhaps the most neglected of the summer residents were the women who arrived from the North of Scotland, from the Western Highlands and from Ireland to gut herring and pack them in barrels. Few of the women had cabin accommodation on the 200 mile journey north. In calm weather they usually slept on deck while in rough weather they were given a space to stretch out in the hold. Upon arrival at Lerwick, cold and often miserably seasick, they had to open up the damp wooden huts that had stood closed all winter, light the bogey stove and prepare their first meal since leaving home.

When the season started and the herring began to arrive the gutters had to work in the open in all weathers, their fingers rough and reddened from constant contact with the salt. A moment's carelessness when tired after a long stint at the farlins meant another cut that was slow to heal in spite of the thick swathes of bandage.

An attempt to provide first aid facilities was made in 1912 when a fisher girls' Rest Hut was provided at Holmsgarth by the Committee on Christian Life and Work, of the Church of Scotland, on land gifted by Sir Arthur Nicolson. When bad weather curtailed landings the hut was used for recreational purposes.

For the fishermen too recreational and first aid facilities were inadequate. A notable improvement occurred in June, 1912, when the R.N.M.D.S.F. Institute was opened in the Tolbooth, newly vacated by the G.P.O. It had two large rooms on the ground floor and a dormitory on the first floor with beds for convalescent fishermen.

The lack of proper hospital accommodation was the most serious problem of all. The town's only general hospital, the Gilbert Bain Memorial Hospital, was a tiny building with beds for four male and four female patients and with commendable foresight and determination the fish trade itself set out to improve the situation. At a meeting in August, 1911, at which John W. Robertson was as usual a prominent speaker, a Fish Trade Hospital Committee was set up to achieve their ambition. The target was an ambitious one considering the foundation on which they had to build — they aimed to provide two six-bed wards and two private wards containing three and two beds respectively. The whole scheme was expected to cost £1,000.

The target was reached by a levy on fishing vessels at the rate of 10/- (50p) for each steam drifter and 5/- (25p) for each sailing boat, and a levy on fishcurers of 2/- (10p) for each employee. The sum raised by this means was £1,331 and the additional wing was built during the spring of 1912 and formally handed over in July. Arrangements were made with local doctors to visit the hospital each day to attend both in and out patients, while medical advice and treatment was free to all members of the fish trade. It was soon in use and between 16th May and 16th September, 1912, 46 in-patients and 78 out-patients benefited from the facilities.

Having financed its erection the fish trade also contributed towards its maintenance by an annual levy of 6d. (2½p) on each fishworker, 5/- (25p) on each steam drifter and 2/6 (12½p) on each sailboat. A levy was also laid on shipbrokers and coal merchants.

LOCAL FIRMS

Although most of the curing and fishselling concerns came from outwith Shetland several local firms played an important part. Mr Laurence Laurenson, Mr McGowan Moffat, Mr James Johnson and the firm of John W. Robertson were active as salesmen competing for a share of the trade with such well known firms as Bloomfields and Norford Suffling Ltd. Another English firm that became closely identified with Lerwick was the Lowestoft Steam Herring Drifters Co. Ltd., whose managing director, Mr Thomas Sargeant and his successor, Major H. B. Jackson, both took a deep interest in Lerwick's fishing industry. For many years its local representative was Mr Frank Smith.

Of Lerwick's fish merchants at the time of the herring boom most important was Andrew Smith, victor in the Sinclair's Beach case. Mr Smith had a varied business career. He came to Lerwick in 1868 and began in business as a grocer and general merchant. When the decline of the 1880s affected his business he acquired a stake in the Faroe cod fishing, his first purchase being the welled smack "King Arthur" and when the herring industry revived he added several large sailboats to his fleet. In 1897 he disposed of his grocer's business and became a ship-broker and commission agent, later adding herring exporting to his list of activities.

In 1895 Mr Smith purchased Garthspool Docks where he extended and improved the main pier and filled in the Vadill and the dock to the east of the sail loft. He erected dwelling houses on the reclaimed ground, let part of his property as curing stations, and between 1905 and 1907 he built Islesburgh House, the largest private dwelling house in Lerwick.

In 1912 Andrew Smith took into partnership Mr J. T. J. Sinclair and his eldest son A. J. Smith. By this time the firm had become associated with Max L. Schultze & Co. of Peter-head and in the same year it was decided to amalgamate under

the name of Andrew Smith & Schultze. The firm became one
of the largest in the trade, exporting herring to Germany, Russia
and America. Mr Smith retired from all his business activities
in 1914 and he died in 1917.

At Freefield, Hay & Co. still played a prominent part, both
in the herring industry and in the general economic life of
Lerwick. Their foreman, David Leask, was succeeded by John
Shewan whose skill as a carpenter and boatbuilder was soon
recognised all over Shetland. John Brown's business, too, was
still thriving and he was now a shipowner as well as a blacksmith and fishcurer with his three-masted schooner "Linus"
trading as far as Africa. He had extended his station at the
North Ness by taking in the site of the old battery and here
he cured herring in summer and dealt with haddocks in winter.

At the North Ness, James Mitchell & Sons had an extensive
curing business with a barrel factory which employed up to 70
hands throughout the year. The two older North Ness herring
stations had by this time been thrown into one, being leased
by Messrs H. MacDonald & Co.

No discussion of Lerwick in the years before World War
I is complete without a description of John W. Robertson's
activities. In 1910 he took over the Malakoff boatbuilding yard
at the North Ness and built carpenters' workshops, net stores
and a shipchandler's shop. For years his burning ambition was
to provide at Lerwick a hauling slipway where fishing vessels
could be repaired instead of having to go to Stromness or ports
on the mainland.

In 1910 he proposed to build a slipway on the north side
of his property at the North Ness next to Messrs MacDonald
& Company's station but once again there were complaints from
neighbouring properties about infringement of their right of
way,

In February, 1914, Mr Robertson tried to get Lerwick
Harbour Trust to provide a slipway at John Brown's station
where the old battery had stood. Mr Brown expressed his willingness to accommodate this development and the Rose Street
Foundry and Engineering Co. Ltd. of Inverness agreed to prepare plans and specifications. From the four sets of plans provided Mr Robertson recommended one that would accommodate
four drifters and one cargo vessel or torpedo boat, its cost being

estimated at £30,000. It was agreed to seek a grant from the Admiralty but once again the Trust's plans to provide a slipway came to nothing.

CHANGES IN LERWICK'S FLEET

As the number of steam drifters increased the number of sailboats declined. First to go were the older vessels that had arrived in the 1870's and 1880's — obsolete even before the advent of steam. Their fishing days were over but they often found a job as flit boats carrying offal to the manure factory at Bressay or transporting barrels of herring from the stations to cargo vessels anchored in the harbour. The larger and newer vessels such as the "Swan" and John Brown's "Gracey Brown" and "Joey Brown" kept going a little longer.

But in Lerwick as elsewhere there were men who realised that the steam drifter was going to dominate the industry, who realised that they would have to adapt to the changes of the period or go out of business. First steam drifter to be purchased by Lerwick owners was the "Content", purchased from Yarmouth in January, 1907. She was put under the command of Thomas Isbister, formerly skipper of the "Swan". About the same time Alex Watt sold his share in the "Joey Brown" and placed an order for a new steel drifter to be built on the Clyde. Named "Mayflower", she arrived at Lerwick in time for the 1907 season. Other arrivals that year were the "Dolphin". skippered by James Gatt, and the "Consolation", owned by Joseph Mair and skippered by John McKay.

Apart from the "Consolation" which met an ignominious end when she took fire and sank while anchored off the North Ness, the steam vessels were successful and their success encouraged others to follow their lead. In 1910 John W. Robertson purchased an English vessel which he renamed "Fitful Head" and two years later he purchased the "Superb" which he renamed "Sumburgh Head". More vessels arrived in the early part of 1914 bringing Shetland's fleet of steam drifters up to ten. These included the "Rova Head", owned by John W. Robertson, and the "Hamnavoe", in which Mr Robertson had a share.

The sailboats did not surrender without a fight and with the coming of the internal combustion engine a marine engine was invented that enabled many of them to prolong their fishing careers.

Mr Joseph Gray, son of Gifford Gray, was associated with the internal combustion engine both ashore and afloat. After serving his time with John Brown at Freefield Iron Works, he first went into business with Mr William Goudie when they set up as engineers and blacksmiths. In 1903 Mr Gray decided to step out on his own. The first motor car had appeared on Shetland's roads in 1902 and by 1911 there were sufficient of them to persuade Mr Gray to start a motor garage to cater for them.

In 1907 the first Shetland vessel to have a motor installed proved the success of this new device and about the same time the first private motor launches were brought north to ply between Alexandra Wharf and the stations in the North Harbour. On 6th April, 1911, Lerwick Harbour Trust found it necessary to amend their rates of dues bringing motor boats into the same category as sailing boats with steam capstans.

In 1912 the motor boat "Thelma" brought an improved service to the "milk run" between Bressay and Lerwick and in the same year the Trustees ordered for the use of the Harbour Master a fine new motor launch. She was built by Hay & Co. at a cost of £36, and a 7 h.p. Kelvin engine costing £69 was installed by Joseph Gray. On 24th May, 1912, the Trustees had an hour-long cruise through the harbour in their new boat and they reported that everything seemed satisfactory "so far as they were able to judge".

A few weeks later the Trustees received a letter from the Town Clerk of Glasgow suggesting that the harbour should be decorated on 31st August to commemorate the centenary of the launch on the Clyde of the world's first steamship "Comet". The Trustees complied with this suggestion and the harbour front and fish market were decorated with bunting, while flags flew from the Town Hall and County Buildings.

Steam drifters and even sailboats were decked with flags celebrating an event that had brought such mixed fortunes to Britain's farthest North. For although steam applied to communications had brought great improvements, steam applied to fishing had brought changes to which few island fishermen could adapt.

Chapter Nine

THE SMALL BOAT HARBOUR

Although the herring fishery was the major activity of the year being prosecuted by boats and men from all over Britain, the winter haddock fishery between October and April was also of considerable importance and it was carried out entirely by Lerwick's resident fishermen. The Shetland haddock boat could be hauled ashore when bad weather threatened but the heavier and beamier haddock boat introduced by Scottish "immigrants" required year round dock facilities which Lerwick Harbour Trust had not been able to provide. There was also the question of providing accommodation for the pleasure craft displaced from the area below Fort Charlotte when Alexandra Wharf was built. The Trust felt obliged to cater for these vessels too.

The problem was first raised in July, 1906, when Mr Barron, engineer, was asked to provide a plan for a small boat harbour in the problematic area between Alexandra Wharf and the Gas Pier, where earlier it had been suggested that a slipway or floating dock could be provided. On 19th September, 1907, the Trustees actually agreed to proceed with the construction of a harbour for small boats in this area — a project to cost £1,100. One of the reasons for urgency at this time was that it seemed that Alexandra Wharf and the fish market were going to cost less than the first estimate of £13,500 and the Trustees would then lose part of the grant promised by the Treasury. Of course the total expenditure amounted to almost £19,000 including stores, and the plans for a small boat harbour were shelved for the time being.

There was some doubt in the minds of the Trustees as to whether the site was really suitable for development. John W. Robertson was opposed to this project, maintaining that this was the only place where a dry dock could be provided. In any case, he pointed out, the harbour entrance as shown on the

plan would be unsafe during bad weather and in his opinion a
far better site would be found south of Victoria Pier.

The merits of Mr Robertson's suggestions were obvious to
many members of the Trust. Here was a chance to ease congestion on Victoria Pier and provide a more sheltered berth
for the mail steamers besides providing shelter for small vessels.
Enthusiasm mounted and their ideas crystallised in new proposals
put forward at a meeting on 30th December, 1908. These
included the extension of Albert Wharf to meet Victoria Pier
by filling in the existing slipway and the construction of a new
one, the lengthening of Victoria Pier and, most important, the
building of a breakwater out from Hay's Steps towards the
point of Victoria Pier, leaving an entrance 100 feet wide.

Even these proposals did not satisfy John W. Robertson
and at the January meeting he produced his own plan showing
a breakwater 30 feet wide running out from Craigie's Stane
in a N.N.W. direction for 300 feet, then turning N.W. for a
distance of 280 feet. The second arm would be 40 feet wide
to accommodate stores if required. The resulting area enclosed
for the shelter of small boats would be 10,544 square yards as
opposed to a mere 2,777 square yards on the other plan.

In March Mr Robertson's plan was adopted with, in addition,
the extension of Albert Wharf in both directions to meet Victoria
Pier. A memorial was sent to the Treasury for a grant in aid
of the proposed works and preparations were made for a Provisional Order to increase the borrowing powers of the Trust.

But Mr Robertson's ambitions continued to develop and
in June he succeeded in getting the Trustees to incorporate
a floating dock in the proposed works. He had contacted a firm
on Tyneside who suggested that a floating dock suitable for
Lerwick could be got for £10,750.

The Trustees received a great deal of support for their
proposals. Mr Cathcart Wason, M.P., did a great deal of canvas-
sing among other M.P.'s interested in fisheries' development,
while Provost Smith of Leith, a Shetlander by birth and a
champion of the fishermen, succeeded in getting Leith Chamber
of Commerce and the Committee of the Convention of Burghs
to petition the Treasury in support of the Trust's application.
The County Council in lending their support to the scheme,
appointed a committee with Mr J. W. Robertson as convener
to draw up a memorial to submit to Parliament. But in Novem-

ber, 1909, when the Council chose their representative to the Trust, Mr Robertson was surprisingly replaced by Mr J. Jamieson. So the Trust actually lost the member who had done most to promote the scheme.

In January, 1910, the Government turned down the Trust's application for a grant on the grounds that the scheme was too ambitious. And a word of advice came from the Trust's legal adviser, Mr S. F. Sutherland, in Edinburgh. The Trust had been under the impression that they did not require authority from Parliament to build the proposed work. They had believed that they could do as they had done in the case of Alexandra Wharf and extend the works within their rating limits with the sanction of the Board of Trade only, and that a Provisional Order if required would be merely to extend the borrowing powers of the Trust. Mr Sutherland pointed out however that the Act of 1877 laid down certain limits of deviation and while the works carried out previously might reasonably be regarded as modification of the works approved in 1877 the latest scheme was something entirely different.

The Trust accepted this advice and set about drawing up detailed plans to accompany the Provisional Order and on 5th May, 1910, the main points were finalised. To give more room at the neck of the pier, Albert Wharf would be extended southwards to meet Victoria Pier, Victoria Pier itself would be lengthened by 100 feet, while the breakwater would run out from Hay's Steps to a point opposite the tip of the extended Victoria Pier from where an arm would turn inwards for 100 feet not quite parallel to the pier but leaving an opening 100 feet wide at the point and 80 feet wide at the inner end.

In October the draft petition to the Secretary of State for Scotland and the Draft Provisional Order were approved by the Trustees and the Clerk was instructed to submit them to the law agents in Edinburgh for completion. Unfortunately the agent blundered badly and failed to advertise the notice of the Provisional Order in due time. The misunderstanding meant a delay of several months since the Provisional Order could only be brought forward in April — a delay that almost proved fatal to the scheme.

In November, 1910, John W. Robertson was returned as a Trustee representing shipowners. His ambitions for Lerwick were in no way diminished and he was furious that his scheme,

of which the Trustees had once approved, had been pruned so
drastically. He attacked the smaller scheme as one that would
prevent all further improvement of the harbour. It would cost
£15,000, so why not spend another £2,000 and get three times
the wharfage and three times the area of sheltered water?

In February a special meeting was called to discuss Mr
Robertson's motion that the harbour scheme be amended. Mr
Barron had costed both schemes and came to the conclusion
that the larger scheme would cost £27,500 and provide only
9,211 square yards of sheltered water, so that for an extra 2,200
square yards of shelter the cost would be £10,000.

Mr Robertson disagreed with Mr Barron's calculations and
pointed out that in his scheme the breakwater ran almost north-
south and would divert the heavy seas during southerly gales. In
the smaller scheme, on the other hand, the breakwater ran out
at right angles to the shore and this would cause a heavy backwash during stormy weather and create problems for the owners
of property to the south.

Mr W. A. A. Tulloch supported Mr Robertson's motion
but other members of the Trust argued that a great deal of
expense had already been incurred and to amend the Provisional
Order would involve added expense and considerable delay. It
was decided by five votes to four with three abstentions to
proceed with the Provisional Order as decided at the meeting
of 5th May, 1910.

The fishermen of Lerwick were unhappy with certain aspects
of the scheme and on 21st April, 1911, a deputation called on
the Trustees with their grievances. But the fishermen did not
object formally to the Provisional Order and it was passed as
Lerwick Harbour Order Confirmation Act, 1911. It gave the
Trust powers to levy, for the first time, dues on certain classes of
shipping within the conservancy limits of the harbour. Vessels
transhipping herring inside the conservancy limits would in future
pay a charge of 2/6 (12p) a trip or 2d per register ton, while
the dues on fresh fish would be raised from 1d to 3d per cran
and for the first time dues would be levied on coal hulks. Another
important change inaugurated was that instead of holding office
for one year a Trustee would serve for three years, but that
one seat in each of the four categories should be contested each
year in rotation.

The Trust decided to proceed with the works as authorised

and Mr Barron was again requested to prepare working plans and specifications which were ready in April. They showed a 25 ft wide breakwater to be built of concrete running out from Hay's Steps. Victoria Pier was to be extended and the existing slipway on the north side of Victoria Pier was to be filled in and a new one erected in line with the face of Albert Wharf. In May the sanction of the Board of Trade was received and the Development Commissioners were approached for a grant of £10,000. To ensure a supply of stone the most northerly of the South Ness quarries was rented by the Trust.

In August the Development Commissioners approved a grant of £7,500 and a loan of £2,500. The Trustees were delighted by this offer and letters of thanks were sent to Mr Cathcart Wason and Provost Malcolm Smith for their help. The Chairman who was going south on holiday was instructed to arrange a meeting with the manager of the Union Bank in Glasgow to arrange the necessary advance to get the works under way.

As often happens, amendments were made to the plan before work started. It was agreed to abandon the proposed slipway at Albert Wharf and to run a seawall from the south east corner of the wharf to a point 30 feet west of the east end of the existing slipway where the Harbour Master kept his boat. On the other side of Victoria Pier two slipways were planned — one southwards from Victoria Pier and one from Hay's Pier northwards along the Esplanade. Each would be 70 feet long. It was also agreed to make the return arm of the breakwater parallel to Victoria Pier — not angled as shown in the original plans — while the entrance between the breakwater and Victoria Pier would be a uniform 85 feet.

In December, 1912, tenders for the scheme were invited and that of Messrs Kinnear, Moodie & Co. of Glasgow was accepted. The contract price was £31,401 — a considerable increase from the first estimate of £17,000.

Although the Provisional Order had gone through Parliament unopposed, the real opposition was only encountered after the building contract had been signed. Local fishermen drew up a petition which they sent both to the Development Commissioners and the Scottish Fishery Board objecting to the scheme. They pointed out that the cost had soared to over £30,000 and would in all probability reach £45,000 when engineers' fees, etc., were taken into consideration, and yet the public had not been consulted. More specifically the fishermen declared that the site chosen was unsuitable as a fishing harbour. Most fishermen resided in the North Road area and it was a long way to have to carry lines and gear to and from the South Esplanade. In their opinion the fishing harbour should be constructed somewhere north of Victoria Pier. Finally, the entrance to the harbour as shown would be unsafe in bad weather, when it was needed most, because of the mooring chains of mail steamers berthed at Victoria Pier. The petition was signed by 121 men—practically all the fishermen of Lerwick.

Public feeling was aroused and a public meeting called by the Town Council was held in the Town Hall on 22nd January, 1913. This was an unprecedented move on the part of the Town Council and many of the Trustees regarded it as unwarranted interference in their affairs.

The meeting highlighted the split both in the community and among members of the Trust. Speaker after speaker condemned the scheme, but although the opposition was overwhelming there was a lack of unanimity as to the grounds for objection. Some people maintained that the scheme was too expensive and would be a drain on the slender resources of the Trust. Another group, solidly behind John W. Robertson, maintained that the scheme did not go far enough and would stifle all future development. The fishermen had their supporters, maintaining that nothing short of a new site north of Alexandra Wharf would satisfy them. On one point all were agreed — the Trust must pause and reconsider the scheme.

On 31st January, 1914, the Trustees met to consider a letter from the Fishery Board concerning the fishermen's petition. In his reply the Clerk pointed out that the petition was prepared and circulated after the tender for the new works had been accepted and that the site which the fishermen said was too far from their homes was only 400 yards from the spot which they themselves preferred. Furthermore it was untrue that the public had not been consulted since the plans had been adopted at a meeting of 5th May, 1910, and were confirmed at the monthly public meeting of the Trust and discussed at 28 subsequent meetings. At every stage the changes and modifications had been discussed fully in the local press.

The Development Commissioners, pressed by the Town Council to hold a public enquiry, wrote asking if the Trust were irrevocably committed to the construction of a small boat harbour south of Victoria Pier. The Clerk was instructed to reply that work had already started.

In the midst of all this controversy Messrs Kinnear, Moodie & Co. began to assemble their material. In February they began to build a cement store below the Post Office and the first consignments of timber arrived on the s.s. "St. Magnus". Considerable interest was aroused when a power house with gas engines was erected in front of Messrs Goodlad & Coutts premises on the South Esplanade. Three electric cranes were erected, one beside Albert Wharf, and one at Hay's Pier, while the largest was erected at the point of Victoria Pier, and to enable work to start immediately an old fashioned steam-powered crane began dredging operations. Finally the smack "Bertie" arrived with a cargo of explosives to enable blasting operations to commence at the South Ness quarry and at the concrete deck of the Esplanade south of Victoria Pier where it had to be removed in constructing the new slipway. While work proceeded on the extension to Victoria Pier the "North of Scotland" Shipping Company was given use of Alexandra Wharf and the Smith Dock Trust Company's store until May, 1914, when the demands of the herring industry made a return to their normal use imperative. Clerk of Works was Mr William Low of Aberdeen.

In the meantime in June, 1913, there had been another change in the clerkship of the Trust with the death of Arthur Sandison. His successor, Peter Brown, who for three years had been Assistant Clerk to the Harbour Master, was appointed on 31st July. Soon afterwards a Board Room and office for the Clerk was provided in the Harbour Master's office and this became the meeting place of the Trustees.

At first work on the scheme went ahead at a satisfactory rate, then it slowed down alarmingly. The contractor blamed the late delivery of materials, which was apparently a common complaint at that time in all parts of Britain. In February, 1914, there were two unforeseen delays, the first caused by the breakdown of the gas engines, and for several weeks it was possible to operate only two of the cranes at one time. Further delay was caused by a strike among the 50 or so workmen who demanded a pay rise of 1d an hour. They agreed to resume work when the contractor offered a rise of ½d an hour, bringing their hourly rate up to 5½d.

G

But February also produced progress when the Public Works
Loan Board offered a loan of £20,000. This was accepted upon
security of a mortgage of all the property and income of the
Harbour Trustees to be repaid with interest of 4¼% per annum
by half-yearly instalments by way of an annuity in 50 years.

Events in the summer of 1914 caused further delay in the
completion of the scheme. It had been intended to deck the
surface of Victoria Pier in Caithness flags but no shipping was
available to convey them and the Trust agreed to settle for
concrete instead, with a pipe track covered in granite setts from
Nesting. The contract period expired in December and the
Trustees threatened to enforce the penalty clause. But the contractor pointed out that the outbreak of war had made it difficult
to obtain materials.

The final stage of the operation was marred in January,
1915, by the drowning of two men in a boating accident while
erecting a profile at the return arm of the breakwater.

By July the work was practically complete and the contractor began to dismantle his plant. In December of that year
dues were fixed on vessels using the small boat harbour. For
steam trawlers the rates were £1 for the first day and 10/- (50p)
per day thereafter, for steam drifters the dues were lighter at
£1 10/- (£1.50) for the first four weeks and £1 for each four-
week period thereafter. Small boats under 20 feet long would
be charged 1/- (5p) per day or 15/- (75p) for a period of six
months, while for those over 20 feet the rates would be 1/6
(7½p) and 25/- (£1.25) respectively. Boats not engaged in fishing
would be charged at the rate of £1 for six months if under 20
feet long, and those over 20 feet £2 for six months, while small
boats calling from Bressay, Nesting and other places would pay
6d (2½p) per trip.

These rates on small boats caused a furore in the town
with the owners of pleasure craft complaining that since Lerwick
Harbour Trust had embarked on their schemes of improvement,
the owners of small boats had been chased from place to place.
The Trustees had an obligation to provide accommodation in
the small boat harbour either free of charge or at a nominal
rate, and if the proposed rate was enforced the owner of a small
boat costing £5 would pay in three years in dock dues the whole
initial cost of his vessel.

Inshore fishermen complained that they would find it impossible to operate from the new harbour and the town's people in general feared that they would lose a valuable source of fresh fish if instead of selling direct to the public the fishermen were forced to go north to the Docks and dispose of their catches to the curers. The Town Council discussed the question of dues at their January meeting and urged the Council's representatives on the Trust to have the matter reconsidered.

The Trustees heeded the protests of the inshore fishermen and made a concession whereby they would be allowed to sell their catches in the small boat harbour without charges being levied, on condition that they leave it immediately afterwards. The others were unsuccessful in their protests and they remained resentful — especially the owners of pleasure boats who were indignant that large vessels such as steam drifters were permitted to berth in what had been planned as a harbour for small boats. In fact the owners of pleasure craft fared very well since for the next three years no charge was levied on their use of the dock.

The small boat harbour was a successful scheme from many points of view and although inadequate for Lerwick's fishing fleet it was the first real dock provided by the Trust. There was an unfortunate sequel to its construction for, just as one of the Trustees had predicted, the backwash from the breakwater during south-easterly gales produced an outwards suction which had a disastrous effect on the adjacent property —the Queen's Hotel. This was overcome by building a protective wall which the Trustees were forced to provide after a protracted legal battle that went on from 1915 to 1917 and known in legal circles as Miss Hay versus Lerwick Harbour Trust. But this paled into insignificance when compared to a far more serious conflict that raged world-wide throughout this period.

Chapter Ten

LERWICK AT WAR

After the stirring days of the Napoleonic wars, Lerwick adjusted to an era of peace without prosperity. There was so little opportunity at home that many island seamen retained their links with either the Royal Navy or Merchant Service. In the winter of 1861-62 a unit of the Royal Naval Reserve was established at Fort Charlotte and by 1870, 400 reservists drilled there. In 1875 when the County Buildings were erected the room in Fort Charlotte formerly used as a court house became vacant. It was transformed into a large drill hall and the number of reservists steadily increased until between 1,000 and 1,400 men reported every winter.

At first gunnery practice was carried out at the Fort with 32-pounders, the target being at Cruister in Bressay but the people there were alarmed and in 1868 a new battery was erected at the North Ness. When gunnery practice was being carried out a floating target was anchored in the North Harbour and on the following day the fishermen of Lerwick would earn a few extra shillings by dredging for the balls.

After the erection of the North Ness battery two 6½ ton Armstrong guns were emplaced at the Fort for demonstration purposes and in 1883 John M. Aitken erected another battery there. In February, 1905, by which time they had been replaced by more modern guns, the 6½ tonners were sold. Only the carriage fittings were considered worth salving and the guns themselves were dumped into the embankment being formed for Alexandra Wharf.

The influx of reservists every winter was a great source of income to Lerwick's landladies. A well meaning attempt to improve accommodation was made in 1877 when property was acquired on the South Esplanade to be turned into a Seamen's Home. But the scheme was unsuccessful because the reservists actually preferred the old system which was cheaper and the home was closed in 1879. Most of the "dreelers" lodged in

Burns Lane and Reform Lane and their basic diet was sillocks "pocked" at Victoria Pier.

Lerwick's interest in the Royal Navy was undeniable but there was great disappointment locally at the lack of interest shown by the British government in Lerwick Harbour. Kirkwall and Scapa Flow were considered far more important while Lerwick was regarded merely as a minor port. Lerwick was visited by the Channel Fleet in 1861 and two years later the Duke of Edinburgh visited Lerwick while a midshipman on board H.M.S. Rangoon. The Reserve Squadron visited Lerwick in 1883 but again this was merely a courtesy visit such as was made regularly to minor ports in all parts of the country. On one occasion the Admiralty was requested to send down a portion of the Channel Fleet but Their Lordships stated that they could not do so because there was insufficient room in the harbour to accommodate the fleet.

As had happened before in the history of Lerwick another nation — this time Germany — began to show an interest in the harbour. In May, 1894, a German squadron of five ships arrived under the command of Vice - Admiral Koester whose flagship was the "Baden". In May, 1900, the Germans sent nine ships to Lerwick, two of them being the largest in their navy. They made a magnificent spectcle as they entered the harbour. First came the cruisers "Jagd" and "Hela", followed by the battleships "Sachsen", 'Wurtemberg", "Kaiser Friedrich III", "Kurfürst Friedrich Wilhelm", "Brandenburg", "Wessenberg" and "Woerth". The two cruisers proceeded to the North Harbour where the "Jagd" narrowly missed grounding on Loofa Baa, while the seven battleships anchored in line, the most southerly lying off the Ham, Bressay. The visit was extremely successful and was marred only by the desertion of two sailors from the "Kurfürst Friedrich Wilhelm".

In the House of Commons, Sir Leonard Lyall asked why R.N.R. men in Shetland did not have a chance of seeing a British fleet and had to derive their ideas about battleships from German fleets. Mr Goschen replied that although Lerwick had not been visited recently it was possible that a squadron, or part of one, would visit the port when again in that area.

But the next important fleet to visit Lerwick was again a German one when 32 vessels of the German Active Fleet arrived on Saturday, 23rd July, 1904, and stayed for several

days — the most impressive display of maritime might ever seen
in Shetland although exceeded in numbers by King Haakon's
fleet in 1263. Ashore the Germans were correct in their behaviour
although many people were annoyed by the number of cameras
and the desire to photograph practically everything in and
around Lerwick.

On Monday the fleet began to disperse but it was not
until after 10.00 pm that the last vessel, the Admiral's flagship
"Kaiser Wilhelm II" got under weigh. Even then the proceedings
were not over. About midnight the sound of gunfire was heard
and ironclads were seen in the Bay of Quarff as part of a mock
attack on the approaches to Lerwick. About 2 am a number
of torpedo boats entered the harbour by the north entrance
and left the same way—a feat that caused surprise locally that a
foreign fleet should possess such accurate knowledge of Lerwick
Harbour. Once inside the harbour the torpedo boats set off
coloured rockets signalling the success of their "surprise
attack".

Many British newspapers expressed their disgust that a
friendly visit should have ended in a night attack on the town
where they had been entertained as guests. But the Germans
were delighted with the success of their visit. They had learned
a lot about Lerwick and its approaches, its safety and its dangers.
As the fleet dispersed eastwards they ripped through the nets of
the Sandwick herring fleet resulting in nine claims for damage
amounting to £19. Except in one case the Germans admitted
liability and compensation was paid to the claimants by the
German Vice Consul in Lerwick. It was a cheap price for
Germany to pay for knowledge which might well be useful to
her in the future.

It seemed that at long last the eyes of the British government were opened and it was announced that Lerwick would
be favoured with a visit from the Channel Fleet in September,
1904. Great preparations were made in town and country to
make the visit a success and Lerwick Harbour Trust had repairs
effected at the landing steps of Victoria Pier, Albert Wharf and
the South Esplanade. But instead of the 15 ships expected only
four arrived. The rest had gone to Kirkwall, the explanation
being that the weather was too rough and Lerwick Harbour
too small to accommodate the whole fleet. Very few men were
allowed ashore and an officer was rarely seen. No attempt was

made to learn anything about Lerwick or its approaches so the visit was of no practical value to the British Naval Authorities as well as being a keen disappointment to the people of Shetland.

However the navy atoned in full for this disappointment when in September, 1905, 13 ships of the Channel Fleet arrived at Lerwick and carried out a full programme of naval exercises, sporting engagements and public functions. Lerwick rose to the occasion and provisions were found for 8,000 extra men. There was a feeling of satisfaction that Admiral Wilson had proved once and for all that Lerwick could provide anchorage for a large fleet of modern warships.

In the next few years naval vessels made occasional visits to Lerwick. In April, 1909, Lerwick Town Council wrote to the Admiralty reminding them of the facilities Lerwick could provide and as if to prove their continuing interest in the port, H.M.S. "Dreadnought", flagship of the Home Fleet, broke off her exercise in the Orkney area to visit Lerwick in May. But in 1910 Lerwick received a setback when it was decided that all R.N.R. shore bases should be closed. It was claimed that much of the training given at these bases was devoted to gunnery practice which few reservists would be required to put into practice. Shipboard knowledge, on the other hand, would be a decided advantage and thereafter periods of training would be done at sea.

Relations with Germany rapidly worsened. In January, 1912, members of Lerwick Town Council discussed a circular from the Lord Mayor of London asking if the Council could do anything to remove the cause of misunderstanding between Great Britain and Germany. The Provost stated that Lerwick had always been friendly with Germany and Bailie Goodlad moved that the Council express their most friendly feelings towards the German nation. But this expression of goodwill from Britain's farthest North could do nothing to stop the deterioration in Anglo-German relations and by the summer of 1912 Shetland was being described as "the stopper in the bottle" to hold the German fleet in the North Sea.

The first sign of the growing strategic importance of Lerwick was the construction of a lookout station on Anders Hill in Bressay — Lerwick's early warning station from where news of the approach of enemy vessels could be signalled to the town.

In March, 1914, work began on a large wireless station near

the Loch of Trebister on part of the Scattald of Sound resumed from crofting use by its proprietor, Sir Arthur Nicolson. The contract was awarded to Alex Hall of Aberdeen who also built the new Post Office at Lerwick. In April the people of Lerwick were given their first glimpse of a motor lorry — that used by the contractor to carry material from the harbour to the site.

On 19th May, 1914, Lerwick Harbour Trust discussed an application from the contractor for permission to store sand and gravel on a site behind the fish market. The application was refused on the grounds that there was insufficient room. The Trustees could not have realised that this was the last occasion for some time on which they were at liberty to refuse an application of this nature.

THE OUTBREAK OF WAR

June, 1914, had all the signs of normality. A large British fleet was engaged in the herring fishing and foreign vessels called regularly for shelter and for stores. The German fishery cruiser "Zeiten" spent three days at Lerwick and in one week 33 German drifters called at the port to tranship their catches to Emden. Another caller was the German fishery cruiser "Poseidon" studying the effects of trawling on North Sea herring stocks.

But underneath the appearance of normality international trust was crumbling and events elsewhere in Europe dictated the course of events in Lerwick too. On Saturday, 2nd August, notices were sent to all R.N.R. men in Shetland ordering them to report to Lerwick and next day the Territorials were called out. On the 4th Britain declared war on Germany; young Germans engaged in the herring trade left in a hurry, and fishing operations came to a premature halt.

On 6th August, Lieutenant Colonel Evans arrived at Lerwick to assume control of the islands and of the few hundreds of reservists and Territorials who in those early days constituted the islands' only defence. He announced changes in the conditions of service in the R.N.R. Reservists would be allowed to continue their civilian occupations but must be ready to report to Fort Charlotte at short notice.

During the next few years Lerwick found itself in the front line of activity as a steady stream of naval vessels and merchant ships called at the port. Battle-scarred vessels frequently limped into harbour and survivors of torpedoed ships were given food and clothing before continuing their journey south. And Shetland's own contribution to the war effort was soon to be evident as contingents of R.N.R. men marched through the streets to the harbour and the troopships waiting to take them away. On 13th June, 1915, local Territorials followed in the troopship "Cambria". Many of them never saw their homes again.

In November, 1914, Lerwick was established as an examination base and a base for auxiliary patrol vessels under the command of Captain Startin as Senior Naval Officer, his headquarters being the yacht "Shemara". During the ensuing winter all fishing vessels on passage to and from Iceland, Faroe and the White Sea had to call at Lerwick for instructions. In the first 11 months of 1914 only 99 steam trawlers had called at Lerwick but in December alone the number was 250.

In March Captain Startin was relieved by Commander H. G. Alston as S.N.O. and an office was established ashore in the north end of the Fish Market. In the meantime under the Defence of the Realm Act the Admiralty had taken over the northern portion of Alexandra Wharf and the Fish Market while the stores let to the fish trade were sub-let to the Admiralty.

On Monday, 12th April, 1915, a fire broke out in the net loft of the building leased by the Lowestoft Steam Herring Drifter Co. Ltd. and Peacock and Co. Ltd. Bystanders must have been surprised at the efforts of the naval authorities to evacuate the area. The spectators did not know of the deadly contents of the store below which contained several hundredweights of T.N.T. stored there without the knowledge of Lerwick Harbour Trust.

At 12.58 pm (just before lunch-time) the whole town was shaken by a tremendous explosion which lifted the store bodily into the sea while debris flew in all direction. Seven people were killed including four Shetlanders, one of them a 15 year old boy who had been watching the fire from the Esplanade behind the building. 20 people, some of them badly injured, were carried on stretchers to the Gilbert Bain Hospital.

Extensive damage was done to surrounding property within a wide radius of the deep crater where the store once stood. The adjacent building leased by the Smith Dock Trust Company was wrecked. Almost every window in the Fish Market building was shattered and the roof was badly damaged while Brentham

Place also suffered severely from the explosion. The staff of the Customs and Excise, then occupying a room at the front of Brentham Place, had a fortunate escape being warned in time that an explosion was expected. Naturally the disaster caused indignation that explosives should be stored in a residential and commercial area but there was relief that the death toll was not higher.

The demands on the Trust's property continued. In the summer of 1915 the Harbour Master's boat was rented to the Admiralty at £1 a month. The whole of Alexandra Wharf was taken over by the Admiralty and a Church Army Hut was erected at the back of the Fish Market where torpedoed crews were given dry clothing and accommodation if needed. The auction hall of the Fish Market assumed a new role being used for church services by ratings on the trawler patrol service.

On 29th August, 1915, H.M.S. "Brilliant" arrived at Lerwick and took over the duties of guard and depot ship at the base. She remained at Lerwick until 27th January, 1918. In September, Lerwick became examination centre for neutral ships sent in by the 10th Cruiser Squadron. This work was carried out on a large scale and in the quarter July-September, 1916, 269 ships were examined. The sight of so many fine ships at anchor brought delight to many people in Lerwick. On one occasion there were seven full-rigged ships anchored in the harbour. This work achieved good results and in one year alone 150 suspects, many of them Germans, were removed from intercepted vessels.

In February, 1916, under the provisions of the Military Service Act, all single men between the ages of 18 and 41 were conscripted. Some the Trustees maintained that Peter Brown, Clerk to the Harbour Trust, should be exempt from military service on account of the vital work he was doing. But some of the Trustees decided otherwise and at a special meeting in March they claimed that there were older men available to do his job should he be called up. Mr J. T. J. Sinclair moved that the claim for exemption be recalled and this was seconded by John W. Robertson. Mr Robertson said he was confident that a qualified man could be found to act as Clerk. The position would only be temporary, Mr Robertson continued, and Mr Brown's job would remain open to him after the war — if he was spared to come back.

So Mr Brown found himself in the army and Mr W. A. A.

Tulloch, a partner in the firm of Laurenson & Co., resigned from the Trust to take on the duties as Clerk. He did not take on the task of collecting dues, this difficult job falling as an extra burden on the Harbour Master.

THE GREAT CONVOY SYSTEM

In March, 1917, the convoy system was introduced to overcome the alarming loss of allied ships due to action by U-boats, a loss then estimated at a million tons a month. Under the new system merchant ships were convoyed in groups from other British ports to Lerwick from where they were escorted by naval vessels and armed trawlers across the North Sea. In less than one year 4,500 vessels of 5,000,000 tons were brought into Lerwick harbour. The port saw unprecedented scenes of activity since in addition to the concentration of merchant ships a large number of naval vessels, drifters and trawlers were engaged in fighting the submarine menace. The greatest concentration of vessels is said to have occurred on 23rd September, 1917, when 139 vessels were in port including 55 merchant steamers.

On 17th October, 1917, occurred one of the great dramas of the war. A convoy of 12 neutral ships being escorted to Lerwick under the protection of the anti-submarine destroyers H.M.S. "Mary Rose" and H.M.S. "Strongbow", was attacked from the rear by three German cruisers. Without hestitation the two destroyers turned to face the enemy in full knowledge of the fate that awaited them and they fought until they were completely crippled by the heavy German armament. Having sunk the destroyers the cruisers pursued the fleeing merchant ships and exacted a fearful toll. Only three of the twelve escaped, their safety purchased by the delaying action of the destroyers. 88 officers and men of the "Mary Rose" and 47 of the "Strongbow's" complement were killed. The disaster left a deep impression on Lerwick where the destroyer's crews had many friends.

This was only one of many such dramas enacted in the waters around Shetland. On 30th June, 1917, the destroyer "Cheerful" was blown up by a mine off Heliness, the tragedy being witnessed by many people in Lerwick and Bressay. Only 18 of her complement were rescued.

On 12th December, 1917, another frightful tragedy occurred when a convoy on its way to Lerwick was attacked and the destroyer "Partridge", four armed trawlers and six merchant ships were lost. On yet another occasion two convoys, one incoming, the other outgoing, collided almost stem on in the darkness of a stormy night. Each convoy believed it was under attack and chaos ensued. Several ships were sunk including the destroyer "Marmion".

On 8th October, 1917, there was yet another change in command at Lerwick and the flag of Rear Admiral Greatorex was hoisted at Fort Charlotte. The new S.N.O. took over Brentham Place which was quickly transformed into naval headquarters.

Although Lerwick was protected by submarine-proof boom defences, U-boat minelayers frequently laid mines right up to the rock nose at Bressay lighthouse in the path of incoming or outgoing convoys and every morning at dawn a flotilla of sweepers left Lerwick to clear a channel two miles wide and 12 miles long. One of the minelayers, U 55, was sunk outside the harbour when she developed a fault and had to surface. Eight of her crew were rescued and brought to Lerwick.

Early in 1918 Lerwick ceased to be a convoy port but in May the Northern Patrol Force was established instead. This consisted of H.M.S. "Implacable", H.M.S. "Gibraltar" and a large number of sloops, hydrophone trawlers and attendant destroyers, all engaged in extensive anti-submarine operations.

On 7th February, 1918, another tragedy at Alexandra Wharf shocked the whole town. A naval electrician and several ratings were working on the stern of the trawler "Tenby Castle" trying to rectify a fault in a depth charge when it exploded, killing four men. The stern of the trawler was shattered and again buildings in the vicinity of the wharf were damaged.

No discussion of Lerwick at war is complete without mentioning the contribution made by John W. Robertson. His coaling business was commandeered by the Admiralty and he ran the business on their behalf. By this time he had two repair shops under his control for in 1916 he acquired the Iron Works at Freefield on the death of John Brown and he ran this in conjunction with the Malakoff yard. Most outstanding of all was Mr Robertson's contribution in the field of marine salvage. Among the remarkable feats he carried out was the refloating, using the technique of coffer damming, of the 4,000 ton steamer "Margarita". She had struck a mine outside Lerwick Harbour and while being towed in sank at Twageos. Another feat was the refloating of the 5,000 ton Roumanian steamer "Juil", ashore at Sound. After repairs had been effected by Mr Robertson's workmen she was able to proceed to the Tyne under her own steam.

FINANCIAL PROBLEMS FOR THE TRUST

The drop in revenue as a result of the war was a serious problem for the Trust. The revenue for 1915 was only £3,556 — a decrease of £2,473 compared to 1914. Shore dues from goods carried by the "North of Scotland" Company's steamers showed a drop of £244 and tonnage dues on their vessels dropped from £629 to £427 due to the discontinuance of the direct steamer to Aberdeen during the summer months and the reduced number of trips to the North Isles.

The fall in revenue came at a difficult time since the Trustees were struggling to complete payment to the contractor for the small boat harbour scheme whose cost had risen to over £36,000. To add to these difficulties there occurred the destruction of the two stores at Alexandra Wharf and serious damage to the fenders of the wharf caused by continual use by large naval vessels.

The Trust sent the Admiralty, a claim for £3,582 for damage caused by the explosion, but the Lords Commissioners of the Admiralty responded with a cheque for £1,186 "purely as an act of grace and without any admission of liability on the part of the Admiralty". The accompanying letter explained that payment must be accepted as a final settlement and no correspondence would be entered into with regard to it. The Clerk was instructed to acknowledge receipt of the cheque which sum had been placed to account of the Harbour Trustees' claim against the Admiralty.

Because of the deficit for 1915 the Trust found it impossible to meet their liabilities to the Public Works Loan Board and by March, 1916, three instalments amounting to £1,104 remained unpaid. The Trust sought authority to suspend repayment to the P.W.L.B. or alternatively to be allowed to offset the sum owed by the Admiralty against money due to the P.W.L.B. The Board sympathised with the Trustees in their difficulty but would not agree to suspend repayment while there was still a large Reserve Fund to draw on. There was indeed a sum of

£3,000 held in reserve but this was due to be paid to the contractor although retained as a guarantee until minor defects in the extension to Victoria Pier were repaired. As regards the suggested offsetting of money the Board would not even consider it.

In the circumstances the only way to increase the Trust's income was by raising the rates payable by users of the harbour. In May, 1916, the tonnage rate on the "North of Scotland" Company's vessels was raised by 1d to 3d per ton. At the same time it was decided to raise the compound rates for steam drifters to £3 for the summer season and £2 for the winter season. Sailboats and motor boats were overlooked at the time but they too were subject to a 50% rise in dues a few months later.

At the end of 1916 the Trustees, again unable to meet their repayments to the P.W.L.B., were forced to realise their Sinking Fund and although it stood at £2,300, it realised only £1,589.

In August, 1917, the Trustees again increased the rate of dues to the maximum level authorised of 4d per registered ton. The rate on herring landed at the harbour was fixed at 2d a cran and for white fish 2d a score. Nevertheless, the income for 1917 was only £3,513, a drop of £200 over the previous year because the Admiralty had failed to make any payment for their occupation of the works that year whereas in 1916 they had paid £354.

In March, 1918, the Trustees were faced with the added expenses incurred by the case of Miss Hay versus Lerwick Harbour Trust. The Trust would have been in serious difficulties had not the Bank stepped in and agreed to an overdraft of £4,000 to tide them over until the expected compensation was paid by the Admiralty. In August the position eased slightly when the Board of Trade authorised the levying of an *ad valorem* rate of fish landed at the harbour works of 5d per £1 value on herring, and 4d per £1 on white fish, purely as a wartime measure.

THE EFFECT ON THE FISHING INDUSTRY

When the war broke out in August, 1914, there was a large fleet of over 400 vessels at Lerwick but immediately fishing operations ceased. It had been a short season and earnings suffered. Shetland's eight steam drifters averaged only

£610 compared to £1,500 the previous year, while sailboats earned from £400 down. The curers were extremely worried since they had 36,000 barrels on their hands at a time when the German market was closed and the Baltic unsafe as an access to Russia. Yet before the end of the year most of these had been shipped to Russia via Archangel.

During the war fishing was strictly regulated by the Senior Naval Officer who could dictate where or where not to go. In August, 1915, it was decreed that no boat except rowing boats should be afloat anywhere within the three mile limit around Shetland except by permission of the S.N.O. The following April two Lerwick men were fined the large sum of £10 each for travelling to Mid Yell and back without a permit. Small boats were restricted to day time fishing and had to be ashore within 30 minutes after sunset. In May, 1917, piltock fishers sent a petition to Lerwick Town Council asking them to approach the authorities and point out that piltocks only began to take after sunset.

The price of fish rose to a record level. Most of the white fish catch was shipped to Aberdeen to take its chance on the open market. Inshore and part-time fishermen at Lerwick found a ready demand for their catches and sold them direct to the public until as the demand increased they began selling to the highest bidder. Under these conditions there began another innovation — the selling of fish by retail. Early in 1916 Mrs Simon Smith and Mrs Jessie Hay were allocated stances at Albert Wharf by Lerwick Harbour Trust at a rental of 1/- (5p) a week.

The new system was far from popular at first and the retailers were regarded as speculators coming between the fishermen and the customers. In April, 1916, the Trustees discussed the allegedly exorbitant prices being charged by the retailers and resolved to warn them not to commandeer the catches of small boats. In June, 1918, when there were three retailers at Albert Wharf the Trustees were urged to review the situation with the possibility of removing the stalls. The Trustees, however, decided that the retailers were doing a valuable service but they imposed conditions in having the area around the stalls tidied and in raising the rent to 10/- (50p) a week. The price of fish continued to rise. In January, 1918, haddocks realised £3 16/- (£3.80) a cwt. and the retail price rose to a "scandalous" 11d. (4½p) per pound.

The herring fishing suffered most from the war. In 1915 the greatest number of boats to fish from Lerwick was only 44 and the islands' catch was 20,778 crans worth £49,217, most of this being landed at Lerwick. The perils of fishing in wartime were highlighted in June, 1915, when two German submarines like marauding wolves among a flock of sheep terrorised the fleet of steam drifters fishing off Skerries. They sank 16 of them, leaving one or two to carry the survivors ashore. Most of them were landed at Lerwick and accommodation for 140 men was found at the Town Hall.

The 1916 season, on the other hand, was outstandingly successful. The fleet reached a maximum of 210 vessels at the end of May then declined to around 100 for the rest of the season. The fishing continued well into October and earnings were unusually high. The total catch was 129,800 crans worth £199,800. Shetland's fleet included 71 sailers, 12 steam drifters and 12 motor boats. Top boat was the steam drifter "Hamnavoe", belonging to John W. Robertson and skippered by Alex Watt, which grossed £4,000.

The 1917 season was another complete failure, the total value of winter and summer herring fishings being only £39,000. Many of the steam drifters had been taken over by the Admiralty while the "Hamnavoe" was sunk by a German submarine.

The 1918 season produced a total of 27,900 crans of which 10,288 crans were kippered. Late in the season the U.S. government began to allow imports of cured herring and prices rose to an average of £2 a cran, reaching a maximum of £6 6/- a cran in September. It was a successful season for the local fleet with the most successful motor boat grossing £2,850.

THE END OF HOSTILITIES

Early in 1918, when the problem of the U boats was finally overcome, Lerwick ceased to be a convoy port. Gradually it became clear that the allies were winning, although much loss of life was still to come before the end. On 12th February, 1918, the "North of Scotland" Company's "St. Magnus" was torpedoed off Peterhead and a Lerwick crew member was killed at his post in the stokehold and two passengers were killed by the explosion.

Then on 11th November, 1918, the howling of sirens in the harbour signalled for Lerwick the end of hostilities and very soon the harbour front was decorated with bunting. Nevertheless it was many months before the harbour returned to normality.

The winter was fairly quiet at Lerwick, then the following spring the port became an intermediate base for British operations in the North of Russia. A steady stream of troopships, colliers and cargo vessels called at Lerwick on their way north. Then came the evacuation of Archangel and Murmansk and all the traffic came hurriedly back again.

In the summer of 1919 American minesweepers were based at Lerwick for several months as they began clearing the northern minefields. The Americans brought with them their own social organisation, "The Knights of Columbus", which organised dances, boxing tournaments, etc., in the Rechabite Hall. The Lerwick branch of the organisation was based in premises at 135-139 Commercial Street, now occupied by Messrs Hepworths.

Part of Alexandra Wharf was released by the Admiralty to enable the herring fishing to get under way on lines once again approaching normality. Then Rear Admiral Greatorex announced that Lerwick Naval Base would be closed on 13th December, 1919, and that the remainder of Alexandra Wharf would be released from that date.

From January to July, 1920, the salvage steamer H.M.S. "Recovery" was engaged lifting anchors, chains and mooring buoys used in the boom defences and also in July the Admiralty sent s.s. "Isleford" to collect ammunition from the magazines at Fort Charlotte and at the Knab. She was given permission to come alongside Alexandra Wharf on the condition that the Admiralty would recoup the Trustees for any damage done.

The end of hostilities marked the end of an era for Lerwick in more ways than one. So many changes had taken place, so many familiar faces had passed away both at home and on the battlefield. In June, 1915, Mr John Brown, a Trustee for 13 years, and Captain Allison, the first Harbour Master, both died. In December, 1917, the death occurred of Andrew Smith, a man whose personal interests had once been at variance with those of the Trust. He was one of the initial Trustees appointed in 1877 and was the victor in the prolonged and costly Sinclair's Beach case. These were men who had lived long and useful lives with a record of public service remembered long after their deaths. Far more tragic was the loss on war service of young

H

men like Captain John W. Brown, only son of John Brown, drowned at Dunkirk in December, 1916. He should have succeeded his father in his business at Freefield but due to the war a promising life and an important business together came to an end. In every corner of Shetland there were many similar cases to regret as the islands mourned their 600 sons who had died in the service of their country.

Chapter Eleven

BETWEEN THE WARS

The property of Lerwick Harbour Trust had taken a terrific battering during the years of hostilities, most obvious being the scar at the north end of Alexandra Wharf where the net stores had stood. In addition the Fish Market and offices were in a deplorable state, the floors uneven, some of the walls threatening to collapse and the whole building badly in need of redecoration. More serious still was the condition of the sea wall at Alexandra Wharf, especially at the north end where it had been weakened by the explosion on the "Tenby Castle". There was never a time in the history of the Trust when money was so badly needed, but the trade of the port was paralysed with the fishing industry only starting to recover. Income was low and even the legitimate claim against the Admiralty was being rejected.

There was a great deal of work to be done before Alexandra Wharf took on the appearance of a fishing quay. The wharf was littered with temporary stores, canteens and workshops, all playing their part in the running of a naval base, but generally unsuited to peace-time use, at least on the sites then occupied. There were exceptions since the large canteen became a recreation room for fishermen run by the Mission to Seamen (Flying Angel) and in 1920 it was removed to a new site at Holmsgarth. The Salvation Army purchased the Church Army hut for holding services, the Trust giving them the occupancy of the site until Whitsun 1920.

The former Clerk, Mr Peter Brown, was demobbed early in 1919 and applied to be reinstated in his old job. The Trust were in a quandary since they were under an obligation to re-employ Mr Brown but Mr W. A. A. Tulloch was doing such valuable work for the Trust that it was considered unfair to displace him. In the end it was decided that Mr Brown should be given the post of collector of dues.

The Trust were in no position to promote development for some considerable time to come but many small changes

were made, especially in the area of the North Esplanade. In
1917 Mr Corothie's shop in Messrs Gansons' premises on the
Esplanade took fire and the whole building was badly damaged.
The building was purchased by Messrs J. & J. Tod & Sons who
rebuilt it and extended it by incorporating neighbouring premises.
In June, 1919 Ganson Brothers informed the Trust that they
had also transferred their whole right and interest in the store
and steps immediately to the south of the Co-operative Coal
Company's store to Messrs Tod.

The Trustees agreed that it was time the position regarding
this property was regularised. Ganson Brothers had had the use
of the store for a rent of one shilling a year but for the previous
eight years no payment had been made. On the other hand the
Trust had never paid Ganson Brothers the sum of £5 agreed
as part of the bargain for the firm renouncing their rights in
Leask's Jetty. Messrs J. & J. Tod & Sons were anxious to buy
the stores and steps but the Trust discovered that they had no
power to sell and it was agreed to let the store at terms to be
negotiated.

One of the most important changes of this period was the
growing importance of the internal combustion engine both
ashore and afloat. In Lerwick a large number of firms were
set up to keep them in repair and supplied with fuel. In April,
1920, the Trustees agreed to give the Anglo-American Oil
Company a site in the ballast yard north of the coal stores
for the storage of barrels of paraffin. A month later a rival
company, the Scottish Oil Agency Ltd., was granted temporary
use of the site of the old net stores, but in June they obtained
a more suitable site when they rented the more northerly of
the two coal stores. A few months later they purchased a 12,000
gallon tank from the old seaplane base at Catfirth and had a
motor tanker supplying fuel to boats at Alexandra Wharf.

In April, 1921, the Co-operative Coal Company was wound
up and Lerwick Harbour Trust purchased their two stores. The
larger was let to the Scottish Oil Agency Ltd. who then vacated
the other store and in the meantime the Anglo-American Oil
Company were granted the use of the old urinal adjacent to
the ballast yard as a petrol store. Another of the Trust's stores
was let to Mr C. Thomson as a motor garage and in February,
1924, this firm was given permission to erect a second garage
and repair shop north of the first.

The quays and roadways were not designed for motor cars so congestion soon became a problem. The situation was most difficult at Victoria Pier, especially when a steamer was due, and opposite the bottleneck caused by Tod's premises, the oil stores and Thomson's garage. The former trouble spot was improved when regulations were introduced to control traffic on the pier. It was decided that only vehicles carrying invalids or injured persons should be allowed on the pier prior to the arrival or departure of mail steamers, and that at all other times motor cars had to use the stances provided in front of Messrs Goodlad & Goodlad's shop and on the upper side of the South Esplanade below the Post Office. The other hazard was more difficult to tackle and it soon became apparent that the only solution was the widening of the quay. Unfortunately many years were to pass before this could be carried out.

There was a speed limit of 10 m.p.h. within the boundaries of the burgh but it was often ignored. As early as April, 1916, the Trustees were concerned that cars were hurtling over the cobbled surface of the Esplanade at speeds approaching 20 m.p.h. In August, 1922, the Chief Constable decided to secure a prosecution as a warning and armed with a stop watch he stationed himself in the door of the Harbour Office. He did not have long to wait since a young taxi owner, Mr Peter Moar, in a hurry to get home, was charged with exceeding the speed limit. The court was shocked to hear that he had covered the measured distance at 17.3 m.p.h. He was fined ten shillings, in spite of his contention that the timing procedure had not been carried out properly.

In 1923 to improve access by motor lorries the Trust carried out considerable improvements to the steamers' store. The old office at the west end of the building was removed to give more storage space and a new office was erected as a lean-to at the east end. The main entrance door at the west end was then moved to a central position to facilitate the entrance and exit of vehicles and allow goods to be stored along both sides of the building.

The pier itself was subjected to a much-needed "tidy-up" campaign. The shipping company was ordered to remove the sprawling pile of bunker coal used by the "Earl of Zetland", returnable boxes had to be shipped weekly and casks of paraffin were in future to be stored on Albert Wharf. In addition the company was ordered to remove the old gangway once used by the paddle steamer "St. Magnus" together with the old anchors and other scrap that littered the pier.

PERSONALITIES

At the end of the war the Trustees were Messrs John Leisk (Chairman), Sinclair Johnson (Vice Chairman), F. H. Pottinger, P. S. Goodlad (then Provost of Lerwick), J. A. Mair, W. Sinclair, J. T. J. Sinclair, R. D. Ganson, S. W. Fordyce, George Leslie, A. Ratter and John W. Robertson. The next few years however were to see more changes than any comparable period in the history of the Trust.

In January, 1919, the membership was broken by the death of Mr Frank H. Pottinger, one of the County Council's representatives. At the election of 1919 Sinclair Johnson, a Trustee since 1901 and Vice Chairman for 16 years, resigned, since he intended leaving Shetland for New Zealand, and he was replaced as Vice Chairman by John W. Robertson. A newcomer in 1919 was Mr Edwin S. Reid Tait, son of George Reid Tait, one of the original promoters and guarantors of Lerwick Harbour scheme of the 1880's and a Trustee in 1882 when elected by the Commissioners of Supply. Other newcomers in 1919 were J. J. Pottinger and James Laing.

About this time there arose an unfortunate dispute between the Trustees and Mr Russell, Town Clerk of Lerwick. It began when Mr S. W. Fordyce applied to the Trust for the use of the ex-Admiralty carpenter's shed, then used by the Town Council in connection with the supply of water to Alexandra Wharf. Lerwick Harbour Trust requested the Council to vacate the shed and this prompted the reply from Mr Russell that in his opinion it was illegal, if not immoral, to oust a public body merely to accommodate one of their own members.

The Trustees were highly indignant and one of their members, Mr John W. Robertson, felt compelled to resign. He too, was a tenant of Trust property and wished to place himself absolutely beyond suspicion. Fortunately he was not long absent from the meetings of the Trust, being re-elected by the shipowners in 1923.

At the A.G.M. of 1920 Mr John Leisk retired from the Trust, completing a record of 43 years service that has never been equalled. He was one of the original Trustees appointed in 1877 and throughout the long period of 30 years had served continuously as Chairman. He admitted that he had intended to retire three years earlier but the financial position of the Trust was then critical and he was worried in case the public should liken him to a rat leaving a sinking ship. Since then however the fortunes of the Trust had recovered and his only regret was that he had not succeeded in getting the Admiralty to pay compensation for the stores that had been destroyed. He urged the Trustees to press on with their claim. In his place Mr John T. J. Sinclair, first elected in 1916, became Chairman and Mr E. S. Reid Tait became Vice Chairman.

1921 saw more changes, starting in June when Mr Henry Mouat was co-opted to fill the vacancy caused by the resignation of Mr James J. Pottinger. Later in the year the death occurred of Mr J. S. Tulloch, brother of Mr W. A. A. Tulloch, and Legal Adviser to the Trust since 1912. He was succeeded as Legal Adviser by Mr John Small, solicitor. In October the death was reported of another member of the Trust, Mr S. W. Fordyce.

In April, 1922, the Assistant Harbour Master, Sinclair Black, resigned, being replaced by Adam Manson, formerly employed as berthing master, and at the election of 1922 two new members were appointed to the Trust with the election of Arthur Coghill and James Garriock. In September, 1923, tribute was paid to another well known personality, on the death of Mr John M. Aitken, contractor, planner, architect and builder of so many of Lerwick's prominent buildings.

Finally in July, 1924, when he was 72 years old, Captain Gray resigned from his position as Harbour Master, which post he had held for 16 years. In September Captain Gilbert Harrison was appointed to succeed him at a salary of £225 per annum, plus free house and light. He already had an indirect association with the Trust since his father, John Harrison, had been one of the original promoters.

REPAIRS AND MINOR IMPROVEMENTS

The problems that beset Britain in the post-war years were felt as keenly in Shetland as anywhere, with unemployment and low wages combining to cause industrial unrest. Lerwick experienced a strike in 1920 when for 4½ weeks the trade of the port was hampered as 203 men, including engineers, blacksmiths, shipwrights, sawyers, sailmakers and dockers came out on strike for higher wages.

It is indicative of the demand for work that in June, 1920, when it was decided to advertise for a berthing master at £4 a week, 17 applications were received. Fifteen applications were received for the post of mart caretaker and Charles Edwardson was appointed to this job which was now worth £172 a year. In common with national trends Lerwick Harbour Trust began to make the conditions of their employees a little less harsh when in September, 1920, it was decided to institute a weekly half-holiday.

First of the Trust's property to be repaired was the Fish Market building whose octagon was strengthened with buttresses at several of the corners while part of the walls was taken down and rebuilt. In March, 1920, the rebuilding of the net stores was discussed and it was considered essential to have them ready for occupation during the coming season but no contractor would bind himself to complete the work in such a short time.

The question of rebuilding the net stores was discussed again the following year but on the advice of the Chairman it was decided to wait since building costs were then prohibitive and they were still awaiting a settlement of their claim against the Admiralty. The situation was partially relieved in October, 1921, when the Trust accepted the sum of £1,695 for the use of Alexandra Wharf by the Admiralty for the period up to 31st March, 1917. Early in 1922 the Admiralty forwarded a further sum of £1,500 as tonnage dues for the same period and £500 to account in respect of dues incurred after that date.

This came at a fortunate time since the Trust's revenue for 1921 was only £5,335, a decrease of £1,726 compared with 1920. Shore dues were only £1,574 compared with £3,718 the previous year, mainly because the *ad valorem* dues on fish had now been abolished.

In December, 1921, it was decided to proceed with dredging of the quays and small boat harbour, John W. Robertson having offered to remove 16,000 cu. yds. of material at 6/6 a cubic yard. A few weeks later Mr Robertson reported that serious damage had been done to the north-east corner of Alexandra Wharf. He was requested to have the foundations here dredged out to enable a detailed survey to be made.

It was during this operation that the most fascinating discovery ever made in Lerwick Harbour came to light. In 1915 Mr Low had noticed the remains of an old ship embedded in the sand 30 yards north of Alexandra Wharf. In August, 1915, it was examined by Mr John Robertson, diver, who prepared a report for the Trustees. When the question of its removal was being discussed Mr Sinclair caused considerable mirth when he remarked "it may be a treasure ship and well worth lifting".

In February, 1922, it was decided to remove the wreck and Mr J. W. Robertson's dredger "Green Head" was anchored over the spot. It was soon discovered that the obstruction was not merely an old wreck. As the mud was cleared the diver was surprised to find four large cannons, the largest of them being 8½ft. long.

The discovery caused a great deal of interest in Lerwick and a great deal of discussion followed as to the identity of the vessel. The riddle was solved by local historian R. Stewart Bruce who remembered an account of a battle that had taken place in Bressay Sound in 1640 when a Dutch warship and three Dutch armed merchantmen lying peacefully at anchor were surprised by 10 Spanish privateers from Dunkirk. After a violent fight two of the Dutch vessels "De Haan" and "De Reiger" were run ashore on the Lerwick side of the Sound. It was almost certain that one of these was the wreck lying off Alexandra Wharf.

There were numerous signs of the violent action that had taken place. Cannon balls were scattered around the wreck and some were still in clusters (although now held together by barnacles) suggesting that they had been stacked in pyramid fashion for serving the guns. When one of the guns was examined an obstruction was found in the touch-hole which on being removed had the appearance of lead. This suggested that before the ship was abandoned by her crew the guns had been "spiked" to render them useless should they fall into enemy hands.

Confirmation that the vessel was indeed "De Haan" caused a great deal of interest in Holland. The Trustees decided that only one of the guns would remain in Lerwick. It was mounted on a timber platform and put on display at Albert Wharf. The other three were sent to Holland — one to a shipowner in Scheveningen and one each to museums in Rotterdam and Amsterdam.

The excitement obscured for a time the real purpose of
John W. Robertson's investigation on the seabed which was
to examine the state of the north face of Alexandra Wharf.
The diver reported that the sea wall was cracked from top
to bottom and that the foundations were shattered and unsafe
to build on.

There was little doubt that the damage was due mainly
to the explosion that had occurred on the "Tenby Castle" and
as Mr Robertson commenced repair work the Trustees submitted a claim against the Admiralty. But at a special meeting
of the war compensation court in October, 1924, the claim
was finally rejected.

There was a happier conclusion to the Trust's other claim
against the Admiralty. In September, 1922, the latter agreed
to pay the sum of £2,000 in full and final settlement of the
Trust's claim for compensation for the loss of the net stores,
in addition to the sum of £1,186 previously paid. In agreeing
to accept this the Trustees paid tribute to the efforts of Sir
Malcolm Smith, then M.P. for Orkney and Shetland, for the
valuable assistance he had rendered.

Almost immediately Peter Thompson, architect, was instructed to prepare plans and specifications for the new stores.
In February, 1923, Messrs Robertson & Johnson's tender amounting to £2,980 was accepted and Peter Thompson was appointed
Clerk of Works to supervise the building.

Between 1923 and 1925 minor but very effective improvements were made to the North Esplanade between the oil stores
and the junction below Harbour Street. Part of the wall at
the north end was removed to give traffic coming down Harbour
Street a better view of the north-bound traffic on the Esplanade,
the high wall being replaced by an iron railing set in a low
concrete wall. Further south the steep wooden steps linking
Commercial Road and the Esplanade were removed in the
interests of safety and the opening was closed.

On the other side of the road a retaining wall and pavement
were erected between the Fish Market and the Gas Pier. The
timing of this scheme was deliberate since it was carried out
to provide work for the large number of unemployed men in
the town.   Three-quarters of the wages bill was met by the
government's Unemployment Grants Committee.

DEVELOPMENT PLANS

Soon the Trust's financial position brightened sufficiently for major schemes to be considered. As early as June 1923 the Chairman, Mr J. T. J. Sinclair, had laid before the Trustees his suggestion for the widening of the roadway south of Alexandra Wharf by constructing a new sea wall to connect Albert Wharf and Alexandra Wharf. The scheme was also intended to provide much needed additional accommodation for the large fleet of drifters that again fished from Lerwick.

As usual the Trust's ambitions were set in motion and soon a second part of the scheme was being discussed for the widening of Victoria Pier by a roughly triangular section 60 ft. wide at its base tapering to 8 ft. at the point of the pier. After discussing these proposals with Sir Robert Hamilton, who had displaced Sir Malcolm Smith as M.P., it was decided to concentrate on the Albert Wharf — Alexandra Wharf scheme.

A new firm of consulting engineers, Messrs. Henderson & Nicol of Aberdeen, was appointed to advise the Trust and in February, 1924 Mr. Archibald Henderson visited Lerwick to discuss the scheme. Plans were drawn up and the cost was estimated at £18,500. The Fishery Board and the Development Commissioners were both approached for assistance and both replied favourably, the former offering a grant of £1,000 and the latter one of £5,200.

But before the necessary legislation could be inaugurated to raise the Trust's borrowing powers the Trustees were faced with the far more serious problem of further repair work required at Alexandra Wharf. The seriousness of the situation was first recognised in April 1925 by the diver John Robertson, who effected temporary repairs at the south corner of the wharf. Messrs. Henderson & Nicol drew up plans for permanent repairs to this section and estimated that the job would cost £3,200.

Preliminary survey work went ahead with John Robertson, the diver, doing probing work to determine the length of sheet piling required. But as the evidence from the seabed accumulated it became obvious that there was something very far wrong with the entire length of Alexandra Wharf and eventually the consultants declared that the whole of the seawall would have to be rebuilt. From the nature of the seabed as shown by probing, the consultants decided that sheet piling was unsuitable and that the new wall should be of stone and concrete.

There was a delay in starting work but eventually in February, 1927 a committee consisting of Messrs. Ganson, Shearer and Laing was appointed to supervise repairs. A quarry was opened in the Gilbertson Park by arrangement with Lerwick Town Council and soon afterwards the Scapa Flow Salvage and Shipbreaking Company Ltd., of which Mr. John W. Robertson was a director, began dredging at Alexandra Wharf to prepare the excavations for the new wall.

While this work was going on another interesting old wreck was discovered at the south end of Alexandra Wharf. A 38 ft. long section of a ship's keel was brought ashore and again local historians began thumbing through their files. The wreck was identified as the Dutch ship "De Reiger" run ashore at the same time as the "De Haan".

Following the commencement of repair work the Trustees turned their attention to the Draft Provisional Order which was necessary to extend their borrowing powers. Among powers sought were permission to connect the two wharves, to levy dues on aircraft and seaplanes, to levy dues on fish cured or preserved on board vessels and on fresh fish loaded within the harbour limits. Haste was essential since the Trust had to meet Parliament's March deadline and besides the gloomy reports on the state of Alexandra Wharf made it imperative to raise a loan to finance repair work with the minimum of delay.

Unfortunately the hasty start almost proved fatal for the Provisional Order since a serious error was incorporated in the preliminary notices. Although the Trustees intended raising the entire scale of dues by 50 per cent the Clerk was under the impression that this income would apply to cargo dues only and not to tonnage dues. Perhaps the Trust's Legal Adviser should have spotted this discrepancy in the preliminary notices and queried it. Nevertheless the Clerk, Mr. W. A. A. Tulloch, accepted full responsibility for the mistake and felt compelled to resign. In his place Mr. Peter Brown was once again appointed Clerk. Fortunately the Trust were not denied Mr Tulloch's services for long since he was reappointed a member of the Trust in 1929.

The Legal Agents found it impossible to make any alterations in the order and even recommended that it should be withdrawn and a new one introduced in the autumn session of Parliament. But the urgency of the situation with regard to Alexandra Wharf made this suggestion untenable. The Association of British Chambers of Commerce suggested a legal formula to overcome the difficulty by proposing that the standard revision clause should be included in the order to give the Trustees powers to raise their schedule of dues.

But as had happened so often in the history of Lerwick Harbour Trust, objections were raised against these proposals. This time Messrs. James and Charles Mitchell, representing a large group of fish merchants and others, insisted that the proposed amendment of tonnage rates be abandoned and that the Trust's borrowing powers be restricted to £20,000. In the face of all these pressures the Trustees had to abandon their attempts to raise the rates merely to save the Provisional Order which became law on 21st December, 1927.

Towards the end of 1927 there was a change in the chairmanship of the Trust. Mr Sinclair resigned although remaining as a Trustee and his place was taken by Mr E. S. Reid Tait while Mr Henry Mouat became Vice Chairman.

Repair work commenced and by the end of February, 1928, 280 feet of sea wall had been built at a cost of £9,270. The new sea wall ran from the north end to a point opposite the south end of the Fish Market building from where it ran off at an angle to meet the old southern section at a point 50 feet south of the pronounced "kink" thus hiding thereafter this prominent feature of the original face.

The overdraft with the Union Bank now stood at £15,000 and accordingly plans were made for application to the Public Works Loan Board for a loan of £20,000. The Fishery Board helped with a grant of £1,000 then in August 1928 the P.W.L.B. offered a loan of £12,212 on condition that the Trustees would agree to raise the compound rates on all vessels engaged in the herring fishing as from 1st May, 1929. The Trustees had no choice but to accept this condition and accordingly raised the rate on steam drifters by £1, on motor boats by 10/- (50p) and on sailboats by 5/- (25p).

Renewed protests came from the fishing industry. Major Jackson of the L.S.H.D. Company protested that the fishing industry was being asked to bear the burden of repairs on behalf of all users of the wharf. Mr R. Ollason, Secretary of Shetland Fishermen's Association, backed him with the protests of his members. In December 1928 a deputation of boatowners met the Trustees to try and persuade them to retain their rates at the old level. The fishermen were reminded that the Trust had intended to raise all their dues by 50 per cent but the fishermen and others by their objections had forced the removal of this clause. Now the Trust had no choice but put the increase into operation if they wished to avail themselves of the loan offered by the P.W.L.B. and without a loan the wharf would simply fall into the sea.

Alexandra Wharf was saved but the new sea wall cost a total of £21,000. Thanks to the objections raised against the Provisional Order the sum which the Trustees were authorised to borrow was sufficient only for the cost of these repairs. The proposal to widen the roadway south of Alexandra Wharf had to be dropped and the bottleneck at Tod's premises continued for many years afterwards.

CHANGES IN THE FISHING INDUSTRY

On 3rd June, 1919 the sale of herring was resumed at the Fish Market after a lapse of four years while the building was occupied by the Admiralty. The fleet gradually built up until 205 vessels fished from Lerwick at the height of the season. The total catch that year was 145,000 crans worth £196,000, much of it being sold for kippering.

The steam drifters commandeered by the Admiralty during the war were returned to their owners and in 1920 the first of the Admiralty drifters to be sold to ex-servicemen came to Lerwick. Under this scheme Mr. John M. West purchased the drifter "Glacier" and renamed her "Girl Joey" and John Watt, formerly skipper of the "Gracey Brown", purchased the drifter "Grey Sky" newly built by Forbes of Sandhaven.

The lack of suitable dock accommodation remained a problem since the small boat harbour was obviously far too small even for the fleet of haddock line boats that berthed there. In May 1920 Mr. E. S. Reid Tait moved at a meeting of the Trust that "nothing bigger than a Burra Isle fishing boat" should be allowed inside the dock but the Trustees decided that they could not refuse any sector of the fishing industry since the dock had been built with a grant from the Fishery

Board. In November 1923 the Trustees decided to heed the protests of small boat owners by giving the owners of steam drifters and flit boats one month's notice to remove their vessels from the small boat harbour. At the next meeting however this decision was overturned and instead the Harbour Master was authorised to organise berthing inside the dock .

The number of sailboats continued to fall although their loss was compensated for to a certain extent by the growing number of motor boats. In 1920 when 358 steam drifters were based at Lerwick the number of sail boats and motor boats were 80 and 65 respectively. Of local vessels only nine were steam drifters whereas there were 71 sail boats and 42 motor vessels.

The closure of both the German and Russian markets was a serious blow to the herring industry, and although the market for salt herring gradually improved it never regained the position it had held in pre-war years. In 1921 10 cargoes of roused herring were sent to Hamburg and Altona thus opening a market that had been closed for many years. This outlet increased in importance and in 1926 there were three firms engaged in freshing, as this activity was known. The freshers rented part of the breakwater, Albert Wharf and the north end of Alexandra Wharf and paid between £20 and £30 a month in addition to normal scheduled dues on cargoes of herring.

The Lowestoft Steam Herring Drifters Co. Ltd. were still prominent as boatowners and fishsalesmen. Soon after his return from the war Mr. Bertie Robertson succeeded Mr. Frank Smith as local manager while the company's directors, Messrs. Jackson and Sargeant along with Wilfred Haynes, salesman, were familiar figures at Lerwick during the summer season. In 1934 Mr. Alex. J. Gear joined the firm as junior clerk soon becoming active in the actual selling of fish. Mr. Gear was to play a prominent part both in his company and in the affairs of Lerwick Harbour Trust.

The herring industry declined throughout the 1930's yet Lerwick retained the position as one of the great herring ports of Europe. To help visiting crews locate the yard of the curer who had bought their catch the stations were given numbers running consecutively from the North Ness to Grimista and then south along the Bressay shore. The numbers were displayed prominently either on a notice board or painted on the walls of the curing sheds.

The haddock line fishery remained the chief occupation of the winter months, the new motor boats proving specially suitable for this type of fishing. In 1926, seining, a new type of fishing, was introduced to Shetland but many years passed before it ousted line fishing from its position of importance. Most of the catch was purchased by firms in Lerwick and packed in ice for shipment to Aberdeen where it was sold on the open market.

There was a small outlet for local consumption and the retailers had by this time become an accepted part of the community, although Lerwick Harbour Trust found it difficult to decide on the best position for their stalls. In 1922 they were removed from Albert Wharf to the open space south of the Fish Market and in 1926 they were moved again to a site behind the Fish Market south of the latrine on the east side of the retaining wall. In February 1927 the occupants of the stances were Miss Aggie Smith and Messrs. James Fraser, H. M. Johnson and John Sales. This site was never satisfactory and in 1943 the stalls were moved again to Albert Wharf.

Prominent among promoters of the fishing industry as of so many related fields was John W. Robertson. By 1921 he was Convener of the County and in the preceding 15 years he had built up a large business as ship and boat owner, boatbuilder and engineer. He was also a salvage contractor soon to be heavily involved in salvage operations at Scapa Flow. In addition he was a dock owner with 10 acres of property at Garthspool formerly owned by Andrew Smith, a builder and contractor, a coal and general merchant, and a fishcurer and fishsalesman with 70 boats on his books in 1921.

The hub of this vast business was the Malakoff yard where he had built carpenters' sheds and engineering works housing the latest appliances including air compressors and pneumatic tools while his oxy-acetylene plant, installed in 1917, was the first in Shetland. The whole property including net lofts and general store was lit by electricity generated on the premises.

At the Malakoff yard Mr Robertson built a patent slip, a project that for many years he had urged Lerwick Harbour Trust to undertake. The opening ceremony was performed on 25th February, 1921 when the steam drifter "Sumburgh Head" was hauled clear of the water. Thereafter the slipway was in constant use and not only by local vessels. An interesting visitor from Faroe, the old smack "King Arthur" formerly owned by Andrew Smith, arrived at Lerwick in October, 1921 with a cargo of wet salted cod for Hay & Co. and her skipper was glad of an opportunity to have his vessel slipped for overhaul.

ASPECTS OF SAFETY

The years following World War 1 saw several attempts to make Lerwick Harbour and its approaches safer. In 1921 the wireless station near the Loch of Trebister was transferred to the Air Ministry and converted into a meteorological station. The following year Lerwick Harbour Trust suggested that the Met. Office in London should provide daily weather forecasts in the national press. The director replied that arrangements were being made to include reports from Lerwick in the sheet of observations issued to the press each evening. The Chairman of the Trust commented that what was wanted was prospective not retrospective reports. Fortunately the station at Lerwick was soon to play its part in the steady improvement in forecasting weather conditions in the entire Shetland area.

Improvements were made in the harbour itself when in 1926 submerged rocks off Gordon's Station, Bressay and at Mitchell's Station, Hays' Quay and Holmsgarth were marked by red conical buoys. About this time the Commissioners of Northern Lighthouses agreed to alter the coloured areas of Rova Head Light to assist navigation in the vicinity of the Skibby Baas.

In 1925, H.M.S. "Beaufort" was engaged in hydrographic surveys in the Shetland area and at the suggestion of Lerwick Harbour Trust the Admiralty agreed to take the opportunity for a re-survey of Lerwick Harbour on a larger scale than had previously been done.

Although not a compulsory pilotage port, Lerwick had several pilots licensed by the Trust who offered their services to stranger vessels. In July, 1927 the Board of Trade suggested that the Trustees should consider the desirability of reorganising this service on lines generally adopted by other pilotage authorities in the U.K. The Board suggested the introduction of a Pilotage Order and By-laws including a revised schedule of pilotage rates in accordance with the Pilotage Act of 1913. This course was followed and new rates were fixed for pilotage within the limits of the harbour between Bressay lighthouse and

I

Rova Head. Inward rates were fixed at from £1 10/- (£1.50) to £10 depending on the size of the vessel while outgoing vessels were charged at half the inward rates.

1930 was a year of tragedies around Shetland. On 29th March the Aberdeen trawler "Ben Doran" was wrecked on the Ve Skerries, a dangerous ridge of rocks lying north-west of Papa Stour. Lerwick Life-Saving Company and the crew of the Burra Isle fishing boat "Smiling Morn" made valiant attempts to rescue the crew but the situation was hopeless and as the "Ben Doran" broke up her crew were drowned. It came as a shock to many people in Britain to realise that there was then no lifeboat stationed in Shetland, the nearest one being at Stromness in Orkney. This vessel was indeed called out to assist the "Ben Doran" but she arrived on the scene three days after the stranding occurred. Later in the same year the mail steamer "St. Sunniva" ran aground on the island of Mousa on her way to Lerwick. No lives were lost but the vessel became a total wreck.

These accidents highlighted the need for proper lifeboats to be stationed on both the east and west sides of Shetland. Lerwick station was opened in July 1930 when the lifeboat "Lady Jane and Martha Ryland" was commissioned. Her first task was carried out on 21st February, 1931 when she went to the aid of the Faroese ketch "Nolsoy" and towed her to Lerwick. She only had time to refuel before being called out again, this time to the aid of the steamship "Everline" of Riga, disabled by an 80 m.p.h. gale off Ramna Stacks. The crew were taken off and brought to Lerwick. By the end of 1931 Lerwick Lifeboat had saved 34 lives.

THE YEARS OF FRUSTRATION

The 1930's were frustrating years for the Trustees. As the herring industry declined the Trust's income fell and although several schemes were proposed they came to nothing. The main problem was still congestion on Victoria Pier and the North Esplanade which was now having to carry the bulk of the traffic from Victoria Pier to practically the whole of Shetland.

There were two proposals — the widening of the roadway and the building of a new sea wall to link Alexandra Wharf and Albert Wharf. The Trustees applied to the Ministry of Transport for a grant but the M.O.T. replied that only if the roadway were to be taken over by the local highway authority would they even consider the possibility of a grant. In June 1930 the Secretary of State for Scotland visited Lerwick to see at first hand the problems faced by the Trust. The result was the offer of a grant by the Treasury but the Trustees considered the offered sum inadequate considering the state of the Trust's funds.

In this period of general stagnation a welcome diversion took place on 7th January, 1933 when the old gas lights along the seafront were replaced by electric lamps served from the municipal scheme. The switching-on ceremony was performed by Mrs. Reid Tait, wife of the Chairman. The new lighting system consisted of eleven 200 watt lamps from the breakwater along the Esplanade to Alexandra Wharf and two 300 watt lamps at the point of Victoria Pier and at the point of the breakwater. It was claimed that this scheme made Lerwick one of the best-lit ports in the North of Scotland.

But not even the brightness of the harbour lights could dispel the gloom that pervaded Lerwick at this period. The main overall problem was unemployment with all the social ills that follow in its wake. As a special concession the Trustees gave permission for card games to be played in the Fish Market in the evenings but this concession was withdrawn in February, 1934 when one of the net stores was let as a workmen's club at a rent of 12/6 (62½p) a week. The club was governed by stringent rules and it was closed at 11 p.m. on week nights and remained closed all day on Sunday .

Another diversion occurred in August, 1933 when the Lindberghs, the famous pair of pioneer aviators, called at Lerwick after a flight from Faroe. And a month later an R.A.F. flying-boat landed in the harbour.

There were minor changes in the operation of the port. In 1934 by-laws were approved by the Trustees to put a stop to the practice of pumping out bilge water into the harbour. Inevitably changes occurred too, in the membership of the Trust and many familiar figures passed away. In December, 1935 Mr. J. T. J. Sinclair died. He first became a Trustee in May 1916 and in 1920 he succeeded Mr. John Leisk as Chairman. In March 1936 the Trustees paid tribute to Mr R. D. Ganson, a member for 31 years and in October they recognised the service of the late Mr. W. P. Harrison who served on the Trust between

1912 and 1918. Another former member, Provost P. S. Goodlad passed away in November the same year.

On 23rd June, 1936 a ceremony was held to commemorate the 50th anniversary of the opening of Victoria Pier. The s.s. "St. Sunniva" and s.s. "Earl of Zetland" were dressed overall for the occasion. The former was a new vessel built to replace the former holder of the name wrecked on Mousa but the latter was the same old "Earl of Zetland" that had lent dignity to the occasion 50 years before.

A cake and wine banquet was held in the Town Hall when tribute was paid to John Leisk and others who had paid such a prominent part in the development of the harbour. One of the current Trustees, Mr. W. A. A. Tulloch, had been present at that memorable occasion in 1886 when as a Free Mason he bore the vase of oil at the laying of the foundation stone. It was also mentioned that one of the subscribers to the preliminary expenses fund, Mr. Thomas Ogilvy was still alive although unable to attend.

Sheriff Wallace, in his speech, referred to the problems of the herring fishing and the practice of dumping large quantities of unsold herring into the harbour while in the south consumers were being charged 2d for "a small flabby herring hardly worth cooking." He urged the industry to devise some means of bridging the gap between producer and consumer.

In November, 1936 Mr. Reid Tait resigned from the Chair being replaced by Mr Mouat while Mr W. A. A. Tulloch became Vice Chairman. In June 1937 the clerk, Mr Peter Brown, died after a long illness and Miss M. M. Reid became Interim Clerk, at a wage of 30/- (£1.50) a week but in July Mr. Arthur Laurenson was appointed Clerk at a salary of £175 a year. Other changes occurred the following year when Mr. Tulloch became Chairman and Mr. James Laing, Vice Chairman.

By 1937 the Trust's financial position had improved considerably since the initial loan of £20,000 had been fully repaid and a fairly large Reserve Fund had accumulated. Again the Trustees began to plan the developments that would alleviate congestion in the harbour area. For some time they were under the impression that having repaid the loan of £20,000 they were thus entitled under their existing powers to raise a fresh loan to this amount but the Scottish Office explained that each Provisional Order related to a specific scheme and that a new order would be required for the scheme being contemplated.

Mr Nicol of Henderson & Nicol was commissioned to draw up plans for the widening of Victoria Pier at its base with a "fillet" 164 ft. long to accommodate the new inter-island steamer which the shipping company was then having built. It was also intended to widen the North Esplanade by joining Alexandra Wharf and Albert Wharf. At the same time negotiations began with Zetland County Council with a view to their taking over the North Esplanade to relieve the Trust of the burden of its upkeep. The whole scheme was estimated to cost £37,000 so the Trustees agreed to seek authority to extend their borrowing powers to £40,000.

The pattern of shipping had changed drastically since pre-war days and goods for the entire North Mainland were now passing through Lerwick in addition to those for the South Mainland and North Isles. It was decided to seek powers to widen the Trustees' franchise to enable merchants all over Shetland to have a say in electing ratepayers' representatives, but Lerwick Town Council insisted that this right should remain the town's alone and by formally objecting they succeeded in having the offending clause removed from the Provisional Order.

Tenders for the new works were invited and that of Mr W. J. Anderson of Aberdeen amounting to £36,632 was accepted. But the Lerwick Harbour Order was not confirmed until 29th September, 1939, by which time Britain was again at war and all works of improvement were suspended. It seemed for a time that the widening of the Esplanade would be permitted, using the Reserve Fund, but the Secretary of State for Scotland refused to grant permission for even this to proceed.

Chapter Twelve

WORLD WAR TWO

Throughout the spring of 1939 as relations with Germany steadily worsened there were ominous signs that conflict was inevitable. An R.A.F. flying-boat base was established at Lerwick and naval vessels began to call in increasing numbers. In April, the month that recruiting started, the s.s. "Eurylochus", of the Blue Funnel Line, docked at Alexandra Wharf to unload a large cargo of general stores. 430 feet long and of 5,723 tons gross, she was the largest vessel ever to have berthed at Lerwick.

But the summer took on a semblance of normality with a large fleet of drifters and motor boats engaged in the herring fishing while Deufrika, the German firm of freshers, were heavily engaged in running cargoes of roused herring to Altona. One of the freshers' staff made no secret of the fact that he was an ardent Nazi. He was also an enthusiastic photographer and went nowhere without his miniature Leica — a practice that caused a certain amount of disquiet among his friends in Lerwick.

August saw the arrival of the new "Earl of Zetland" and the departure of the old vessel that had served the North Isles for a remarkable 62 years. But within a few weeks the old vessel had returned to serve another six eventful years while the new vessel was put into service as a troopship running across the Pentland Firth.

In September, Europe was once again plunged into war and it was soon clear that Shetland was again in the front line of the war at sea. Early in October the Swedish steamer "Vistula" and the British steamer "Sea Venture" were torpedoed south-east of Muckle Flugga. The crew of the latter took to the boats and Lerwick lifeboat left her base to search for them. The torpedoed seamen saw the lifeboat's searchlight but did not respond since they assumed wrongly that the U-boat had returned to complete her job of destruction. The lifeboat put into Baltasound and eventually the survivors from the "Sea

Venture" landed on a beach at Skaw where the lifeboat picked them up and brought them to Lerwick.

German aircraft were soon familiar visitors over Lerwick keeping close watch on developments there, but their mission was not confined to surveillance alone. On 22nd November, 1939, six Heinkel bombers appeared so suddenly that the air-raid warning was not given until the planes were directly over-head. They came in low over the rooftops and circled the town several times before attacking a flying-boat anchored in the North Harbour.

At least eight bombs were dropped on the solitary flying-boat but all missed. Then one of the planes swooped down and machine gunned the flying boat until it was ablaze. The crew members were seen to jump overboard and almost immediately two haddock boats, the "Olive", skippered by John T. Watt, and the "Nellie", skippered by Joseph Watt, put off to the rescue. They picked up six men clinging to the sides of the burning plane while the seventh swam ashore to a herring jetty about 500 yards away.

In December a new kind of warfare started as German aircraft attacked British trawlers on the fishing grounds east of Shetland and several damaged trawlers were brought into Lerwick to have temporary repairs effected. One of the worst of the early incidents of this type involved the Aberdeen trawler "Star of Scotland" while fishing east of Fetlar. A bomb landed between the wheelhouse and the funnel, killing two of her crew and wounding five.

Like Orkney, Shetland was practically sealed off from the rest of Britain, becoming what was known as a protected area, and no one was able to enter or leave the islands without per-mission. Communications with the south became very erratic since the steamers "St. Sunniva", "St. Magnus" and "St. Clair" were all commandeered by the Admiralty, being replaced by smaller vessels such as the "St. Fergus". Vessels sailing from Shetland had to sail in convoys which entailed considerable delays for those who had to travel.

THE FALL OF NORWAY

In April, 1940, Germany invaded Norway, being anxious to obtain seaports north of the bottleneck between Shetland and Scandinavia. British troops were sent across to assist the

Norwegian forces and both the s.s. "St. Magnus" and s.s. "St. Sunniva" took part in this campaign. But resistance was futile since the Germans had planned their attack carefully and were firmly entrenched in Norway. Battered British destroyers limped into Breiwick to have repairs effected while the remnants of Norway's own navy and mercantile fleet also sought refuge in Shetland's voes.

At the end of April when the campaign in the south of Norway was over the small destroyer "Sleipner" made a dramatic entry at a speed of 18 knots into Lerwick harbour, to escape from the German cruiser "Nuremberg". She was desperately short of fuel and water after being at sea for three weeks. During the space of two weeks she had been attacked every day by German aircraft and on one occasion had had 20 bombs dropped around her. But she had successfully fought off all attacks and had even shot down a Heinkel.

On 3rd May the small Norwegian cargo vessel "Borgund" arrived at Lerwick and in addition to her crew she carried a number of Norwegian soldiers guarding 42 German prisoners who had been captured during the early part of the campaign. As the prisoners marched under an armed guard to a place of detention one of them was recognised as having been employed by Deufrika at Lerwick the previous summer. He was none other than Karl Viet, the chap who had carried the Leica. The friendly banter that passed between him and some of the by-standers caused raised eyebrows on the part of the Naval authorities.

In the first two weeks of May about 15 Norwegian fishing vessels and cargo vessels arrived at Lerwick with servicemen and civilians and no fewer than 56 British soldiers left behind at the evacuation of British troops. Many of the Norwegian servicemen remained at Lerwick, becoming attached to a British unit and waiting patiently for a chance to return to their own country. 17th May is an annual holiday in Norway, commemorating that country's independence from Denmark in 1814. In 1940 it was celebrated in Lerwick by a parade of Norwegian service-men and a dinner in the Grand Hotel at which Lieutenant Juliebø presided. The principal speech was delivered by a seaman, Mr Kvalheim, in civil life an insurance agent, who referred to the German occupation of his country and the role to be played by the small band of exiles. "Let us hold together", he declared, "and do our duty, so that we may once again become a free people in a free land".

In the next few months there came a steady stream of refugees from Norway. They came in rowing boats and fishing boats, many of them poorly prepared for their journey across the North Sea. How many were lost in the attempt we shall never know. It is estimated that more than 5,000 civilians escaped to Britain, most of them via Shetland, the peak periods for escape being May, 1940, and the autumn of 1941. In 1941, 1881 refugees passed through Lerwick, the peak month being September with 518. A Home Office camp for refugees was set up at Holmsgarth where for most of the time Mr and Mrs James Adie were in charge.

LERWICK AT WAR

Within a few weeks of the outbreak of war Lerwick had the appearance of an armed fortress. Protective walls of sand bags were built around the G.B. Hospital, the power station, the County Buildings and other important buildings, while a first aid centre was set up in St. Clement's Church. Soon units of the Royal Artillery, Royal Engineers, Royal Army Medical Corps, Royal Signal Corps, Black Watch, Gordon Highlanders and H.L.I. were stationed in and around the town. Gun emplacements were erected at the Greenhead, the Knab and the Ness of Sound, while the harbour was protected against submarines by boom defences. The Home Guard were much in evidence doing guard duty at the pier barriers, the Knab and the Docks.

As in the first world war Lerwick's civilian population played a great part in the war effort. Hay & Co. and Robertsons (Lerwick) Ltd. played an important role as suppliers of coal and their respective coal hulks "Havana" and "Creteground" still occupied prominent places in Lerwick Harbour. The "Creteground" was actually a relic of World War I, one of a class of concrete-hulled freighters hastily moulded in America in a desperate attempt to compensate for the heavy loss of ships by enemy action.

In this war the oil companies had an important part to play. Scottish Oils had by this time vacated their premises at the North Esplanade and had moved to a yard at the North Ness, oil being supplied by pipelines to Alexandra Wharf and to their own private fuelling jetty at the North Ness.

It was there that an accident occurred which might have had serious consequences. On 30th May, 1940, the flitboat "Lilybank" was loading petrol for Grutness when she went on fire. Her crew tried to scuttle her but the water proved too shallow. The situation was saved by Mr James Hall, a sailor, who swam to the blazing vessel and attached a line to her. She was towed out into the harbour by a drifter and was eventually beached in the North Harbour.

In June, 1941, Mr John W. Robertson was appointed to act as salvage contractor for the Admiralty and for the R.A.F., and his drifter "Maid of Thule" was actively engaged in raising sunken aircraft and vessels and salving valuable cargoes. Mr Robertson performed some remarkable feats, using his combination of experience and ingenuity, often with the simplest of materials. On one occasion a Sunderland came down in the sea three miles north-west of Herma Ness and drove ashore at Wood Wick on the west side of Unst. "J.W." had the plane filled with 500 herring barrels and towed her to Cullivoe where she was beached and repaired sufficiently for her to be towed to Sullom Voe.

The crew of Lerwick lifeboat spent long hours at sea searching for survivors of ditched aircraft and torpedoed vessels. In December, 1939, they spent a difficult night at sea searching for the Swedish tanker "Gustaf Reuter" which struck a mine south of Shetland. In spite of mountainous seas and Arctic-like conditions nine survivors of the stricken vessel were rescued and taken to Lerwick, some to receive treatment in the G.B. Hospital.

The entire population of Shetland helped the war effort in some way or other. During November and December, 1940, by holding dances, whist drives and house to house collections, the sum of £6,000 was raised to buy a Spitfire. A much more ambitious target was set for War Weapons Week of October, 1941, when the public was asked to invest their savings to help the war effort. The target was £60,000 but in fact the total raised in this way was £282,363. The campaign was marred by a tragedy in the skies over Lerwick when two Blenheims taking part in a flying display came too close together. Their wings touched and one crashed at the Knab, killing three men, while the other crash landed in Bressay without loss of life.

German planes continued to be a threat to civilians, attacks being made on a variety of targets including the "Earl of Zetland", schoolchildren at Whiteness, and the Scalloway bus, while the lighthouses of Skerries and Fair Isle were attacked on several occasions. At both of these places the wife of a keeper was killed.

A still greater threat however came from the sea in the form of mines washed up on the beaches. On 25th November, 1941, a mine exploded below Lerwick's new cemetery killing a Lerwick man, Mr Allan Laurenson, and two ratings from the nearby Knab Camp who were assisting him.

Mr Laurenson was one of the most popular young men in Lerwick, well known as a businessman, yachtsman, a member of the lifeboat's crew and, not least, for his interest in the work of the G.B. Hospital which led to his appointment as Hon. Treasurer in 1937. When war broke out he volunteered for service in the navy and obtained a commission as sub-lieutenant in the R.N.V.R. attached to the naval base at Lerwick, subsequently being promoted to the rank of Lieutenant. His death cast a tremendous gloom over the whole town.

At 7.30 p.m. on 23rd January, 1942, a night of snow with a gale from the south-east, a mine exploded at Breiwick damaging nearby houses, knocking off chimney pots and stripping slates from the roofs of houses in Breiwick Road. Work began to secure the damaged houses when a second mine went off killing a warden, Mr Walter Jamieson, who had been busy boarding up windows. These mines wrecked the houses around Slates Road and lower Breiwick Road.

With daylight Breiwick Road presented a dismal picture without a single whole window in the fronts of the houses. Many of those at the rear of the houses had also been smashed and huge rocks thrown up by the exploding mines had fallen through some of the roofs. Forty houses had been evacuated as had the G.B. Hospital.

Mr Jamieson was another extremely well known and popular figure in Lerwick. His death was all the more disturbing since the mines were reported to the naval authorities on Friday afternoon and they apparently did nothing to prevent the tragedy.

THE NAVAL BASE

Throughout the six years of war a steady stream of vessels

called at Lerwick to refuel, for repairs or for shelter. Almost every day a fresh surprise greeted the townspeople as troopships, tankers, supply ships, destroyers, corvettes, mine layers and mine sweepers anchored in the harbour or berthed alongside Alexandra Wharf.

Submarines were especially numerous as they broke off their hunt for enemy shipping to refuel and rest their crews. In November, 1941, that successful pair of hunters, "Trident" and "Tigress", called briefly to refuel after sinking eight German ships in Arctic waters. Their numbers increased throughout 1942, British vessels being joined by Norwegian, Polish and Dutch submarines. In January, 1943, a great deal of interest was shown in a different type of submarine, an ex-German U-boat captured a short time before by the crew of a British flying-boat. Russian subs began to arrive and in May, 1943, an American vessel made her first appearance.

The submarine war gained momentum throughout 1944 with a large number of these vessels being based at Lerwick. For a time it seemed that they added to their score on every mission —the "Sceptre" had ten kills by April, 1944, while the "Ula" flaunted eight bars and two daggers, signifying eight vessels sunk and two successful commando raids on Norwegian soil.

THE NORWEGIANS FIGHT BACK

In the autumn of 1942 a flotilla of Norwegian motor torpedo boats was stationed at Lerwick. These were very fast vessels built of wood, highly camouflaged and fitted with torpedo tubes and anti-aircraft guns. In addition to attacks on German vessels they carried out the same kind of operations as the special naval unit at Scalloway — laying mines, landing agents and military equipment, organising escapes and carrying commandos for attacks on specific targets. They were joined by a flotilla of British M.T.B.'s engaged in similar activities.

The people of Lerwick could always sense the growing excitement among the Norwegians that heralded an attack on Norway. Then they watched as the vessels slipped their moorings and wondered how many would return. Usually the Norwegians arrived in jubilant mood, sometimes flying the Jolly Roger to denote a kill, while bandaged heads and arms in slings were a cheap price to pay for success against the enemy. On other occasions there was less jubilation as badly wounded men were transferred to the G.B. Hospital, some to die from wounds received in their homeland. On one occasion the entire crew of a M.T.B. were captured by the Germans and shot.

Most of the M.T.B.'s were based at the south end of Alexandra Wharf, while others berthed at the North Ness at Mitchell's Yard and the Anglo-Scottish Station. Here a camp of wooden huts was erected to accommodate the men while the old Anglo-Scottish herring jetty was extended. On 14th April, 1943, an explosion occurred on an M.T.B. berthed at the North Ness, killing one man and injuring four.

A greater tragedy occurred at 8.30 a.m .on 21st November, 1943, when a British M.T.B. lying alongside a Norwegian vessel took fire and her cargo of high octane fuel exploded, killing eight men. Both vessels blazed furiously until sunk by gunfire. In view of the danger of further explosion the area was evacuated and Commercial Road was closed to traffic. This proved a wise precaution since about 9.20 a.m. a much more violent explosion shook the town, causing widespread damage. At least 50 plate glass windows were blown in between MacLeod & MacLean's premises and Freefield Pharmacy.

From August, 1943, a number of smaller Norwegian vessels, originally whalers, were stationed at Lerwick to provide escort service between Lerwick and the Scottish mainland, to work on patrols around the islands and to act as mine sweepers on the approaches to Lerwick harbour. On other occasions they were given the more exacting job of towing M.T.B.'s towards Norway. The M.T.B.'s with their powerful engines and high speeds used an enormous amount of fuel so were often towed across the North Sea so as to have full tanks when they entered Norwegian waters.

THE END OF HOSTILITIES

Sunday, 3rd December, 1944, was the official date for the stand down of the Home Guard. It was marked by a parade in Lerwick with a march past the County War Memorial. Shetland's Home Guard unit had been one of the best armed in Scotland and at its maximum strength it numbered 1501 men — a creditable figure considering how many Shetlanders were on active service. On Monday, 7th May, 1945, came the news which the country had so long awaited, when the B.B.C. announced that Germany had surrendered unconditionally.

Victory was celebrated next day with bunting flying along the seafront from Alexandra Wharf to Victoria Pier, while the s.s. "Blyth" was dressed overall. Norwegian flags were much in evidence and there were even one or two American flags. As darkness fell the sky was lit up with Verey lights and rockets and on the square at Ronald Street an effigy of Hitler was burned on top of a bonfire.

Next day Provost Magnus Shearer sent a congratulatory telegram to Air Chief Marshal Tedder who as Deputy Supreme Commander signed the surrender terms in Berlin. The telegram ended "Many of the older citizens remember you in your early days in Lerwick". Lerwick was proud of its association with Air Marshall Tedder. Indeed many townspeople had been class-mates of his at the Anderson Educational Institute while his father was supervisor of the Inland Revenue at Lerwick between 1894 and 1898 and the family lived at Braeside, Law Lane.

The following Sunday, thanksgiving services were held, and in a victory parade the various Navy, Army and R.A.F. units and the Home Guard, Police and Civil Defence services marched through the streets. Members of the Royal Norwegian's 54th M.T.B. Flotilla and the 52nd Flotilla of the Royal Navy took part in the parade but left soon afterwards for Norway. They were determined to be in Norway for Norwegian Independence Day on the 17th which, that year, had a special significance.

On Saturday, 19th May, great interest was shown in two surrendered U-boats that called at Lerwick for fuel escorted by the Canadian frigate "St. Pierre". They were part of a group of 15 U-boats being escorted to Loch Eriboll. Refuelling completed they set off to rejoin the others and people in the villages along the east side of Shetland had a marvellous view of the procession as it continued southwards.

After their welcome in Norway the M.T.B.'s returned to Lerwick for the last time. Their crews had learned what provisions the people needed most after their years of privation and hundreds of pounds were spent in Lerwick's shops on flour, oatmeal, coffee, sauces and condiments. Then in ones and twos they took their leave of Lerwick. The largest group of six M.T.B.'s left on Sunday, 3rd June, their crews lined up on deck as they passed close by the front of Alexandra Wharf which was crowded with their many friends in Lerwick. They proceeded slowly out into the south harbour, gathered speed as they passed the South Ness and soon they disappeared eastwards around the Bressay Lighthouse thus bringing to a close another exciting chapter in the history of Lerwick.

Gradually Lerwick began to take on its usual summer appearance as local boats began fishing for herring. The "St. Magnus" arrived from Aberdeen sporting her peace-time colours of black hull, white topsides and yellow masts and as for the first time since 1939 her whistle sounded to signal her arrival it was clear that Lerwick was returning to normality.

Three months after the end of the war in Europe Lerwick joined in the celebrations to mark the victory in the Far East. The "St. Magnus" was dressed overall and the seafront was again decked with bunting while the celebrations on Commercial Street went on for most of the night.

A few days later the 220 ft long German submarine U-776 arrived at Lerwick in the hands of a British crew and went on show at Alexandra Wharf. It was one of this class that penetrated the defences of Scapa Flow in October, 1939, and torpedoed the "Royal Oak". But U-776 was a new vessel with only two cruises to her credit and none of her torpedoes had made a kill.

The s.s. "St. Clair" returned to civilian life after an exacting role as a rescue vessel accompanying North Atlantic convoys and the new "Earl of Zetland" after serving as an Army transport ship across the Pentland Firth returned to the route for which she was intended between Lerwick and the North Isles. The old "Earl" was finally sold but the most exciting chapters in her life were only just beginning. She was soon to be employed in running illegal immigrants to Palestine and was finally broken up on a beach in Israel.

Chapter Thirteen

POST-WAR RECONSTRUCTION

The drawbacks of Lerwick's harbour front had long been apparent to the Trustees and general public alike. The Esplanade, built in the days of horse-drawn vehicles, was hopelessly inadequate for the motor traffic of the mid twentieth century. The situation had become even more desperate since from 1939, when the west side steamer service was withdrawn, Lerwick had been left to handle virtually all the incoming freight required by a population of 20,000 people besides exports of livestock and fish. Congestion became acute on Victoria Pier and delays occurred in the sorting and delivering of goods.

For the fishermen the problems were just as serious. Alexandra Wharf, built in the days when a short summer season was the main part of the year's activities could not provide the year round shelter which the larger motor boats and the remaining steam drifters required. The small boat harbour was inadequate even for the haddock boats of the 1920's and could hold only a small number of the larger vessels that had replaced them.

The inter-war years had been sterile as regards the development of the harbour and although numerous schemes had been proposed none of them had come to fruition. There was no clear indication of what the future might hold. It was assumed by many people that the herring fishing would recover to the level attained prior to 1914 but it failed to do so and its eventual decline in the 1930's was a bitter blow to the harbour and to the town. Then of course war broke out and for the second time in a quarter of a century European markets were closed.

It became clear the days of the expensive coal-burning steam drifters were over and that a cheaper and more efficient form of vessel was required. It became clear, too, that the days of unlimited demand for large quantities of salt herring were

17. Her Majesty Queen Elizabeth after the opening of the new harbour works on 10th August 1960. On the right is Mr George H. Burgess, O.B.E., then Chairman of the Trust.

18. The Royal yacht Britannia at anchor during the 1969 royal visit to mark the quincentenary of the mortgage of the Shetland Isles to Scotland.

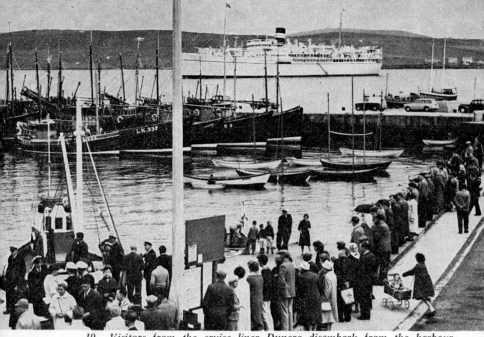

19. *Visitors from the cruise liner Dunera disembark from the harbour launch Budding Rose at the Bressay slipway in the small boat harbour.*

20. *A frequent visitor to Lerwick in the 1960s, the Faroese passenger vessel Tjaldur. On the left of the picture is the Norwegian lifeboat J. M. Johansen while the vessel in the centre is the Dutch fishery protection vessel Panter.*

21. *An unusual photograph showing three 'North of Scotland' boats in harbour at the same time. The Earl of Zetland and the larger St. Clair are berthed at Victoria Pier while the St. Ninian prepares to berth on the outside of the pier arm.*

22. *The harbour in July 1966 crowded with Norwegian purse seiners.*

23. *A sailing race in progress during an inter-club regatta.*

24. *Local purse seiners discharging herring at Alexandra Wharf. On the left is Laurenson Quay and the new white fish market opened in April 1975.*

over and that new ways of processing smaller quantities would have to be found.

Even before the war was over Mr John W. Robertson was considering the problems of the fishing industry. He was now Chairman of the Trust having succeeded Mr W. A. A. Tulloch when the latter died in 1943. In July, 1943, Mr Robertson outlined to his fellow Trustees his proposals for a new fisheries complex at Leraness Voe in Bressay incorporating freezing and cold storage facilities, a fish meal factory and a dry dock. But like so many of "J.W.'s" proposals they came to nothing — not because of any weakness in his plans but because there were so few people in Shetland who equalled him in enthusiasm and had sufficient capital to invest.

Fortunately for Shetland the government began to take a long hard look at the problems of the fishing industry in the whole of Scotland. On 1st September, 1945, Mr F. A. Bell, Chairman of the Herring Industry Board and Captain F. H. Wilson the Board's secretary, visited Shetland and during their stay met members of Lerwick Harbour Trust.

Mr Bell stressed the uncertainty of the herring industry with 75% of previous markets under Russian control while a further 20% in Germany was occupied by British and American forces and outlets there would depend on how much Germany was allowed to buy. Mr Bell saw the future of Shetland's fishing industry as being based on quick freezing for the home market with consignments being shipped weekly to reach Billingsgate in time for Monday morning sales. Overhead charges for herring alone would be crippling but other fish could be handled throughout the year. Finally Mr Bell intimated that the H.I.B. were arranging to have moved to Lerwick the freezing plant that had been used for experimental purposes at Fraserburgh. He hoped that this would become the nucleus of a much larger plant financed locally with assistance from the Board.

On 13th November a meeting was held in Lerwick attended by representatives of Lerwick Town Council, Lerwick Harbour Trust and the H.I.B.'s engineers Mr Tawse and Mr Sproule when it was agreed that the best site for the proposed freezing plant was the Anglo-Scottish station at the North Ness.

While the Herring Industry Board was turning its attention to the problems of the fishing industry Lerwick Harbour Trust had their own problems to tackle. The Fish Market building

K

had suffered badly from neglect during the war and in March,
1946, Mr Dryburgh, county road surveyor, advised that the
building was too far gone to be saved. Mr Reid of Blyth and
Blyth also inspected the building and had the foundations
opened up. He confirmed what many people had suspected for
almost forty years — the building had been built to specifications
but the infill materials was unsuitable. In his opinion the building
was worth shoring up rather than rebuilding but he admitted
that the walls could never be made plumb.

In spite of Mr Reid's relatively optimistic report it was
found necessary to remove the building. First part to go early
in 1948 was the central octagon that housed the sale ring, being
followed soon afterwards by the north wing which was removed
as part of the Trust's reorganisation of quay space when more
room was urgently required by firms engaged in the export to
Germany of large quantities of fresh herring.

Another problem to be tackled in those early post-war
years was the question of traffic congestion on the Esplanade.
Parking space was at a premium and there were numerous
complaints from the owners of property, both private and
commercial, that cars and buses were blocking the entrances
to their buildings. A joint meeting was convened between the
Trustees and Lerwick Town Council to try to devise a scheme
for orderly parking. A scheme was agreed but was never
implemented and thereafter the Trust decided to to allot the
ground at their disposal to the owners of country buses and
hiring cars leaving the problem of private cars to the Town
Council. Stances were allocated by the Trust at the Market
Cross, behind Stove & Smith's, behind the Clydesdale and North
of Scotland Bank and south of Messrs J. & J. Tod's premises.
The stances were then advertised for let at charges varying
from two guineas (£2.10) per year for a taxi to four guineas
(£4.20) a year for a large bus in accordance with a plan which
reserved areas for access to the various properties.

All the stances were allocated and the scheme proved
satisfactory to operators and the general public alike. But it
was resented by those taxi drivers who had had cars for hire as
early as 1919 and who believed that continuous use for almost
30 years had earned for them the right to their stances without
paying rent.

One taxi driver refused to pay the rent demanded and

continued to park in front of Messrs. Goodlad & Goodlad's shop at the Market Cross. He maintained that the Trust had no right to the ground in question since it belonged to Messrs. Anderson & Co. whose rights extended to low water mark, or at least to the point which had been low water mark when the shoreline of Lerwick was in it natural state. It was with considerable reluctance and trepidation that the Trustees agreed to resort to legal action to enforce their claim since the memories of Sinclair's Beach and the case of Smith versus Lerwick Harbour Trust still haunted the Board Room.

But there were certain important differences between those two cases and this one as Sheriff Wallace pointed out when he gave his decision. The property of Anderson & Co. was not a udal holding since a feudal title had been derived from the Crown and because there was no recorded title to the adjoining foreshore, no competing or preferential title arose against the Crown Grant acquired by the pursuers in 1878. Therefore he had no hesitation in upholding the claim of the Trustees.

Next the Trust turned their attention to the North Esplanade whose upkeep had for long been a serious drain on their resources. It was a busy thoroughfare used by people from the whole of Shetland and it required a great deal of maintainance although it contributed nothing to the income of the Trust. The problem was eventually solved in 1952 when it was taken over by Zetland County Council marking the end of negotiations between the two authorities that had been started in the late 1930's.

There were other significant changes in this post-war period. In December, 1946, the Trust became responsible for supplying water to shipping when the Town Council handed over all the necessary equipment. Thereafter water was supplied at the quays at the rate of 2/- (10p) a ton, half of this sum being retained by the Trust, the other being paid to the Town Council. In the same month the Police gave up their tenancy of the rooms in the Harbour Office and moved to more spacious accommodation behind the County Buildings.

The flat above the Harbour Office soon had a new occupant for Captain Harrison resigned and from 105 applicants Captain Wm. Inkster was appointed Harbour Master. In 1948 when it was decided that he was having to undertake far too much routine work on account of the advanced age of his assistant,

Adam Manson, a new assistant was found in Robert J. Robertson.

In 1947 the surface of the Esplanade was much improved when the granite setts were removed and the roadway was covered in tarmacadam. Inevitably there were some people who warned that a new danger would arise since until then motor vehicles had had their speed restricted by the roughness of the road surface and could be heard rattling as they approached. With the new surface of tarmacadam they could not be heard so readily and the smoothness of the surface actually encouraged speeding, or so it was claimed.

All along the Esplanade minor improvements were carried out. In October, 1947, permission was given to Messrs Aitken & Wright, on behalf of the Anglo-American Oil Co. Ltd., to lay a pipeline from the oil store to the oiling berth at Alexandra Wharf. The wharf itself was repaired with concrete slabs and north of the refreshment rooms, on the site of the old watering trough, a weighbridge was constructed to fill a long standing need.

June, 1948, saw improvements in the harbour when it was decided to lay down a buoy off the pier at Heogan to warn shipping of the shoal north of the "north" buoy. In the same month the Northern Lighthouse Board decided to adopt the new uniform system of buoyage and to alter the two buoys they maintained. Lerwick Harbour Trust responded by altering the marking of the six buoys under their control to conform to the new system. In August, 1954, the Northern Lighthouse Board made an important contribution to safety when their previously unlit "North" buoy was converted to a lighted buoy.

HARBOUR DEVELOPMENT

Although plans for development had been far advanced at the outbreak of war, following the confirmation of the Lerwick Harbour Order of 1939, authority to construct the works had expired since a start had not been made within the stipulated two-year period. In 1944 the Trustees tried to have the period extended but their Legal Advisers pointed out that these powers could only be revived by means of a fresh Provisional Order. The Trustees enlisted the aid of Major Neven-Spence, M.P., but he could do nothing to help.

So it was decided to proceed with a fresh Provisional Order embodying all the main points contained in the prevous one with in addition the provison of a sheltered harbour for the fishng fleet.

A great deal of discussion centred on the form the new works should take. Most Trustees were in favour of the widening of Victoria Pier and the construction of a new sea wall linking Alexandra Wharf and Albert Wharf to allow widening of the Esplanade. But the question of a harbour for the fishing fleet was more difficult and some members even maintained that the only place for such a harbour was somewhere in the North Harbour in the lee of the North Ness. In January, 1945, Mr R. J. H. Ganson submitted his own scheme for a dock at Freefield big enough to hold 50 of the 60 ft long class of vessel which it was expected would be ordered by Shetlanders after the war. Although landowners in this area expressed interest in the scheme the Trustees decided it would be more satisfactory to develop part of their own area if at all possible.

Soon after his appointment as Harbour Master, Captain Inkster produced his own suggestions for solving Lerwick's berthing problems. Most revolutionary of his ideas was the proposal to construct a solid breakwater from the north end of Alexandra Wharf running eastwards for 260 ft then turning south to run parallel to Alexandra Wharf for a distance of 680 ft leaving an entrance of 160 ft between the end of the new breakwater and the point of Victoria Pier which he also visualised being widened and extended. His plans also included a dry dock at the extreme northern end of Alexandra Wharf.

On 8th October, 1946, Mr Archibald Henderson, the Trust's Consulting Engineer, visited Lerwick and met the Trustees. He complimented Captain Inkster on his scheme which he commended as ambitious, wide and comprehensive and covering commercial as well as fishing interests. Moreover it was revenue producing and would provide excellent shelter for the existing works. He promised to incorporate these suggestions in the plans he would produce after taking soundings and probing the seabed.

But the Trustees received a shock in April, 1947, when they were informed of Mr Henderson's death. It seemed possible that a new consultant would have to be appointed and that he would have to start from scratch. The firm, however, was reorganised as Archibald Henderson & Partners and in July Mr Ian F. Henderson and Mr Malcolm H. Morrison came to

Lerwick to satisfy the Trustees as to their ability to carry out the work.

On 12th August a select committee of Trustees consisting of Messrs John W. Robertson, Joseph Mair, L. W. Smith, James G. Peterson, George H. Burgess and William Thomson was appointed to consider the proposed developments from both commercial and fishing points of view in order to obtain as much financial assistance as possible from the respective government departments.

In September, 1947, Mr Henbest, finance officer to the Admiralty, visited Lerwick to discuss with the Trust the settlement of their claim against the Admiralty for the use of the works during the war. After two meetings the Admiralty offered £4,000 for the use of the wharves by naval craft, quay rental for the storage of boom defence gear and other machinery, accommodation charge for the floating dock that had been anchored in the North Harbour and abnormal damage to Alexandra Wharf. The Trustees accepted the offer but protected themselves by reserving the right to claim for the dredging of the small boat harbour where silting had occurred due to naval vessels dumping ashes overboard.

Two important visitors met the Trustees in September, 1947, when Mr Tom Fraser, Under-Secretary of State for Scotland, and Mr Aglen of the Fisheries Department visited Shetland to examine problems in the fishing industry. They studied models of the proposed developments at Lerwick and promised to consider the case sympathetically when it was time to seek grant aid. The scheme was also discussed by the Advisory Panel for the Highlands and Islands who promised to support it.

The Trust were grateful for the help given so willingly by Mr F. B. Dryburgh, County Road Surveyor, who was consulted on numerous occasions over plans, reports and estimates. In December, 1947, he was invited to submit his account for services rendered and he responded with an account for £15 in respect of his services since April, 1943. The Trustees decided that this was inadequate and offered to pay him the more realistic sum of £135.

The Trust's plans were studied by many more influential groups of people. In April, 1948, officials of the Transport Group of the Advisory Panel for the Highlands and Islands, of which

Mr R. J. H. Ganson was a member, visited Lerwick. As expected the group expressed their admiration for the scheme but they pointed out that it would be a costly development and they reminded the Trustees that harbour schemes in other parts of the country were being much restricted and curtailed.

The consultants went ahead with detailed plans and drawings and the Legal Advisers set about drafting a new Provisional Order. Consideration was given to the revision of harbour dues which had not been raised since 1911. It was also agreed to continue the line of deviation for the proposed works northwards on the landward side as far as the North Ness since it seemed likely that the property north of the Gas Pier would soon come on the market and the Trustees felt that they might be in a position to purchase it.

In July, 1948, the Trustees had a visit from the Fisheries Group of the Advisory Panel and from Mr Wallace, Harbour Engineer to the Scottish Home Department. But there was still no sign of action on the part of the Scottish Office. In February, 1949, the Trustees appointed a deputation consisting of the Chairman and Vice Chairman, Harbour Master and Clerk to proceed to Edinburgh to urge the necessity for the full scheme to proceed or at the very least part of the fisheries breakwater and the remainder of the scheme. The Chairman, Mr Robertson, unfortunately became ill and Mr L. W. Smith was appointed as fourth member of the deputation. The outcome was inconclusive but the Trust were strongly advised that the scheme should be tackled in two stages with the promotion of two Provisional Orders.

In the meantime the Trust had begun to tackle the problem of providing office and storage accommodation to replace that removed with the demolition of most of the Fish Market building. They purchased a large hangar which had stood during the war beside the airfield at Scatsta and erected it on Alexandra Wharf opposite the foot of Harbour Street. The Trustees next turned their attention to the need for a larger transit shed on Victoria Pier and for this purpose they purchased a second hangar from the aerodrome at Sumburgh which they intended to re-erect on the site of the old transit shed.

In August, 1949, the Trustees were pleased to meet Mr John J. Robertson, a Shetlander and a Member of Parliament, at that time Joint Under-Secretary of State for Scotland. There was no doubt as to his own personal attitude to the scheme but obviously his enthusiasm was tempered by the guarded approach of a politician .

By this time it had been decided to eliminate from the scheme the large breakwater from the north end of Alexandra Wharf although it was hoped that a small breakwater could be incorporated running north from the end of Victoria Pier. There were however two new proposals for incorporation in the overall plan — the erection of a new transit shed and the conversion of the partly - erected hangar on Alexandra Wharf into a permanent building with walls of concrete blocks.

In July, 1950, when there was still no decision by the Scottish Office as to whether the scheme would attract financial assistance, the Trustees outlined the situation to the new Member of Parliament, Major Joseph Grimond, who promised his support.

At the A.G.M. in November, 1950, Mr John W. Robertson resigned from the Trust due to failing health. He was replaced as Chairman by Mr George H. Burgess while Mr Laurence W. Smith became Vice-Chairman. At this meeting reference was made to the long years of service given to the Trust by Mr John W. Robertson.

The news that the Trust had awaited so long was conveyed to them at a special meeting held on Tuesday, 6th March, 1951, when the Clerk, Mr Arthur Laurenson, read a letter from the Secretary to the Treasury giving approval to practically all the Trust's proposals. Approval was given for the extending and widening of Victoria Pier with an extension of the old break-water, the widening of the Esplanade, the erection of the new transit shed and the conversion of the hangar on Alexandra Wharf into stores and offices. The cost of the whole scheme was estimated at £285,000 and it was proposed to meet this by way of a loan of £100,000 repayable with interest fixed at 3% over 30 years and a grant of £185,000 from the Development Fund.

There were certain conditions which the Trustees must accept. A new schedule of dues must be fixed; the materials used should be of British manufacture wherever possible, and where direct labour was employed the rate of wages should not exceed the local authority rates to council workmen or the recognised rate should that be lower.

In expressing his delight at the Government's decision, the

Chairman pointed out that a grant of £185,000 towards a scheme in Shetland was something unique in the history of the islands. It was however a matter of sober reflection that in undertaking the obligation of a loan of £100,000, the Trust were facing a commitment equal almost to the total amount spent in the development of the harbour by previous Trustees since 1877.

In moving acceptance of the offer Mr Arthur Johnson commented that the benefit would be twofold — the scheme would achieve the improvements so long desired and it would also provide work for the large number of unemployed men throughout the county. Mr James G. Peterson seconded the motion and it was adopted unanimously.

The Trustees were anxious that work should begin immediately since at a time of rising costs a scheme estimated to cost £285,000 might cost £350,000 if delayed for two or three years. Furthermore they wanted to make an immediate start on the conversion of the hangar at Alexandra Wharf since the offices and stores would be required whenever construction work should begin.

But the government put a damper on their enthusiasm and refused to sanction an immediate start or even an early start. The Secretary of State explained that it had been found necessary to restrict the amount of payment to be made annually from the Development Fund for harbour projects during the period 1951 - 53 and he advised the Trust to plan their work so that no very substantial demand would fall on the fund until 1953-54. It was also pointed out that in any case no work could begin until the required legislation had been carried through in the form of a Provisional Order giving the formal consent of the government to the scheme.

Work on the Draft Provisional Order occupied most of 1951. The new schedule of rates was modelled on that in use by Stornoway Harbour Commissioners and it was agreed that the rating limits of the harbour should be the same as the conservancy limits. Among powers sought was authority to acquire the properties of the Feuars and Heritors of Lerwick at the North Ness and also the stores below the Medical Hall at Greig's Pier which had belonged to the late Mr James Stout. Finally the Prayer for Presentation to Parliament signed by the Chairman, Vice-Chairman and Clerk was lodged in the Scottish Office on 27th November, 1951.

In this period of waiting there was time for a great deal of preliminary but essential work to be done. The tenants of the two fish stalls at Albert Wharf, Messrs J. & M. Fraser and Mrs A. Jones, were advised to find new premises and thereafter their tenancy was continued on a week to week basis. In January, 1952, tenders were invited for the conversion of the hangar at Alexandra Wharf into stores and offices. The lowest tender was that of Messrs Pearson & Tawse for £19,486 which came as a shock to the Trustees since the previous estimate had been £8,000 and they feared that it might cause the Scottish Office to have grave doubts about the final cost of the whole harbour scheme.

In March, 1952, the Town Council opened their new car park off Commercial Road as their contribution to solving parking problems along the Esplanade. It had cost £7,000 and the only way to recover this sum was to force the bus operators, then renting stances from the Harbour Trust, to move to the new car park. This put the Trustees in a quandary. They were reluctant to terminate an agreement with the bus operators and, besides, by paying rent for stances the bus operators had established a certain right to them. Nevertheless the bus operators were invited to a meeting with the Trustees where it was pointed out that although they would not be moved immediately, every available part of ground, including their stances, would be required by the contractors for storing materials when work on the harbour scheme should begin.

Late in 1952 Lerwick Harbour Act was given the Royal Assent and almost immediately work began on two important parts of the scheme — preliminary site investigations and the conversion of the hangar. The former contract was awarded to Messrs George Wimpey & Co. Ltd. who commenced work in January, 1953. The work was interrupted by the exceptionally severe storm of 31st January, when the firm lost some valuable equipment. Nevertheless the borings were completed by mid-March so enabling the consultants, Arch. Henderson & Partners, to produce the actual working plans.

In September, 1953, the estimates for the entire scheme were revised and since costs in general had risen considerably a new figure of £330,427 was estimated. The Scottish Office urged the Trustees to curtail the Victoria Pier extension with a corresponding reduction in the breakwater arm thus saving

£40,000. There followed a complete review of the whole scheme and in the interests of economy it was agreed to curtail the planned extension of Victoria Pier and abandon altogether the idea for a projecting arm on the old breakwater.

While the scheme was being reconsidered a proposal came from the Education Committee of Zetland County Council that a swimming pool should be incorporated in the scheme. An ideal site would have been found on reclaimed ground north of Albert Wharf but the plans for the area involved the construction of a new sea wall of concrete anchored back at 30ft. intervals and this precluded the possibility of incorporating a swimming pool.

In July, 1954, when tenders were invited for the work eight offers were received and the contract was awarded to William Tawse Ltd. of Aberdeen, although several months were to elapse before the firm could actually begin work. These months were not wasted, since several changes were made in the harbour area, all preparing the ground for the new scheme and in their own way marking the end of another long chapter in the history of Lerwick harbour. The remaining wing of the fish market building was demolished, the old crane was removed from Albert Wharf and the Dutch cannon, recovered from "De Haan" was removed to the safety of Fort Charlotte.

Out in the harbour, too, a relic from another age was finally removed. Since 1924 the coal hulk "Creteground" had occupied a prominent place off the Bressay shore. Although no longer used for supplying coal she was used by motor boats in summer for the cutching of drift nets. In June, 1956, she began her last journey, being towed to Iceland where she was beached to provide the basis for a quay.

In January, 1955, the Trustees purchased the old Burra Isle fishing boat "Budding Rose" for use as a harbour launch and pilot boat. It was expected that she would also play an important role in the construction of the new works. And a third use was found for her since the Customs & Excise were persuaded to give up their tenancy of the boat shed near the Gas Pier on condition that the Trust would make the "Budding Rose" available whenever Customs Officers were required to board vessels in the harbour. The shed was then let to Lerwick Boating Club as a store for oars and sails.

CONSTRUCTION BEGINS

Early in March, 1955, the Trustees appointed Mr D. G. Anderson to act as Resident Engineer and simultaneously work began on the widening and extending of Victoria Pier. In the former case a survey of the seabed and underlying rock had indicated that a cheaper type of seawall was possible — instead of having to build a mass concrete gravity wall it was possible to build a wall of interlocking sheet piling resulting in a saving of £4,000. And in the extension of Victoria Pier the contractor had discovered that here, too, a saving was possible since he intended to use box piles instead of the pre-stressed concrete piles specified.

As suggested in 1952 every available space along the Esplanade was required for the storage of building material and the country buses were forced to give up their stances. Most of them went to the new car park but the Scalloway buses found stances on Commercial Road below Fort Charlotte where they joined the Dunrossness buses which had parked there since the war years. It was claimed that the Dunrossness buses now had an unfair advantage over the Sandwick buses and in 1957 they were forced to join the others at the new car park.

During the summers of 1956 and 1957 while work on the new south face of Victoria Pier was in progress the "North of Scotland" Company's vessels were moved to Alexandra Wharf and were given the use of a store in the new building there. The face of the wharf was modified with the construction of sponson fenders to make it suitable for these vessels. Meanwhile the white fish vessels that normally landed their catches at Alexandra Wharf were moved temporarily to the small wooden jetty at No. 1 Station but the herring fleet had to manage as best they could at the south end of Alexandra Wharf and part of Albert Wharf.

The arrangement worked extremely well but Alexandra Wharf was exposed and unsuitable for year round operations and in the winter of 1956 the shipping company's vessels were allowed to return to Victoria Pier where a specially constructed fender or dolphin guarded the "green" concrete of the pier from damage.

Even at this late stage the programme was altered. Since the original scheme had been modified it would obviously be constructed for far less than £285,000. The Trustees decided that the "surplus" money should be used as far as possible in constructing a harbour for the fishing fleet. By building a breakwater northwards from the point of Victoria Pier and a spur jetty out from the south end of Alexandra Wharf they would be able to provide about three acres of reasonably sheltered water at a cost of £72,000. The additional works would involve a modification of the point of Victoria Pier so it was essential to get approval for this addition as quickly as possible. While awaiting a reply from the Scottish Office the Trustees were shocked to hear of the death of Mr Anderson, Resident Engineer. The post was re-advertised and Mr George Tatton was appointed.

January, 1956, marked a considerable step forward when the Customs & Excise, among the first tenants of the new block, took occupancy of their offices. They requested the Trust to make a decision as to their new address and after some discussion it was decided to name the block Alexandra Buildings.

A month later the Scottish Home Department turned down the Trust's suggestion for alterations to the scheme. Bearing in mind the appeal made by the Chancellor of the Exchequer for the utmost economy in capital expenditure they wished to restrict investment to what was strictly necessary. The Trustees expressed their complete dissatisfaction with the decision and agreed that they would not accept it without a fight.

In February members of the Highland Panel again visited Lerwick and the Trustees took the opportunity of placing the facts before them. The Trustees were not seeking an increase in the grant and loan offered but merely wished to make full use of the offer made. The proposed breakwater and spur jetty were urgently required by the fishing industry and if delayed to a future date would cost at least £95,000 as compared to the current estimate of £76,000. The Trustees' stubborn attitude yielded results for in August approval was given for the alteration to proceed.

In April, 1957, from four tenders received for the second stage of improvements that of Messrs Wm. Tawse Ltd. amounting to £59,514 was accepted and a few weeks later the contract was approved by the Secretary of State for Scotland.

The arm at the point of Victoria Pier was first to be constructed and as work progressed the Trustees had another of their brainwaves. If the arm were to be extended by a further two bays the "Earl of Zetland" would be able to berth inside the arm thus freeing the remainder of the dock for use by fishing vessels.

The Scottish Home Department were quite amenable to the suggestion provided that the shipping company would give a guarantee that they would continue to operate a service to the North Isles and that the "Earl" would not be replaced by a smaller vessel. To the first question the company would not give a guarantee but they could promise that no smaller vessel would replace the "Earl". However the company objected to the proposed alteration in the "Earl's" berthing arrangements maintaining that loading and unloading would often be interrupted during bad weather owing to the distance of the proposed berth from the steamers' store. The Trustees had no choice but to accept the company's point of view.

Next the Trustees turned their attention to the spur jetty at Alexandra Wharf. Local fishermen asked the Trust to reconsider the siting of the jetty in order to increase the area of sheltered water. The suggestion was approved and instead of being built at the south end of Alexandra Wharf as originally intended it was built farther north at the "knuckle" of the wharf.

The plans for the erection of a hangar in place of a transit shed on Victoria Pier did not materialise. Instead a new steel-framed building was erected by Messrs Tawse who sub-contracted the concrete block work to Messrs Thomas Smith & Son of Scalloway, while the hangar was sold as it lay in sections for £1,800. The transit shed was completed in November, 1957, the finishing touch being an electric clock gifted by Wm. Tawse Ltd. and set in the west gable of the building.

In March, 1958, the various parts of the new works were named. For the extended quay from Victoria Pier to the spur jetty the old name of Albert Wharf was retained while the dock itself was named Albert Dock. The spur jetty was named simply North Jetty but no name other than Victoria Pier arm was given to the breakwater at the point of Victoria Pier.

The appearance of the North Esplanade was entirely altered with the building of the new works. The roadway was widened at the bottleneck and was bounded on the east by a pavement and low boundary wall extending along Albert Wharf. The wall was interrupted by a large new public convenience which was a great improvement on the old one that had stood next to the Harbour Master's Office.

The Scalloway buses returned to the area below the Clydesdale and North of Scotland Bank and the people of Lerwick gave a sigh of relief for in order to reach their stances below Fort Charlotte the buses had had to negotiate the whole length of Commercial Street north of the Market Cross.

With the major developments nearing completion the Trustees decided to carry out a number of much needed improvements. In February, 1959, it was decided to widen and extend Hay's Steps at the south west corner of the small boat harbour and also to extend the slipway. This latter project was urged repeatedly by the people of Bressay who made most use of the slipway. They had been greatly inconvenienced by the loss of the wooden platform on the south face of Victoria Pier, removed when the new quay wall was constructed.

In June, 1959, work began on a new covered fish market for the landing and sale of white fish. Fishermen suggested that it should be provided at the north end of Alexandra Wharf but the Trustees pointed out that this was a valuable deep water berth which could not be spared for any other purpose. The Trustees would have preferred to site the new fish market at No. 1 Station but the area was then used extensively for the handling of dogfish and it was claimed that dogfish would contaminate white fish if landed in the same building. So a site for the white fish market was found on newly reclaimed ground south of Alexandra Wharf.

There was a great deal of excitement in Lerwick in the summer of 1959 since for the first time a reigning monarch was to visit the islands. As part of her engagements on 10th August the Queen had graciously consented to formally open the new works and also to officiate at the naming ceremony of Lerwick's new lifeboat.

As early as March the Trustees had begun discussing how this important visit should be commemorated. It was agreed that a plaque should be incorporated in a traffic island at the head of Victoria Pier. The island would take the form of an equilateral triangle, each side being 30ft. long, while the plaque would be sited on a low wall on the side facing the Esplanade.

Elaborate arrangements were made and the Royal visit was planned in such detail that a week beforehand "The Shetland

Times" could declare "so complete are the plans that it is almost possible to write the story in advance". It was arranged that the "St. Clair" would not occupy her usual berth but would be alongside the outer side of Victoria Pier arm. At 9.30 a.m. on 10th August the Royal Yacht "Britannia" would drop anchor off Victoria Pier and 20 minutes later the Queen and the Duke of Edinburgh would come down the companionway and step on board the Royal Barge.

During the short journey to the shore a 21-gun salute would be fired, the last report timed to coincide with the Royal party's arrival at the Bressay slip. There the guests would be met by Sir Basil Neven-Spence, Lord Lieutenant of the County, and his daughter, and as they walked up the slipway the Queen would inspect a guard of honour provided by local Territorials. From the head of the slipway the Queen and the Duke would walk to the specially prepared platform to unveil the plaque in front of the traffic island. This done the Royal party would proceed to the north side of the pier for the naming and handing over of the new lifeboat.

But all these plans came to nothing for at very short notice the Royal visit was cancelled. The only event to be carried out on 10th August was the naming of the lifeboat, which was performed not by the Queen but by Miss Annette Neven-Spence. The vessel, one of the 52ft. long Barnett class, was named "Claude Cecil Staniforth" and was then formally handed over to the Lerwick branch by the Rt. Hon. the Earl of Howe, Chairman of the Committee of Management of the R.N.L.I.

Members of the local branch were bitterly disappointed at the cancellation of the Royal visit. A platform had been specially made for the naming ceremony by the staff of Lerwick Harbour Trust and at the suggestion of the Trust's Chairman it was decided to present it to the R.N.L.I. for use on similar occasions elsewhere in Britain. Mr Francis Garriock, a director of Hay & Co., offered to convey it free of charge to any port in England that the R.N.L.I. suggested. It was also agreed to affix a small plate giving the information that it had been made by the staff of Lerwick Harbour Trust. As the Chairman pointed out, it would show what Shetlanders could do for a special occasion and also prove that they were not "at the back of beyond".

The disappointment felt at the cancellation of the Royal

25. *Silos on Victoria Pier arm in 1972 marking Lerwick's first involvement with oil exploration.*

26. *The pipe laying barge Viking Piper at anchor in Brei Wick.*

27. *The ro-ro terminal at Holmsgarth.*

28. *The south harbour showing (left to right) small boat harbour Victoria Pier and arm, Albert Basin, North jetty, Alexandra Wharf, Laurenson Quay, the oil depot of Messrs S. & J. D. Robertson and Ocean Inchcape (Shetland) Ltd's oil service base.*

29. *The North harbour with Norscot's service base in the foreground.*

30. Trustees and harbour officials, March 1977. Left to right are Mr Leslie H. Johnson, Assistant to General Manager; Capt. David I. Polson, Harbour Master; Mr James C. Irvine; Mr William A. Smith, B.E.M.; Mr James J. Paton; Mr Thomas W. Stove; Mr Harry Gray, Chairman; Mr Alex J. Gear, Vice Chairman; Mr Arthur B. Laurenson, General Manager and Clerk; Mr Magnus M. Shearer, J.P.; Col. F. L. Dainty; Mr James H. Henry; Mr Alex Morrison; Mr C. W. Aitken, J.P. Inset Mr Joseph G. Simpson.

visit lessened considerably when it was known that the Queen would definitely fulfil her promise on 10th August, 1960. But before that date there were some important events in the affairs of the Trust.

In December, 1959, the harbour pilot, Mr William Smith, retired. He was a man respected not only for his ability as a pilot but also for his rare sense of humour and his ready comments, caustic or otherwise, on all aspects of harbour affairs. He was first granted a pilot's licence in March, 1920, when there were half a dozen pilots all competing for a share of the work. Since 1939 however he had served as the sole harbour pilot and had handled in a praiseworthy manner all the traffic of the war years. In his place Mr Robert Smith was appointed harbour pilot. Early in 1960 came the announcement of the award of the O.B.E. to George H. Burgess, Chairman of Lerwick Harbour Trust in recognition of his many years of service to his native town, both as Town Councillor and Harbour Trustee.

The Royal visit of 10th August, 1960, was a complete success although the weather was atrocious, in marked contrast to that glorious summer day which the Royal visitors would have enjoyed a year earlier. The speech of welcome was given by Provost R. B. Blance who reminded those present that it was 700 years since Shetland had last had a visit from a reigning monarch — and that was a Norwegian king. He called on Mr G. H. Burgess, O.B.E., to invite Her Majesty to open the works.

In her speech the Queen referred to her own disappointment at the cancellation of the previous programme and to her pleasure that she could at last keep her promise. She congratulated the Trustees for their courage in planning and perseverance in carrying through this scheme and praised those responsible for designing and constructing the works. "Their work will live after them," she declared, "and will, I am sure, make an important contribution to the prosperity and wellbeing of these islands." Then she cut the tape to unveil the commemorative plaque and the new harbour works were officially declared open.

It was a fitting climax to more than 30 years of planning by a great number of men who as members of the Trust had worked very hard towards this goal. Some had served as members for many years including John W. Robertson, George H. Burgess, Laurence W. Smith, John R. Linklater, Francis Garriock, Alex S. Fraser, Arthur Johnson, Lt. Col. Magnus

L

Shearer, Provost R. B. Blance, R. J. H. Ganson, Wm. S. Anderson, James G. Peterson and Harry Gray. Others served for shorter periods depending on their membership of the Town Council or County Council — men like Peter Dalziel, Prophet Smith, Tom Henderson and Lindsay Robertson, while Thomas Moncrieff represented the shipowners between 1949 and 1952. In 1954 three fishermen, John Leask, William Duncan and John Thomson were appointed to represent shipowners and they served for several years.

Some men who had contributed a great deal of effort towards the scheme did not live to see its completion. John W. Robertson died in 1958 having been a Trustee for almost 40 years being first elected in 1908. Captain F. B. Tait of Clousta was a Trustee for a short time and a promising association with the Trust was terminated by his death in November, 1958. He was replaced as Z.C.C. representative by Mr W. R. T. Hamilton. Another former Trustee, Mr William Thomson, died in January, 1960. He was ex-convener of the County and a Trustee between 1946 and 1955. In the same month the death occurred of Mr Laurence Laurenson a prominent figure in the fish trade and a Trustee from 1934 to 1945.

But amongst all these men the contribution of Mr George H. Burgess stands out. It can be said that over a long period of time he and Mr Arthur Laurenson, the harbour Clerk, thought of little else but the development of the harbour. It is fitting that Mr Burgess's name appears on the commemorative plaque at the head of Victoria Pier. In the case of Mr Laurenson there was no formal recognition of the heavy burden of work he had carried out but in 1975, several years after his death, a quay was named after him.

Chapter Fourteen

ECONOMIC RECOVERY

The development programme undertaken by Lerwick Harbour Trust showed remarkable courage and a commendable faith in the future of the islands. Prospects were far from bright in the immediate post-war period for local industries had declined alarmingly while the population of the islands soon dropped to under 18,000 — considerably less than the figure of 30,000 when Lerwick Harbour Trust was formed.

Fortunately for Shetland there were numerous other examples of faith and initiative in the post-war years some of them complementary to the Trustees own efforts at Lerwick. All over Shetland developments took place in the fishing, crofting and knitwear industries, although more than a decade would elapse before the islands' economic decline was halted.

The Herring Industry Board kept the promise they had made in 1945 and early in 1946 work began on a large factory on the site of the Anglo-Scottish station at the North Ness. Most of the wooden huts occupied by Norwegian sailors during the war were cleared away and in their place arose a large quick-freezing plant. It was a race against time for the factory had to be ready in time for the coming herring season. Between 60 and 70 men were employed working seven days a week creating a considerable amount of interest locally as the massive red iron beams were lifted into place and the intricate plant and machinery was assembled. By June the quick-freezing section of the project had been completed and work continued on the second large building housing the kippering kilns and dehydration plant.

While these developments took place at the North Ness work went ahead on the island of Bressay to convert the former guano factory at Heogan into a modern meal and oil factory to handle fish offal and fish surplus to market requirements. Norwegian machinery was installed under the supervision of Norwegian engineers and the result was one of the most modern reduction plants in this country.

Yet another important development of 1946 was the construction of an ice factory at Garthspool by Messrs. J. & M. Shearer. This project had been planned as early as 1935 but the war had caused an unavoidable delay. The ice plant met a long felt want in Lerwick since until then crushed ice had been imported from Aberdeen and it was often impossible to cope when heavy landings of haddock were waiting to be shipped south. The merchants were naturally reluctant to hold a large supply of ice on their premises because of loss through melting but thanks to J. & M. Shearer this problem was finally resolved.

THE REBUILDING OF THE FLEET

The reorganisation of the fishing industry was among the most spectacular of post-war developments. In 1945 Shetland's fleet was composed mainly of Zulus and Fifies, boats built for sail but having received a new lease of life with the introduction of the petrol-paraffin engine. Lining was still a common mode of fish capture throughout most of the year although by that time secondary in importance to seine netting for haddock, whiting and flats. Fishing was now a year-round occupation with the herring fishery lasting from June to August and white fish being sought during the rest of the year.

The fleet was ageing and badly in need of replacement but there was some uncertainty as to what type of boat would prove best for Shetland. First of the improved boats were the MFV's built for Admiralty duties during the war but designed with fishing in mind when peace should be restored. Several of these vessels came to Shetland and two of them, the "John West" and "Mary Watt" were bought by owners in Lerwick.

At this time local markets for white fish were limited. The pattern was still one of shipping fish to Aberdeen by the twice weekly direct steamer but rising freight and handling charges soon to reach £1 a cwt. made this a gamble. Many smaller merchants were ground out of business leaving the firm of MacFisheries, who rented part of the H.I.B. factory, with the impossible task of trying to cope with the bulk of the catch. Not surprisingly prices dropped through lack of competition. There were attempts to surmount the problem of freight charges. The S.C.W.S. ran a carrier, the "Equity", to Aberdeen but the venture was not successful.

The fishermen were left largely to their own devices in

attempting to overcome these problems and they came to depend more and more on the Aberdeen market. They would fish all the week then head for Lerwick on Saturday morning to transfer their catches to the M/V "St. Clair". At these times Victoria Pier became extremely congested with piles of boxes waiting to be shipped while on Tuesdays and Fridays the piles of empty boxes returned to their owners were another problem.

High freight charges affected the fishermen too and many of them found it more satisfactory to fish for four or five days than undertake themselves the 200 mile journey to Aberdeen. This factor played an important part in the design of the new boats that arrived throughout the 1950's. They had to be big enough to fish all year round and to make the 400 mile round trip to Aberdeen and back practically throughout the year.

Few of Lerwick's own fishermen invested in bigger boats. They were mainly sons and grandsons of the "Scotch" fishermen who had arrived here at the turn of the century. They were dedicated fishermen who knew the pockets of sandy bottom around Bressay and Noss as well as they knew the streets of Lerwick. Their fishing grounds were mainly inside the three-mile limit where only small boats were permitted to fish and the good catches they made each summer enabled them to make a living in spite of poor prices. They, too, shipped fish for the Aberdeen market but a great part of their catches were sold to satisfy local demand being bought by merchants such as J. & M. Fraser, H. M. Johnson, John Laurie and of course MacFisheries.

Lobster fishing also developed into a major industry during the 1950's prosecuted mainly by part-time fishermen from small open boats. They set their creels along both sides of Lerwick harbour as weather conditions dictated, sometimes to the anoyance of those who used boats for transport. A man especially indignant was Major N. O. M. Cameron of Garth who protested that creels were being set around his private pier at Gardie. It was largely through pressure from the Laird of Garth that Lerwick Harbour Trust brought in regulations in 1962 to ban creel fishing within the harbour limits. Fishing by means of nets had been banned for many years.

This was a period of great uncertainty in the fishing industry and few businessmen were willing to take shares in new vessels. Notable exceptions were Mr James G. Peterson and Mr Alex. Morrison while the L.H.D. Company were part owners of several of the boats that they managed. The Malakoff slipway, which had been acquired by Mr Alex Johnson, continued to provide repair facilities and an important role was played by the marine engineers, Smith & Gear and Thomas W. Laurenson, the latter having set up business in 1950.

In 1956 there was a praiseworthy attempt to revitalise the white fish industry with the founding of a fishermen's co-operative — Shetland Fish Ltd. They commenced operations at Blacksness Pier, Scalloway; and in a shed on Lerwick Harbour Trust's newly acquired property at the North Ness. The Trustees, uncertain of the line of demarcation between their property and that of Malakoff Ltd., sought legal advice and were informed that part of Malakoff's paint store was inside Trust property and that a corner of the Trust's shed was inside Malakoff territory. It was agreed to compromise and amend the plan to show these buildings wholly within the boundaries of their respective owners.

A major part of Shetland Fish Ltd.'s activities centred on the skinning of dogfish for shipment to markets in the U.K. Inevitably the area around the shed at No. 1 Station became contaminated with grease from the entrails of dogfish and this was an important factor in the selection of a site for a new white fish market a safe distance away on the south end of Alexandra Wharf. Conversely one of the regulations that governed the operation of the new market was that no dog fish would be landed there.

But Shetland Fish like so many ventures of this period did not survive for long. In this case the main reason for its failure was the inability to find new markets. The co-operative was started during the years of plenty when markets all along the coasts of Scotland were being flooded with haddock while the dogfish market continued to be dominated by consignments from Norway.

Fortunately a new approach to the problem was about to be made by local businessmen who realised that the solution to the problem lay in filleting white fish and freezing them for shipment in a frozen state. Pioneers of the process in Shetland were undoubtedly the H.I.B. and MacFisheries but the example that was copied was that of Iceatlantic (Frozen Seafoods) Ltd. at Scalloway who built their factory there in 1959. One of the promoters of the venture was Mr Alex. S. Fraser at that time local manager of the "North of Scotland" Shipping Company and a member of Lerwick Harbour Trust.

For a time it seemed that this venture, too, would fail

since its opening coincided with a period of unusual scarcity of haddock and whiting. But by 1962 the haddock stocks had recovered and two years later there were four such factories in Shetland, two of them in Lerwick. MacFisheries withdrew from Shetland in 1962 but soon Shetland-owned firms were able to cope with the landings of the entire fleet. MacFisheries' premises were rented by Mr John Laurie who later formed an association with Young's Seafoods.

Heavy landings of haddock were made in the period 1962-66. Boats were coming ashore with deck pounds full of fish to continue the process of gutting and washing as they lay alongside the wharves. This was in contravention of the harbour by-laws as the fishermen realised but they found it difficult to stop the practice. Space on a small boat is limited and the fishermen found it convenient to have quay space available to ease congestion on deck. At a meeting of the Trust Mr. Alex. Morrison tried to have a pier reserved for boats gutting their catches but he failed to find a seconder and the Trust reaffirmed their intention to stop the practice in the interests of hygiene. They made a concession of a different nature in 1964 when they amended the rules governing the fish market to allow dogfish to be landed there.

The success of Shetland's fishermen is borne out by statistics. In 1961 the value of the Shetland catch was £500,000 but in 1971 it was £2,107,000. Dues on fish landings accounted for a great part of the Trust's income especially after 1968 when a new *ad valorem* rate was introduced. The new white fish market soon became too small for the job it had to do and in 1971 work commenced on the first phase of yet another development — the building of a new quay at No. 1 Station, the first step in the construction of a much larger white fish market.

FOREIGN FISHING FLEETS

A feature of the post-war period was the growing interest on the part of foreign fishermen in the fishing grounds east of Shetland. This was partly due to the richness of the Shetland grounds but it was also partly due to over-fishing in other parts of the North Sea. During periods of bad weather these vessels called in large numbers for shelter while throughout the year they came in a steady stream in less spectacular numbers for water, fuel, ice, stores, repairs or medical aid.

In the immediate post-war period Norwegian fishermen came in large numbers. They were mainly line fishermen fishing for ling and dogfish on the grounds where Shetlanders used to operate in the days of the salt fish trade. Among them were wooden shark fishers, white painted or varnished with a harpoon mounted on the bows, and a few whalers identified by the black band around the white crow's nest. Their crews were well received by Lerwegians, and Shetlanders in general, continuing a friendship forged in the years of hostilities.

Many people admired the drive and the efficiency of the Norwegian fishermen and suggested that they might offer an opportunity for the advancement of these islands, too. In December 1957 a suggestion came from Lerwick Harbour Trust that Norwegian fishermen should be encouraged to operate from Shetland and develop fish processing to help overcome the lack of demand locally. The Norwegians were unable to do so and fortunately they were not needed since Shetland's own fishermen and processors were able to solve their problems in their own fashion.

The Norwegians continued to operate in this area, and in 1959 Mr. K. Brandal was based at Lerwick as Welfare Officer. Three years earlier, a rescue ship, the Willi Wilhelmsen was based at Lerwick being replaced in 1959 by the J. M. Johansen. Another result of Norwegian operations in this area was the formation in 1963 of the Lerwick & Maloy Friendship Committee. In the following years citizens of these towns exchanged visits, parties of Norwegians being at Lerwick in 1964 and 1966.

In 1953 ships of another nation were frequent visitors to the waters around Shetland — ships flying the hammer and sickle of the U.S.S.R. Before long they used Lerwick harbour for shelter and repairs. Rusty old trawlers with cumbersome deck houses and their names painted on their sterns in strange cyrillic letters. They looked mean and sinister in those early days but only because of the role played by the Russian government in the cold war. The men were seldom allowed ashore although in their dealings with harbour officials the Russian officers and crew were courteous and helpful.

Gradually the ice of the cold war began to thaw, at least in this corner of the UK. The Russians were allowed greater liberty in getting ashore and when their spending allowance was increased to £300 per ship they began to visit local shops for gifts to take home. Genuine friendships were formed in spite of language difficulties.

The Russians found Lerwick a convenient port for loading water for distribution among units of the fleet at sea. Water tankers called regularly and the export of water brought considerable income to the town. In 1966, for example, 84,000 tons of water were sold to the Russians. One of the most regular of visitors was the "Vyru" of Tallin and there was considerable regret when in March 1973 she called for the last time being considered too old for her exacting life in the North Sea.

Polish fishermen, too, made frequent visits to Lerwick and they actually set up a base at Mitchell's Station, North Ness, where their catches were landed for shipment by steamer to Poland. Unfortunately handling charges proved too expensive and the scheme was abandoned.

While the Russians and Poles may have contributed to the general depletion of fish stocks in this area, they used conventional trawls which were no more efficient than those used by British vessels. Perhaps the greatest cause for concern was their practice of trawling for herring, a technique which many Shetlanders considered detrimental to herring stocks.

Shetland's own herring industry was entering a period of relative prosperity since the new dual-purpose vessels were able to gross up to £5,000 for the summer and out of this provide fair returns to their crews. The net still in use was the drift net, little changed in form from that used by the Dutch who anchored in Bressay Sound before Lerwick was built. But the long era of the drift net was almost over for developments in Norway were soon to revolutionise this fishery too. Fundamental to the new technique was the use of sonar to locate herring shoals and huge purse seines to trap them.

In 1965 150 Norwegian purse seiners fished in Shetland waters, forerunners of a fleet that soon numbered 500. Immediately the contrast was apparent between the little wooden drifters from Shetland and the huge steel-hulled purse seiners from Norway. The technique was different and so were the results. While a drifter's crew considered 30 crans or five tons of herring a good night's fishing the pursers frequently took 100 tons or more with one cast of the net. While Shetland's vessels landed their catches fresh each morning for human consumption the Norwegian vessels stayed on the grounds until they could hold no more, then deeply laden they set their course for Norway where their catches were pumped ashore into fish meal factories. The factory at Bressay too worked round the clock and additional plant was installed to increase its capacity.

Scottish fishermen soon realised that they would have to adapt to the new technique of fishing or go out of business. The first British purse seiners fished in 1966, a year later the first Shetland-owned purse seiner was purchased from Norway and by 1972 Shetlanders owned four purse seiners out of a Scottish fleet of twelve. At first catches soared to a new record for the post-war period but on a wider aspect the picture was far less bright. As the Norwegian fleet reached its peak and other countries began to copy them the catch rate began to fall and the effects of over-fishing became clear to everyone.

The scenes in Lerwick harbour in the late 1960's as large numbers of Norwegian, Icelandic and Faroese purse seiners sought shelter during bad weather were reminiscent of the peak years of the Dutch fishery in the late 19th century. And in addition to these large numbers of British trawlers and seiners called regularly for shelter, stores and repairs.

With so many vessels frequenting this area difficulty was experienced making contact with Wick Radio. In 1965 it was suggested that a new radio station should be established in Shetland, a suggestion that received a great deal of support from trawl-owners and skippers in Aberdeen, Fleetwood, Grimsby and Hull. The request was refused but a direct result of the campaign was the upgrading of Lerwick Coastguard Station from 1st January, 1966 to maintain continuous watch on 2182 kc/s. From then on Lerwick Coastguard was able to deal with emergencies and help in medical cases while commercial messages continued to be handled by Wick Radio. In August 1969 the port's efficiency was improved when Lerwick Harbour Trust installed VHF radio sets in the pilot boat and in the Harbour Master's Office.

OTHER DEVELOPMENTS

It would be unfair to others in Shetland to give the impression that the fishing industry was the only one to expand in the 1960's. The success story was repeated by crofters and farmers in all parts of Shetland and by the producers of Shetland knitwear.

No less remarkable was the development of tourism as

growing numbers of visitors discovered that Shetland has a great deal to offer. An indication of this growing interest was the setting up of an Information Centre in the building at the south end of Alexandra Wharf leased by Messrs Robertsons (Lerwick) Ltd. In 1968 the lease of this office was transferred to Shetland Tourist Organisation.

The small boat harbour, Victoria Pier and the fish market were all targets for sightseers while the scenes of activity at Alexandra Wharf when drifters and purse seiners discharged heavy catches of herring never failed to attract a crowd of sightseers. There were added attractions such as the arrival of sailing yachts competing in the round-Britain race which included Lerwick as a port of call in 1966. Another attraction, started in September, 1968, was the sea-angling festival which helped to extend the tourist season into what used to be a rather quiet time of year. Cruise liners made frequent calls at the port and the Faroese m.v. "Tjaldur" called regularly for several summers on a route that included Copenhagen, Lerwick, Thorshavn and, less regularly, Kristiansand. Her local agents were Robertsons (Lerwick) Ltd.

Harbour statistics emphasised the improved economic state of the islands. In 1970 imports discharged at Lerwick totalled 73,000 tons of which bulk oil accounted for 26,000 tons and general cargo by the shipping company 27,000 tons. Exports totalled almost 60,000 tons, a figure inflated by the supply of water to Russian water tankers and including 14,000 tons of fish products. In 1969 the revenue of Lerwick Harbour Trust was just under £38,000 — four times that of 1954.

As revealing was the number of motor vehicles on the roads of Shetland — 4741 in 1970. In Lerwick traffic congestion became acute and ambitious plans were set in motion to improve the flow of traffic. Most ambitious was the proposal to construct a new road from Annsbrae down Church Lane to meet the South Esplanade. But the South Esplanade was still the property of Lerwick Harbour Trust and the scheme would fall down unless the Trust agreed to relinquish control over this stretch of road.

The County Council's plans included the widening of the roadway, the removal of the seawall and the construction of a pavement on a cantilever catwalk supported by the spending slope. But many members of the Trust, and indeed the public at large, were reluctant to see the removal of the seawall.

Children could run along the lower step in safety and visitors could sit in comfort on top of the wall to watch the movements of vessels in the small boat harbour. Indeed the wall was a tourist attraction and added considerably to the charm of the South End of Lerwick.

A more serious objection was that the loss of the South Esplanade would result in a splitting of the harbour works, isolating the breakwater and the small boat harbour from the rest of the Trust's property. Should it become necessary to move a mobile crane or other heavy equipment to the breakwater the new owners of the roadway might be unwilling to co-operate.

Negotiations betwen the two authorities were prolonged and intense and even in October 1968 when the new road was ready to be connected to the South Esplanade the transfer had still not been finalised. However it seemed that agreement was near on the grounds that free movement by the Trust's mobile crane would be guaranteed and that the Trust would be paid for the roadway in question.

In October 1969 the District Valuer reported that he would only recommend a nominal sum of £10 as compensation for the roadway but the Trust's legal adviser, Mr. Goodlad, could not advise acceptance of this price nor did he think the Secretary of State would approve the sale on these terms. But he suggested a way out of the difficulty. The Trust could retain the solum of the roadway and hand over the surface to Z.C.C., free of charge. The sea wall and the parapet would be retained without alteration or encroachment and further development of the existing road would have to be negotiated between the two authorities.

It was not until July 1970 that the Trust agreed to hand over the roadway after extracting a guarantee that the harbour crane would have free movement as required and it was not until May 1971 that Zetland County Council formally accepted these terms.

The great increase in traffic was a cause of concern to the Trust too. Motor cars spilling over from the Esplanade on to the quays hampered the movement of commercial vehicles and added greatly to the congestion of Victoria Pier. The Trust had entered into an agreement with the Chief Constable that cars would be allowed to be parked along the boundary wall at Albert Wharf. But motorists abused this privilege and when the stances were full they began to park along the edge of the wharf itself and even above water hydrants making the watering of fishing vessels impossible. Capt. Inkster and his staff spent a great deal of time in trying to regulate motor cars which they found a far more difficult task than the regulation of shipping in the harbour.

Matters came to a head in July 1967 with a protest from Capt. Mainland, Manager of the "North of Scotland" Shipping Company, that congestion on Victoria Pier was so acute that they had had to suspend loading operations while the owners of parked vehicles were located. Inspector Johnson of Shetland's police force was consulted but while willing to help he pointed out that the Trust's by-laws were framed in such a way that the police had no authority to direct or shift anyone on the pier.

During the next few years Capt. Inkster did his best to alleviate the problem by placing temporary barricades to prevent cars parking on Victoria Pier. Then in June 1970 a special meeting was held between representatives of the Northern Constabulary and Lerwick Harbour Trust. It was decided that only commercial vehicles would be allowed on the pier between 8 a.m. and 6 p.m. and that harbour employees would be available to assist the police until the restrictions were accepted. In 1973 the Trustees had the harbour by-laws amended to allow the police to regulate traffic on Victoria Pier. But the regulations agreed in 1970 were not enforced, traffic continued to use the pier and although congestion was at times acute commonsense prevented a recurrence of the crisis of July 1967.

DEVELOPMENT OF NUMBER 1 STATION

By 1965 when the local fleet was growing towards a new record for modern times and when foreign vessels were calling in increasing numbers it was evident that even the quays provided in the period between 1955 and 1960 were no longer adequate. The Trustees then decided to proceed with development of their property at No. 1 Station, North Ness.

In February 1965 Archibald Henderson and Partners submitted their proposals for use of this area by removing the existing timber jetty and constructing a sheet piled sea wall from the south side of the Malakoff pier across the front of the station for 159 ft. then returning shorewards for 28 ft. to meet the Gas Pier. In place of the existing timber jetty a reinforced concrete wharf would be constructed 89 ft. wide and 125 ft. long consisting of reinforced concrete beams and slab deck carried on concrete cylinders founded on the hard. The plans showed a fish market building across the wharf 105 ft. long and 22' 3" wide. At the north end of Alexandra Wharf the plans showed a new pier 200 ft. long and 40 ft. wide to provide additional berthage for large vessels of deeper draught and at the same time to provide shelter from northerly gales.

The plans were subsequently modified to accommodate the wishes of the Trustees by extending both the wharf and the quay while the consultants further suggested that a cantilever roadway should be constructed across the face of the beach to link the two parts of the scheme. This suggestion did not find favour with some of the Trustees who maintained that the beach should be left in its natural state for beaching vessels to clear fouled propellors.

On 9th June 1965 a deputation from St. Andrew's House led by Lord Hughes, Under-Secretary of State for Scotland, visited Lerwick, and found time to meet the Trustees who outlined the developments proposed at No. 1 station and at the north end of Alexandra Wharf. In February 1966 a deputation was appointed to go to St. Andrew's House to stress again the need for this development. Its members included the Chairman, Vice Chairman and Clerk and Messrs A. Beattie and A. J. Gear. They were well received and a few months later Mr. Peter Martin, Senior Civil Engineer of the D.A.F.S., and his assistant visited Lerwick and were invited to meet the Trustees. Mr. Martin expressed his admiration for the scheme but pointed out that his department had limited funds at its disposal and he could not promise an early allocation of financial assistance. He reminded the Trustees that the scheme would require the promotion of yet another Provisional Order and he suggested that it might be advisable to carry out the scheme in two phases.

In May 1967 the Highlands and Islands Development Board expressed an interest in fisheries developments at Lerwick and sent Board member Mr. Prophet Smith and Senior Planning and Research Officer Dr. Ian Skewis to study the Trust's proposals. Again the Trustees pointed out that the continued expansion of the fishing industry had made the development of No. 1 Station imperative.

Although further delays were to be encountered before work could begin on the scheme a considerable improvement was effected by the construction of a new access road from Commercial Road to the Trust's property at the North Ness.

The road was later extended to the oil depot beyond, following an agreement between Zetland County Council, the Trust, Malakoff Ltd., and the oil company.

In January 1970 there came a suggestion from Mr J. P. Moar, County Surveyor, that a suitable terminal for the proposed vehicular ferry to Bressay would be found between Alexandra Wharf and No. 1 Station. But the Trustees turned down the proposal since a ferry terminal here would be in conflict with both fishing and fish processing.

But the need for a ferry terminal was to influence the form of development at No. 1 Station too. It was agreed that the terminal should be sited at the south side of the spur jetty near the south end of Alexandra Wharf and the Trustees argued that if they were to sacrifice a fishing jetty in the interests of communications the government should allow more money to be spent in providing increased quay space at No. 1 station by way of compensation.

In June 1970 the D.A.F.S. announced that they were prepared to offer grant and loan assistance amounting to £121,087 for the first phase of the scheme. Immediate steps were taken to draft a Provisional Order to meet the November deadline for presentation to Parliament. The Order was passed in July 1971 and in December the tender of Messrs. Wm. Tawse Ltd., to construct the work for £178,272 was accepted. Although disturbed by the substantial increase over the approved estimated cost the D.A.F.S. agreed to increase the amount of their financial assistance to cover the cost of the works plus engineers' and other fees.

THE TRUST'S INDEPENDENCE THREATENED

In November 1960 Mr. Burgess resigned as Chairman although he remained a Trustee. He was replaced by Mr. Francis Garriock and Mr. Arthur Johnson became Vice Chairman. Another change took place in November 1963 when Mr. R. J. H. Ganson became Chairman and Mr. Magnus M. Shearer became Vice Chairman. Mr Ganson resigned in 1966 being replaced as Chairman by Mr. Shearer while Mr. A. J. Gear was appointed Vice Chairman. These gentlemen served as Trustees almost continuously throughout the 1960's as did Messrs. Alex. Morrison, W. R. T. Hamilton, Harry Gray and James Paton. In November 1963 the death occurred of Mr. James G. Peterson, first appointed in 1943. He was replaced by Mr. Andrew Beattie.

Another change occurred in November 1965 with the resignation of Mr John R. Linklater and in 1967 Mr W. A. Smith, B.E.M., was appointed a representative of Lerwick Town Council in place of Mr. Arthur Johnson. Others who served for varying lengths of time were Messrs. Alex. Duthie, John R. Smith, John H. Scott and P. B. A. Hunter.

In March 1968 it was decided to hold the meetings of the Trust in the office at No. 2 Alexandra Buildings, while the old Board room became the personal office of the Harbour Master. The new arrangement was an immediate success.

As in the immediate post-war period, a great deal of credit for the progress of the 1960's was due to Mr. Arthur Laurenson, Harbour Clerk. Unfortunately he did not live to see the start of developments at No. 1 station. He died in April 1968, sadly missed by all those connected in any way with the Harbour. In addition to being Harbour Clerk he had served as the German Consul and had been awarded Das Verdienst Kreuz (first class)— the cross of the German Order of Service. He was succeeded by his son Arthur B. Laurenson who had acted as Deputy Clerk during his father's illness.

Many former Trustees, and former employees too, passed away during the 1960's. In September 1960 the death was reported of Mr John Harrison, a Trustee from 1920 to 1926; and in November of that year Mr. Edwin S. Reid Tait died. He had been a Trustee for 25 years and for seven of those years he had served as Vice Chairman while he had been Chairman for nine. In March 1961 Lt. Col. Magnus Shearer passed away. He had been a Trustee for 17 years in two periods between 1926 and 1957. In November 1962 the Trust paid tribute to Mr. Wm. S. Anderson, a Trustee from 1937 to 1950 and a year later, in October 1963, reference was made to the passing of ex-Provost R. B. Blance and the contribution he had made to the Trust between 1950 and 1962.

In 1964 the Trustees lost three of their staunchest friends. In June they paid tribute to Mr. Laurence W. Smith, a Trustee from 1938 to 1960 and Vice-Chairman for 10 years. A month later Mr. Adam (Eddie) Manson passed away. He was appointed Berthing Master in 1920 and later became Assistant Harbour Master — a position he held until his retiral in 1950. Also in July 1964 tribute was paid to Mr. Gilbert (Bertie) Robertson, a man who was never a Trustee but who did as much as anyone towards the development of Lerwick harbour in his capacity as a Director of L.H.D. Ltd. Another loss was sustained in April 1969 with the death of George H. Burgess, O.B.E., a Trustee for 23 years and Chairman from 1950 to 1960. He was replaced as Trustee by Mr. Leslie H. Johnson.

There were happy occasions, too, as in 1969 when Mr Francis Garriock was awarded the Commander Cross of the Order of St. Olaf, the culmination of several awards made by the Norwegian government in recognition of his services as Norwegian Consul at Lerwick. In January 1970 congratulations were offered to the Harbour Master, Capt. William Inkster, on being awarded the O.B.E. and to Mr. Lindsay Robertson, Danish Vice Consul and a former Trustee, who was awarded the Royal Order of the Knight of the Dannebrog. A month later congratulations were offered to Mr. Magnus M. Shearer when he became a Chevalier First Class of the Royal Order of Vasa. Captain Inkster had previously been made a Knight of the Order of St. Olaf in recognition of his services to the Norwegian fishing fleet while operating in this area.

A threat to the independence of Lerwick Harbour Trust came in 1969 with the Wheatley Report on the reorganisation of local government. It was feared that independent harbour authorities would be swallowed up in the enlarged regional councils and if the report were implemented Lerwick harbour might be administered from Wick or Inverness.

It was a similar fear that made many members of Lerwick Town Council and Zetland County Council consider the advisability of amalgamating with Lerwick Harbour Trust into one authority powerful enough to present an alternative to incorporation in a huge Highland region. But the Trust refused to entertain this suggestion. The County Clerk, Mr. W. A. Scott, suggested that a meeting of the three bodies should be held to discuss the implication of the Wheatley Report and that the observations of the three bodies should be submitted jointly. The Trust replied that while they would be willing to attend such a meeting they would prefer to make their own submission to the Secretary of State.

The meeting of the three bodies was held on 20th January 1970 and the County Treasurer, Mr. I. R. Clark, suggested that if Shetland were to be left as an island authority there should be a single Harbour Department having control over all the harbours and piers in Shetland. This suggestion received little support from the Trustees although they were forced to admit

M

that if amalgamation were to become a reality they would prefer to amalgamate with other authorities in Shetland rather than with those outwith the islands.

Fortunately for Shetland the submissions of the three authorities and the protest of many other bodies and individuals were heeded. In the reorganisation of local government Shetland was granted the status of a special island region and at a local level Lerwick Harbour Trust retained their independence — a fitting conclusion to an era of development that had not been equalled since before World War I.

But greater changes were around the corner and the first signs were already evident in the quickening pace of activity at the port. In July 1970 a new post was created to assist the Harbour Master and Assistant Harbour Master — that of Pilot/Deputy Harbourmaster. First holder of this post was Capt. David Irvine Polson, a Whalsay man then residing in Leith.

It was also becoming clear that in spite of post-war developments the old part of Lerwick harbour was unable to cope with the increasing amounts of cargo being handled by the "North of Scotland" shipping company. The company itself was finding it increasingly difficult to handle the growing volume of trade by conventional cargo vessels. It was clear that the answer lay in replacing the M/V "St. Clair" by a new roll on/roll off cargo vessel, discharging her containerised cargo at a new terminal planned with ample storage space and good access roads.

Fortunately land was available on the western side of the North Harbour with Bremner's station and Shetland Seafoods' property at Dunbar's station both on the market. In 1971 steps were taken to purchase these properties and the land in between.

Then a year later oil was discovered in the East Shetland Basin and plans for development at Holmsgarth were dwarfed by developments elsewhere as the Trust sought to cater for the demands of the oil companies.

Chapter Fifteen

THE OIL BOOM

One day in 1965 two unusual vessels berthed at Lerwick. It was obvious that they were engaged in some obscure branch of oceanic research and as such were no strangers to Lerwick. In fact they were engaged in seismic survey work as part of the preliminary search for oil. Other vessels joined them in a systematic coverage of the seabed; only they were not interested in the seabed itself but in the folds and contortions in the rock strata thousands of feet below the bottom of the sea.

The oil industry is one in which secrecy is important. Shetlanders had little information to work on and they could only watch with growing interest as drilling operations came ever nearer the islands. On Christmas Day 1971 they were given a close-up view of an oil-rig at anchor in Breiwick while in March and April 1972 service companies became established at Sandwick and Scalloway. It seemed for a time that Scalloway might become an important oil service base but, as had happened before, Scalloway found itself on the wrong side of Shetland for major developments to occur there. The main reserves of oil were found in the East Shetland Basin — not in the deep water west of Shetland — and Lerwick on account of its fortunate geographical situation and the services it could offer the oil companies became the natural target for development.

SERVICE BASES

The Trustees were not entirely unprepared for the demands of the oil companies. Even before the search for oil intensified they were looking beyond the North Ness to the shores of the North Harbour. In April 1971 the Clerk, Mr Laurenson, drew up a memorandum on the future development of the North Road area, suggesting that Lerwick could play an important role in oil servicing if more land could be acquired in that part of the town. Development of the North Road area could be achieved if the Trust were to build jetties and lease them to the oil companies who would repay the cost in a very short time. In his view the key to the whole development of this area lay in ownership of the land.

In November, 1971, Mr. Stansbury, County Development Officer, was invited to address the Trust following his visit to Scandinavia and to the oil exhibition, Oceanex 71, at Great Yarmouth. He stressed the need for more land to be purchased and claimed that if this was done the oil companies would definitely set up bases at Lerwick.

On 20th December 1971, at a special meeting of the Trust, the Clerk was given permission to negotiate the purchase of the Grimista Estate which was then on the market and in February 1972 he informed the Trustees that their offer had been accepted. This move had been considered for some time by both Lerwick Town Council and Lerwick Harbour Trust but a growing interest by oil companies and financiers now made haste essential. It was a wise move although it caused a great deal of anxiety at the time and there was also the complication of a sitting tenant to be compensated. Fortunately the Trust were able to come to an agreement with the tenant, for had the case gone to Court the delay might well have proved fatal to the development of the area. The proprietrix, Lady Nicolson, and her solicitors, Messrs Tait and Peterson, were extremely co-operative. It was almost as if they sensed the urgency of the situation in view of the pressures to which the Trustees would soon be subjected on account of North Sea oil.

By the spring of 1972 the Trust had acquired most of the land in the North Road and Grimista area — a total of 1,500 acres — and were poised to take advantage of any proposals for the construction of service bases. On account of their commanding position the Trustees were able to negotiate extremely favourable agreements with the major oil companies.

The Trust's first contacts with the oil industry were made with the firm of British Ceca, suppliers of drilling mud and chemicals. Then before the end of 1971 the American company Vista Clara CA expressed an interest in leasing stations 19 and 22 in the North Harbour and Milchem UK were anxious to establish a base in the same area. The Trust, however had still not assessed the full potential of the North Road area and as an alternative offered these three companies sites for temporary silos on Victoria Pier arm.

It was here that Lerwick's first commercial involvement with the oil industry began with a row of seven silos filled with cement and barytes for use in drilling operations. Three of these were owned by British Ceca, while Milchem UK had two and Imco and Advance Supply Bases (formerly Vista Clara) had one each. Throughout 1972 the pier arm was extremely busy as service vessels called regularly for supplies.

Hard on the heels of the cement and "mud" companies came the major oil companies themselves. Towards the end of 1971 representatives of B.P. Development Ltd., and Shell (U.K.) Exploration and Production Ltd., visited Lerwick to make exploratory contact with Lerwick Harbour Trust and declare a definite interest in establishing service bases at Lerwick. At the same time the Trust began to consider the promotion of a Provisional Order to obtain the necessary powers to develop the North Road area.

In February 1972 a meeting was held with representatives of the Highlands & Islands Development Board, then on a visit to Lerwick. The Chairman outlined the events that had occurred and explained that the Trust had already come to an important decision in that they would be prepared to lease sites rather than sell since they wished to retain in their own hands the full control of Lerwick harbour. The Board's representatives expressed their admiration for the Trust's actions but suggested that the North Road area would not be large enough to cope with the expected build up of oil-related activity, and that the Trust would have to develop the Point of Scotland as well.

The unobtrusive guidance of the Highlands & Islands Development Board was an important factor in the success of the ground work being done at this time. The Board was also important as a link between the Trust, the oil companies and the various government departments. Accordingly the Trust were able to plan their campaign of development in full knowledge of what the oil industry required and because of this were able to present their case for financial assistance upon which the whole scheme depended. In addition the H.I.D.B. provided financial assistance through a 70 per cent grant towards the cost of a bore survey of the North harbour area.

More important still was the support of the Bank of Scotland who granted financial assistance and bridging loans when required, while the confidence they showed towards the Trust was a moral boost at a critical time. Early in 1972 Mr. George Murray, then the Manager of the Lerwick branch, arranged for the Trust's Chairman and Clerk to meet the General Manager

at Edinburgh. At that meeting the Trust received the assurance
of further assistance as required.

Following their visit to Edinburgh Mr. Laurenson and Mr.
Shearer proceeded to Lowestoft and Yarmouth where they saw
for themselves oil-related developments at those ports. They
made the most of their visit to the Mainland and before they
returned to Shetland they had meetings with Mr. R. P. Gibbs
of the Department of the Environment and Mr. Lister of the
Scottish Office — two men whose continued interest in and
support for the actions of Lerwick Harbour Trust has been
invaluable. As a result of these preliminary contacts a meeting
was held in Lerwick in June 1972 attended by representatives
of the Department of the Environment, the Scottish Regional
Development Department and the Department of Agriculture
and Fisheries for Scotland, all of whom wished to make sure
that the Trustees were proceeding along the right lines. At this
meeting the Trust received an assurance that loan assistance
would be readily available from the Government.

On 10th July another meeting was held with Mr. Gibbs and
Mr. Lister when the situation was again reviewed. By this time
Shell had accepted in principle the Trust's terms for leasing a
site at Holmsgarth, BP had sent information as to the type of
jetty they required, the Norwegian company, Norsco AS, a
subsidiary of the Fred Olsen group, were interested in purchasing
a site and the P & O group had expressed their interest in
developing a base at Grimista. Apart from these a great number
of entrepreneurs and businessmen contacted the Trust with a
view to developing their piers for them and Trustees and harbour
officials alike found it difficult at times to discover which of them
really had 'the ear of the oil companies' as they claimed.

In spite of so much interest in the port there remained a
lingering fear on the part of the Trustees that events in Lerwick
were moving too slowly. There were rumours of proposed
developments at Baltasound, Catfirth, Scalloway and other
places while construction work had already begun at Sandwick.
Messrs. Gibbs and Lister were asked whether Lerwick was in
fact going to be bypassed. Both gentlemen replied that this was
extremely unlikely. Anyone developing a site elsewhere would
have to provide many of the services that Lerwick could offer
already and it would be a very costly exercise. The general
pattern was for service bases to congregate in one centre and
Lerwick, being the focal point would naturally attract the major

schemes. Moreover it was in Lerwick alone that the oil companies were interested. They agreed with Mr Laurenson that the Trust should 'play it cool' and not accept the first offer that came their way.

Throughout the remainder of 1972 work went ahead with the promotion of a Provisional Order to authorise the building both of the roll on - roll off terminal and the facilities required by Shell and BP. Among the powers sought were powers of compulsory purchase of land should the owners of property in the area refuse to sell land which was essential for these developments. The Trustees also sought, and were granted, authority to increase their borrowing powers to £3 million — a substantial increase on the previous figure of £150,000.

At the same time the Trust liased with Lerwick Town Council over the development of the Grimista estate with areas being zoned for housing, pipe storage and light industry.

The promotion of the Provisional Order brought the Trust into conflict with the North of Scotland Hydro-Electric Board who owned a jetty and mooring dolphin in this area at which tankers berthed to discharge cargoes of diesel fuel for the Board's generating plant. Their objections almost killed the development scheme at Holmsgarth. For although negotiations with the oil companies continued, approval to proceed was delayed until a settlement had been reached with the Hydro-Electric Board. After months of hard bargaining the Board agreed to hand over the jetty and mooring dolphin to the Trust free of charge provided that the Trust would provide alternative facilities and continue the Board's privilege of paying no shore dues on cargoes of oil and of paying in effect only half the normal rate of tonnage dues.

It was at the northern extremity of the harbour that the first development to cater specifically for the oil industry took place when Norscot Services leased from the Trust a 30-acre site at the Green Head, an area still bearing the marks of World War II and scarred with tunnels and the sites of gun emplacements. On Friday 9th March, 1973 the M/V "Sound of Islay" began unloading heavy machinery and within two days the headland was no longer green.

Construction work was carried out by Bovis who had many difficulties to overcome including site problems and severe weather at the end of 1973. In August 1973 oil rig servicing commenced and a few months later Norscot moved their administration centre from Aberdeen to the Green Head.

In the old part of Lerwick harbour the long-established firm of Hay & Co. (Lerwick) Ltd., also took advantage of the new opportunities to cater for the oil industry and formed a partnership with Ocean Inchcape Ltd., known as Ocean Inchcape (Shetland) Ltd. 20,000 sq. ft. of warehousing was made available and to enable the new company to start operating as quickly as possible a 100 ft. long pontoon was moored at the North Ness to act as a temporary quay. The firm received a setback in December 1973 when the pontoon was holed by a service vessel and sank. While it was being raised Hay & Co. offered quay space at Freefield to allow servicing to continue.

In July 1973 work began on the service bases at Holmsgarth to serve Shell and BP, the companies being granted a 15-year lease by Lerwick Harbour Trust. Over this period the companies agreed to pay sufficient rental to repay the cost of building plus interest, plus a discounted cash flow of 15 per cent. The contract, worth £763,000, was won by Sir Robert McAlpine & Sons who had 92 men on the site by the middle of July. The work involved the removal of Holmsgarth Baa which had long been a hazard to shipping in this area. At the end of June 1974 the last pile on the sea wall had been driven in and infilling proceeded to provide 4½ acres of storage space. In addition Shell leased land at Grimista for the storage of drill pipes and other materials.

In 1973 yet another Provisional Order was promoted to allow construction of a service base in the Bight of Gremista should the P & O group decide to carry out their planned development. In addition the Trust sought and were granted powers to amend the plans that accompanied the 1972 Provisional order and by altering the limits of deviation to obtain a larger area of reclaimed ground.

All the equipment required by these projects had to be taken in by sea — all the trucks, mechanical diggers, caravans, portable offices and thousands of tons of steel and cement. Then servicing began from the silos on Victoria Pier arm and cargoes of chemicals and cement arrived to be stored ashore and shipped out to the rigs in smaller amounts. With such an increase in activity further congestion of existing quay space was unavoidable until the new bases were able to share the burden.

An indication of the increased activity was the interest shown in the port by other shipping companies. In September 1972 Ellerman's Wilson Line, already operating between Grangemouth and the west coast of Norway included Lerwick in their schedule, their local agents being Messrs J. & M. Shearer. In the following year Nimmo Offshore Services began trading between Aberdeen, Kirkwall and Lerwick in competition with the "North of Scotland" Company and in September, 1974, Trucking and Shipping Ltd. of Melton Mowbray introduced their new Shetland Line operating between Boston, Lincs, Grangemouth and Lerwick.

To enable Ellerman's Wilson Line to discharge general cargo from Norway the Trust had to make formal application to H.M. Customs for Lerwick to be approved for this purpose. Approval was given on condition that secure storage facilities were provided for uncleared goods, and for examination purposes. The Trust provided a store on a year to year basis in the old building on the south end of Alexandra Wharf.

THE NEW FISH MARKET

The pressures due to oil-related activities did not mean a loss of interest in the fishing industry or in the old part of the harbour. Work continued at No. 1 Station and as the scheme developed it became considerably enlarged. The Trustees had by this time agreed that it was futile to retain the spending beach since boats with fouled propellors could be beached elsewhere in the harbour or engage the help of a diver. In 1972 it was decided to aim for the maximum development possible and build a sea wall in a straight line from the north end of Alexandra Wharf towards the Malakoff Pier. The benefit would be an extra acre of land for processing factories etc., while the extra space would ease congestion on the access road leading down to the North Ness.

The Department of Agriculture & Fisheries for Scotland were at first unwilling to provide the extra money required but the Trust reminded them that unless the project went ahead they would find it impossible to make available the south side of the spur jetty as a terminal for the proposed vehicular ferry service to Bressay.

Reluctantly the D.A.F.S. agreed and work went ahead throughout the remainder of 1972. By the summer of 1973 the quay wall was complete and fishing vessels were able to berth alongside thus freeing part of Alexandra Wharf for the landing of general cargo.

With the building of the new quay Lerwick Boating Club

could no longer use the facilities at the Gas Pier and the shed there. In October 1972 they wrote to the Trust seeking accommodation for at least 15 "Maid" class boats. The Trust agreed to help and a special raised wooden deck was built along the face of the spending beach south of the slipway in the small boat harbour.

The fish market was the last part of the scheme at No. 1 Station to be completed. In August 1973 it was decided that if built as planned it would be too small and it was decided to extend it by 16 metres making it 53 metres long. As early as March 1969 it had been decided that a net loft should be incorporated in the second storey of the fish market building. The decision was taken when L.H.D. Ltd. took over the firm of D. & A. Duthie who had for several years operated a net repair loft in the upper storey of the building at the south end of Alexandra Wharf.

The fish market was ready for use in March 1975 and plans were made for a formal opening ceremony. But before this could take place the trade of the port was paralysed by a blockade of fishing vessels when, for three days in the first week of April, the Shetland fleet blocked both the entrances to Lerwick harbour as part of a nationwide protest against the importation of cheap frozen fish which it was claimed was depressing quayside prices throughout the U.K. The blockade was lifted when the government promised to investigate the fishermen's grievances.

The new market was officially opened at the end of April 1975, when a retired fisherman, Mr. John West, cut a tape to unveil the commemorative plaque. Mr. West had come to Lerwick as a boy in 1898, one of the first of the Scottish "immigrants" who had formed a "colony" in the north part of the town and who had played such a great part in the growth of Lerwick's own fishing fleet. When Mr. West first came to Lerwick, Alexandra Wharf had not been built and the first steam drifter had not arrived. Mr. West was himself a successful fishing skipper and between the wars he was in charge of the steam drifter "Girl Joey", which was replaced by the motor drifter "Maud Evelyn". After the second war he fished for a time as skipper of the "Blossom" and later purchased an ex-Admiralty MFV which was renamed appropriately "John West".

To add to the dignity of the occasion, the scissors used at the opening ceremony were presented to Mr. West in a box

made by Mr. Brown of Wm. Tawse Ltd., from timber recovered
from the Dutch frigate "De Haan" which sank in Lerwick
harbour in 1640.

There remained one final job to be done in connection with
the new quay — a name had to be found in place of "No. 1
Station" which was no longer appropriate. In August 1975 it
was decided to name it Laurenson's Quay in memory of Mr
Arthur Laurenson, father of the present Clerk, who had played
such a prominent part in the development of the harbour from
1938 to 1968.

REORGANISED SEA-ROUTES

Although the increased activity due to oil-related developments made a reorganisation of shipping services urgent, the
plans for doing so had been made long before the dawn of the
oil age. In 1962 Mr. J. P. Moar, County Road Surveyor had
visited Norway to study ferry systems there and his subsequent
report had a direct bearing on the design of the vehicular
ferries considered most suitable for Shetland's inter-island routes.

In May 1967 Mr. Prophet Smith and Dr. Ian Skewis of the
Highlands & Islands Development Board met members of Lerwick Harbour Trust to discuss the question of introducing a
vehicular ferry to run between Lerwick and Bressay at the same
time as the new car ferries were introduced to the North Isles.
The siting of the Bressay terminal was an obvious choice but
the siting of the Lerwick terminal was a different matter. Some
members of the Trust thought it should be sited in the North
Harbour while the Harbourmaster, Captain Inkster, was of the
opinion that it should be sited in the small boat harbour and
that if necessary the vessel should be made smaller than the
North Isles ferries to suit the accommodation available. Several
meetings took place between representatives of the Trust and
of Zetland County Council before it was decided to site the
terminal at the spur jetty.

The first of the North Isles ferries the "Fivla" was
introduced to the Yell Sound crossing in May 1973 being
followed soon afterwards by the ferry across Bluemull Sound.
Gradually the "Earl of Zetland" found herself with less and
less work to do and soon she was serving only Whalsay. On
23rd February, 1975 she completed her last run to Whalsay and
without fuss or ceremony a long era was brought to an end.
The new system was not quite ready since the ferry terminal

at Vidlin was not completed on time and for a few months the vehicular ferry "Grima" served Whalsay from Lerwick. As for the "Earl of Zetland", she bid farewell to Lerwick on 3rd March 1975 to begin a new career in the search for North Sea oil.

In March 1973 the Trustees themselves became involved in inter-island transport when they took over the Bressay ferry. They purchased the little motor boat "Tystie" displaced from the route across Bluemull Sound and operated a service to Bressay until October 1975 when the County Council introduced their vehicular ferry on the new route between the spur jetty and Maryfield.

RO-RO TERMINAL

In the late 1960's the "North of Scotland" Shipping Company decided to re-organise their service to Shetland with the introduction of a roll on/roll off ferry. It was obvious to the Trust that the existing facilities at Victoria Pier could not be modified since the company required 1½ acres of flat land adjacent to their terminal.

In March 1971 Mr. Ian F. Henderson of Archibald Henderson & Partners inspected Bremner's station which the Trust were contemplating purchasing and he reported that it would be ideal for the purpose with deep water close inshore and an acre of flat land which could be increased if the Trust were to purchase more land in this area. The only drawback was the inadequacy of the existing roads and it was clear that a major reconstruction of the whole area was necessary. A meeting was held between representatives of the Trust and of Lerwick Town Council and it was agreed that the two bodies would try to work together and keep each other advised regarding future proposals for the area.

The Lerwick Harbour Order of 1973 gave the Trust powers to proceed with the development but it was some time before the details of the terminal could be finalised. In 1971 the North of Scotland, Orkney and Shetland Shipping Company was taken over by the P & O Group, the company founded by Arthur Anderson. A year later the company decided to place an order for a new roll on/roll off vessel to be completed in the spring of 1975. She would carry 400 passengers and her speed would be 16 knots. Based on the information given, the Trustees consultants began to design a new terminal to cost just under £1,000,000, but largely due to inflation the estimated cost rose steadily and by February 1974 when the contract was awarded to Costain Civil Engineering Ltd., the estimates had risen to £1,822,000.

The order for the new vessel was awarded to Hall, Russell & Co., Aberdeen. But it was soon clear that the vessel could not be ready in time. No steel was available for the project, a predicament for which the miners' strike and three-day week were largely to blame so the order was cancelled and in March the P. & O. Group decided to take the drive on/drive off ferry "Lion" off the Ardrossan-Larne route and convert her for the Shetland run with accommodation for up to 500 passengers. Inevitably this change of plans caused a re-designing of the proposed terminal.

In July 1975 P. & O. altered their plans again by deciding to put a larger vessel, the "Panther" on the Shetland run. Of 4857 tons and with a length of 402 ft. and a beam of 57 ft. she was a much larger vessel than the one for which the terminal had been designed. By this time the expected cost of the complex had risen to £3,400,000 plus consultants' and engineers' fees while further modification to strengthen the terminal pier was expected to cost £100,000.

In October 1975 the contract for the terminal building worth £156,604 was awarded to T. L. Arcus & Co., while the contract for the transit shed worth £42,129 was awarded to Hunter and Morrison. In the same month the old-fashioned name, North of Scotland Orkney and Shetland Shipping Company was changed to P & O Ferries (Orkney and Shetland Services) and early in 1976 the vessels' funnels were re-painted blue to conform with the rest of the line.

THE NEW IMPORTANCE OF THE TRUST

The early 1970's were critical years for Lerwick harbour. It was a time when unprecedented pressures were brought to bear and a time of unprecedented change when the entire North Harbour was altered beyond recognition. It was a testing time for the body of men who governed the harbour but they proved their worth and emerged at the end of the day stronger than at any time in the 100 years history of the Trust. They had many anxious moments when they were forced to take a calculated risk as when they purchased the Grimista estate and so placed a severe strain on their financial resources at a time when there was no guarantee that it would be required in oil-related developments. Again, in January 1973, when it seemed that a shortage of steel might jeopardise the building of the Shell/BP and Ro/Ro facilities, the Trustees took a risk and placed a £90,000 order for steel when they had no guarantee that any of these developments would proceed and indeed before any agreement had been signed with the oil companies and with the Scottish Office.

In November 1970 two new members, Mr. A. I. Tulloch and Mr. A. B. Fraser, were appointed as representatives of the County Council. They served continuously throughout the important period of planning as did Mr. Alex. Morrison, Mr. James Paton, Mr. Harry Gray and Mr. Alex. J. Gear. In November 1972 Mr. W. R. T. Hamilton retired and was replaced as third representative of the County Council by Mr. T. W. Stove. At the same time Mr. James Wiseman was appointed a ratepayers' representative. At the following meeting of the Trust Mr. Harry Gray was appointed Chairman in place of Mr. Magnus Shearer who had guided the Trust during the critical period of the early 1970's and Mr. A. J. Gear was again appointed Vice Chairman.

Inevitably several former Trustees died during this period, their passing noted with regret at meetings of the Trust. In March 1971 a tribute was paid to the late Mr. William Duncan, at one time skipper of the herring boat "Speedwell" and a Trustee from 1954 to 1959. In March 1973 the death occurred of Mr. John R. Linklater, for many years proprietor of the business known as R. & C. Robertson, and a Trustee from 1954 to 1965. In January 1976 reference was made to the outstanding contribution of the late Robert J. H. Ganson.

In November 1973, after considering legal advice the Trustees discovered that the three members representing shipowners, Mr. Francis Garriock, Mr. Magnus Shearer and Mr. A. Beattie were not entitled to stand for election as representatives of shipowners. The Act of 1877 had laid down that such a representative must be the owner of at least 20 tons of shipping. These three gentlemen were directors of limited companies and although one of the two companies in question, Hay & Co. (Lerwick) Ltd., were owners of two fairly large cargo vessels, this was not strictly what Section 19 of the 1877 Act had in mind. Immediately steps were taken to have the Act amended to allow directors of limited companies to stand for election provided that they had sufficient shares in such a company to qualify under the 20 tons ruling.

In November 1974 Mr. James H. Henry, skipper and part-owner of the purse seiner-trawler "Wavecrest", was appointed a shipowners' representative and at the same time Mr A. I. Tulloch resigned being replaced as Trustee by Mr. J. C. Irvine. A year later Mr. Magnus Shearer was back on the Trust as a representative of the ratepayers after narrowly defeating Mr. Wiseman in an election for the post.

Under the reorganisation of local government in 1975 Lerwick Town Council was swept away, being absorbed in the new single authority which governs the whole of Shetland. But it was agreed that the current balance on the Trust should be maintained and of the six members appointed by the Shetland Islands Council at least three should represent Lerwick wards. It had earlier been agreed that the member for Bressay must also be one of the Council's representatives on the Trust, the first appointment under this ruling being that of Mr. J. C. Irvine. It was also agreed in 1975 that members should be paid an allowance for attendance at meetings of the Trust following an example set by the new Shetland Islands Council.

The amount of work carried out by these men is evident from the number of meetings which were now found necessary. It was evident, too, from the amount of legislation found necessary to cope with development. At one time the promotion of a Provisional Order was a landmark, carried out after careful and prolonged consideration once in a decade or two. But between 1970 and 1975 no fewer than four separate Bills relating to Lerwick harbour received the Royal Assent.

The Act of 1974 extended the harbour limits to a line from the Ness of Sound to Whinna Skerry and in the north to a line between Greenhead and Turra Taing. It also gave the Trust powers to borrow up to £5 million. The Act of 1975 left the southern limits of the harbour untouched but it extended the northern limit to new lines joining Score Head, the Green Holm and Hawks Ness.

Some of these Orders in their passage through Parliament raised formal objections from Zetland County Council as that body sought to reinforce the power it had been given under the Zetland County Council Act of 1974. In every case a compromise was reached — a form of words acceptable to both parties — although the Trust was never forced to abandon any of the powers being sought. In September 1973 it was suggested that one pilotage authority should be set up to cover the whole of Shetland but the Trust were not interested and even decided to examine the question of making pilotage within their own harbour limits compulsory.

An even better indication of the increasing activity at Lerwick was the increase in the number of staff. In 1970 the work of the harbour was carried out by the Clerk, Harbour Master, Assistant Harbour Master and eight employees. By 1975 the Trust had 40 employees including berthing masters, crane drivers, maintenance staff, office staff and crews for the two pilot boats "Ord" (formerly "Budding Rose") and the "Bard" (formerly the "Brighter Dawn", purchased in 1972).

In September 1972 it was decided that the title of Clerk was old-fashioned and did not establish clearly Mr Laurenson's position as the Trust's executive. It was decided to change this to General Manager but although it was perfectly in order for the Trust to have such an official it was still necessary under the terms of the Act of 1877 to have a Clerk. So, Mr Laurenson was given the rather cumbersome title of General Manager & Clerk.

In December 1972 it was decided to make a new appointment — that of Personal Assistant to the General Manager and Clerk. From twelve applicants Mr. Leslie H. Johnson was chosen to fill the new post but first of all Mr. Johnson had to give up his seat on the Trust.

On 28th February, 1974 the Harbour Master, Captain Inkster retired on reaching the age of 70. At a function in the Grand Hotel on 7th March reference was made to his outstanding service during the period of post-war reconstruction and economic recovery. He was replaced as Harbour Master by Captain Polson while Captain Robert J. Groat became Deputy Harbour Master. The latter had been appointed a pilot in April 1973.

The premises occupied by the harbour staff were enlarged considerably. The flat above the Harbour Office was converted into offices for the Harbour Master and other staff. In 1974 an extension was added to the south end of Alexandra Buildings and here on the first floor offices were provided for the General Manager and Clerk and for his Deputy while across the central passage an extension was made to the general office.

Apart from the work carried out by the staff of Lerwick Harbour Trust a great deal of extra work was undertaken by consultants and advisers. Archibald Henderson & Partners remain the Trust's Consulting Engineers and Mr. Gordon Henderson is frequently in attendance at meetings of the Trustees. It is interesting to reflect that the entire development of Lerwick harbour since World War II has been designed in the firm's office at Bridge Street, Aberdeen. At one stage Messrs. Henderson found it impossible to cope with the work involved at Lerwick and they formed an association with the firm of James Williamson to whom much of the planning of the Grimista area was entrusted. Messrs Leslie D. Morrison & Partners were appointed architects for the new terminal building and transit shed and since then have been retained for other projects.

The Trust's legal adviser is Mr. James Goodlad of the firm of J. B. Anderson and Goodlad and accountants are Messrs. A. P. Frame & Co., their local partner being Mr John A. Ferris. Both Mr. Goodlad and Mr. Ferris have been of immense help to the Trustees in their many negotiations. The Trust's Parliamentary Agents are Martin & Co.

The growing trade of the port is evident from the statistics compiled for 1975. In that year a total of 4,809 vessels of 1,257,343 net registered tons used Lerwick harbour, an increase of 778 vessels and 443,617 net registered tons compared to 1974. These figures do not include the comings and goings of Shetland's fishing fleet but they include 1,237 foreign fishing vessels and 1,581 vessels engaged in oil research and development.

The breakdown of foreign vessels is interesting. Scandinavian visitors were most common with 476 Norwegian, 319 Danish, 236 Faroese, 106 Icelandic vessels and 36 Swedish calling during the year. The Danish and Swedish vessels were mainly trawlers engaged in industrial fishing for pout and sand eel while the rest were mainly purse seiners fishing for herring and mackerel. Other callers were 30 Polish, 17 Russian, 12 Dutch, 9 French, 3 German and 3 Finnish vessels.

The total weight of goods handled was 661,599 tons compared to 259,987 tons in 1974. Imports amounted to 405,330 tons and included 179,371 tons of concrete-coated pipes landed at the Norscot Base. Exports amounted to 256,546 tons and included 69,320 tons of concrete-coated pipe shipped to lay barges and 86,594 tons of water of which 68,583 tons were required by the oil industry. The islands' traditional industries continue to thrive and no fewer than 45,644 sheep, 2,817 cattle and 645 ponies were shipped during the year.

N

Chapter Sixteen

THE HARBOUR IN 1977

The shoreline of Lerwick shows clearly the main stages in the growth of the port since the 17th century. At the south entrance the cliffs are still in their natural state although surmounted by the white-painted houses of the Coastguard Station and by the attractive bungalows along the lower side of Twageos Road. The Anderson High School is now a massive complex but the original building donated by Arthur Anderson has changed little in appearance since it was built in 1862. Anderson's Homes too, are outwardly the same as when built but they have been modernised and converted into flats and are now owned by the Shetland Islands Council.

Beyond Anderson's Homes, Twageos Road runs down a steep slope past new housing schemes which in their high density form are reminiscent of the old houses they replace. Then it meets Commercial Street and an area of the town that has changed little in 150 years. The original paving stones have been replaced by concrete slabs but the buildings on either side still retain the atmosphere of the early 19th century and behind those on the seaward side lie the private piers and lodberries that contribute so much to the charm of the South End.

The seawall continues northwards until it meets Gillie's Pier and Lodberry, one of the few surviving lodberries that still serves the same purpose for which it was built. In this lodberry the Angus Brothers once had their workshop and here grew the daisy that inspired James Stout Angus to write his famous poem "Da Kokkilurie". Farther north stands Stout's Pier, built by Robert Stout, father of Sir Robert Stout, once Prime Minister of New Zealand.

The dominant building here, No. 10 Commercial Street, is a tall house with stepped gables built by Patrick Scollay about 1730 and at that time the only substantial building on the seaward side of the road. Behind it stands Torrie's Lodberry, named after a later occupant of No. 10. Next comes Murray's Lodberry, once used by Messrs. J. & M. Shearer as a curing station in conjunction with the jetty at Scarfa Skerry which was built by John M. Aitken much against the will of Lerwick Harbour Trust. Ironically this property is now owned by the Trust who intend to develop it in their plans for a marina.

Behind No. 14 Commercial Street, stands MacBeath's Lodberry, once owned by Andrew MacBeath, and immediately to the north stands the building still known as the Steamers Store Lodberry, although it ceased to fulfil this function in 1875. It has two doors, one facing east, the other opening on to massive stone steps just below the beach at Craigie's Stane.

On the north side of the beach stands a group of buildings now known simply as "the Lodberrie" although they were once known as Robertson's Lodberry when owned by Bailie John Robertson who was Joint Agent with Charles Merrylees for the "North of Scotland" Shipping Company until 1878. One of the sheds was used as a fish curing station and it still has slatted windows which allow air to circulate freely inside.

North of "The Lodberrie" runs a stretch of yellow sand known as Bain's Beach where Dutch bomschuits were once beached to allow repairs to be carried out. In recent years small vessels engaged in oil exploration have occasionally been forced to use it for the same purpose.

From here northwards the upper side of the street is lined with the gable ends of houses built by Lerwick merchants in the early 19th century. Lochend House is still prominent, its courtyard now known as Bain's Yett after the father of Gilbert Bain who purchased Lochend House from the Nicolson family.

On the north side of Bain's Beach stands the Queen's Hotel and behind it are two lodberries, one of them owned originally by Francis Yates, a cooper and slate merchant, the other owned by the Hay family. At the north-east corner of the Queen's Hotel a thick wall of concrete connects it to the breakwater. This wall was erected in 1915 by John M. Aitken and it is a permanent reminder of a bitter conflict that raged between the Trust and the proprietors of the hotel when it was discovered that the backwash from the newly - erected breakwater was undermining the building.

The building opposite the foot of Church Lane is the old Tolbooth whose foundations were laid in 1769. When used as a Court House it was complete with prison cells and dungeons.

Then it became in turn a meeting place for Free Masons, a telegraphic office, a schoolroom, and is now used as an old people's rest room and headquarters of the Red Cross.

The small boat harbour behind, although far too small for the large fleet of boats that require dock accommodation, is one of the most delightful parts of Lerwick and at weekends, and at other times, depending on the seasonal pattern of fishing, it is full of brightly-painted fishing vessels. Along the arm of the breakwater Lerwick's lifeboat, the "Claude Cecil Staniforth", lies throughout the year.

Lerwick is proud of its lifeboat and crew. When the maroons go off a crowd quickly gathers at the South Esplanade to watch the start of yet another mission. The lifeboat's record of service is detailed on a board proudly displayed in the lifeboat station nearby. This building has another claim to fame since it was Lerwick's first harbour office.

The Esplanade was part of the initial scheme of development begun by the Trust in 1883. At its south end it is a quiet and restful spot but for most of its length it is now a busy thoroughfare. A new road runs down what used to be Church Lane, cuts right across Commercial Street and merges with the Esplanade behind the General Post Office.

This building too hides a little bit of history. This was the area of foreshore once known as Sinclair's Beach over which the Trustees fought a bitter legal battle and lost. The name is perpetuated in Sinclair's Steps which link Commercial Street with the South Esplanade. These are the "new" steps constructed at the south end of the Post Office in 1910.

Within the last few years the small boat harbour has been denuded of much of its interest and importance. First to go was the Bressay ferry, the terminal being moved to a new site when the car ferry was introduced in 1975. The slipway is still there and is used occasionally by small vessels but it was a busy place when used by the people of Bressay. First to operate a regular service was an Orcadian named Dennison whose sailing boat carried the milk from the Hoversta Dairy. Then came the motor boats — the "Thelma", "Myra", "Norna" and "Brenda" and latterly the "Tystie". It is unlikely that any vessel will ever equal the records of the "Norna" and "Brenda". The former was one of the lifeboats of the S.S. "Oceanic", wrecked near Foula in 1915. The latter was built as a launch for the German navy and survived the dramatic scuttling of the fleet at Scapa Flow in 1919.

A still greater change came to the small boat harbour in 1976 when the vessels belonging to P. & O. Ferries began calling at the new terminal at Holmsgarth. Only then did the people of Lerwick realise the magnitude of the change. No longer would that splendid vessel "St. Clair" berth on the South side of Victoria Pier, her bows overlooking the Esplanade and Commercial Street. The loading and unloading of cargo were operations in which the whole of Lerwick and visitors too were involved. Who was getting a new tractor? — It was a simple matter to look at the label. Now cargo is loaded and unloaded at the ultra-modern, highly-efficient but extremely impersonal terminal at Holmsgarth and for many people things will never be the same again.

At the head of Victoria Pier the Diana Fountain still stands on the position it has occupied since 1959. When originally erected to commemorate the almost miraculous return of the whaler "Diana" in 1867 it occupied a position farther west. But as more room became available for the widening of the roadway it was moved to its present site.

The Esplanade follows closely the old shoreline of 1883. On its seaward side it is flanked by the new quays of the 1960's but its upper side is a treasure house of history. Ellesmere House dates from 1906 and Victoria Buildings from 1905. The latter now houses the Aberdeen Savings Bank and on its first floor the Planning Department and Motor Taxation Department of Shetland Islands Council. The Harbour Office was also built in 1905 and it still bears evidence of the twin roles for which it was designed for the glass panel of the door on the right still bears the legend "Police, Sanitary and Water Office".

North of the Harbour Office the buildings repay closer examination. Many of the stores were once lodberries standing in the sea and here and there an iron ring where boats were moored remains embedded in the wall. Below the old Medical Hall the date 1736 is cut out in a stone on the end of the lodberry. Some of the old names still designate sheds, steps and lanes but others have disappeared. Grierson's Lodberry was incorporated in the offices of the shipping company and Tait's Lodberry is now the Thule Bar. North of the Thule Bar is a square with buildings on three of its sides. On the south side stands the shop of J. & M. Fraser, fish merchants, run by grandsons of Mrs Jessie Hay who was the first to have a stance allocated in 1916. Opening into the back of the square is Harry Jamieson's barber shop, while on the north side are stores used by Messrs J. & J. Tods, wholesale merchants. The buildings here have changed little from the time when they jutted into the sea for this was part of the North Lodberry and can still be recognised from photographs taken 100 years ago.

On the seaward side of the Esplanade with its back to Albert Wharf stands the plain but essential block of public conveniences, while farther north stands the old white fish market now used as stores for the large nets used in purse seining for herring.

Looking north to Fort Charlotte it is difficult to imagine that this was once a citadel perched on a clifftop overlooking the sea. Now the cliffs drop down to Commercial Road, protected on its seaward side by a high stone wall. Below the wall a wide expanse of roadway and quay demonstrate how much has been reclaimed in the last 100 years. North of Tod's steps the triangular area of ground between the Esplanade and the retaining wall was once virtually all the ground that the Trust had to let. Here they allowed the Co-operative Coal Company to build their coal store. That building stood, virtually unchanged, until February, 1975, when it was removed in the redevelopment of Crossan Oil's fuel depot.

North of the oil depot the building once used as Thomson's Garage has been used since 1971 by Messrs L. Williamson as part of their extensive fish-processing business. Thomson's showroom next door was in 1971 taken over by Thulecraft as a showroom for their range of products moulded from glass reinforced plastic.

Farther north there stands a plain building clad in corrugated iron which although humble in appearance has a fascinating history. It began life as a Police Office on the site now occupied by the Harbour Office and it was removed to the North Esplanade in 1905. For many years it was known simply as Mrs Jamieson's and more recently as Lizzie's Lodestar Cafe until in April, 1975, tenancy was transferred to Miss Moira Rendall.

Immediately to the north of the cafe in the wall behind the weighbridge is a curious cave-like compartment once used as an ash depot where refuse was accumulated before being loaded on to a cart and taken to the refuse tip at the Knab. The weighbridge itself is built on the site of the old watering trough used for the watering of horses while their owners were being refreshed in the cafe.

There was once a gap in the high wall farther north where a flight of wooden steps linked Commercial Street and the Esplanade. The opening, although filled in when the stairway was removed, can still be traced in the face of the wall.

Alexandra Wharf is now the main commercial quay in the old part of the harbour. The quay wall is the one added in the 1920's but the line of the older quay wall is still visible in places. At the spur jetty, now the terminal for the Bressay ferry, the outline of the original face can still be seen as well as the outline of the repairs of the 1920s where the quay was angled off to fill in the "knuckle".

The area north of Alexandra Wharf has been entirely changed since 1970. There is no longer a bight with the Gas Pier and spending beach and gone too is No. 1 Station or Gunthers Quay as it used to be known. Instead the new wall of Laurenson's Quay runs straight towards the Malakoff Pier and links Alexandra Wharf with the North Ness.

The North Ness remains an important industrial area. The Malakoff slipway developed by John W. Robertson and owned in turn by Mr Innes Smith and Mr Alex Johnson is now owned by Lithgows (Holdings) Ltd., who purchased it in 1973. On the north side of the slipway is the extensive oil depot belonging to Messrs S. & J. D. Robertson Ltd., on the site occupied by Hugh MacDonald & Co.'s herring station between the wars.

There is no longer a herring station at the North Ness. The large sheds, barrel store and cooperage once run by Mr Mitchell are now used as stores by Hay & Co. and North-Eastern Farmers Ltd. During the early years of oil-rig servicing in this area Ocean Inchcape (Shetland) Ltd. had a service base on what used to be the north part of Mitchell's station where flitboats once used to call for new herring barrels. The barrel factory itself and adjacent offices are now occupied by a building firm.

The factory built by the Herring Industry Board on the site of the old Anglo-Scottish herring station, previously John Brown's station, is still in operation and is now occupied by Shetland Seafoods Ltd. Some of the wooden sheds occupied by

Norwegian naval personnel during World War II are still in existence.

Freefield docks have changed little in the past 50 years apart for the removal of the old sailing vessel "Eleonore von Flotow" which for 80 years served as a salt store on the western side of the dock. The numerous sheds and stores show clearly the important role played by Freefield during the centuries of Lerwick's growth. Hay & Co.'s boatbuilding shed and slipway remain, the former now used as a timber store, while John Brown's once famous engineering works are now part of Hay & Co.'s sawmill.

The coal corner is still a prominent landmark with extensive coal sheds, one of them used now as a cement store, while the old roofless building to the east, once a gear store, is now preserved as a listed building. Along the northern side of the docks stand the old herring market and the store where the salt cod, taken by smacks from Faroe and Iceland, were dried over rows of braziers, while the tall building at the very end of Docks Road was for long used as a sail loft. In view of the changes in this part of Freefield it is reassuring to find a building that continues to fulfil the role for which it was intended. This is Hay & Co.'s shop which has not changed much in 100 years.

At Garthspool the quays and sheds built in the middle of the 19th century by Joseph Leask now fulfil different purposes in the varied enterprises of their present owners, Messrs J. & M. Shearer. Herring curing is no longer carried out here but the fishing industry plays a great part in the firm's activities with two ice plants, one of them supplying flake ice by chute to fishing vessels at the firm's own quay, and a fleet of lorries delivering ice to any part of the Shetland mainland. In 1975 a new quay was built at Garthspool and it is presently being used by ships of the Shetland Line discharging general cargo.

A greater change has taken place at Holmsgarth. Slater's station is still here but no fewer than six herring stations have been swept away to make room for the roll on - roll off terminal. Gone forever are Leslie's, Woods, Sinclair & Buchan's Bremner's, Pommer & Thomson's and Dunbar's — names that evoke nostalgic memories for an older generation of Lerwegians. In their place have come the terminal with its hydraulically operated ramps, the terminal buildings, and the large transit shed with 1,900 sq. metres of storage space. Farther north are the Shell and B.P. service bases that have played an important role in the development of North Sea oilfields.

Greatest change of all has occurred at Grimista Farm which was acquired in 1971 by Lerwick Harbour Trust. The farm house has been demolished to make room for a scrap yard and the surrounding fields are gradually being transformed into the main industrial area for Lerwick. Already developments are on a collossal scale with the Norscot service base occupying the entire area of the old Greenhead and much more besides, while farther north, near Rova Head, is the large quarry operated by A.Q.S. (Shetland) Ltd. These are merely the first of the developments planned for the Grimista area since a site has been earmarked for an industrial estate and already ten firms have announced plans for building factories here.

In the midst of all these developments stands the Böd of Grimista, a large stone building once the office and stores of a company engaged in drying salt fish and revered by Shetlanders as the birth place of Arthur Anderson.

The oil boom is only beginning but it too will pass and a new use will have to be found for the quays and warehouses that have served the oil industry and Lerwick may well start a new phase of development as exciting as any period in its long history. One thing is certain — the challenge to the Trustees of that future date will be as great as any that their predecessors have had to face.

INDEX

Aberdeen, 13, 14, 15, 22, 24, 45, 46, 47, 59, 65, 101, 135, 147, 157, 177, 181, 185.
Aberdeen, Leith, Clyde & Tay Shipping Co., 14.
Aberdeen Savings Bank, 189.
Aberdeen, W., 5.
Accidents, 65, 72, 74, 76, 90, 97, 122, 130, 131, 133.
"Active", 74.
Admiralty, 80, 93, 95, 97, 98, 100, 101, 102, 104, 107, 112, 113, 118, 121, 127, 130, 142,
Advance Supply Bases, 173.
Advisory Panel for the Highlands and Islands, 142, 149.
"Aeriel", 15.
Aitken, J. M., 53, 57, 61, 66, 67, 73, 92, 187.
Aitken & Wright, 140.
Albert Dock, 150.
Albert Hall, 77.
Albert Wharf, 28, 29, 65, 84, 85, 87, 94, 103, 109, 113, 119, 120, 141, 146, 147, 150, 190.
Alexandra Buildings, 149, 168, 184.
Alexandra Wharf, 16, 53-56, 66, 67, 68, 71, 82, 92, 97, 98, 100, 101, 105, 107, 112, 115, 118, 119, 131, 132, 136, 140, 141, 143, 145, 146, 148, 150, 177, 178, 191.
Allan, J. H., 63.
Allan, W., 60.
Allison, Capt. G., 30, 69, 73, 105.
Alston, Commander H. G., 97.
Altona, 119, 126.
America, 80, 129.
American ships, 8, 105, 132.
"Anaconda", 11.
Anders Hill, 95.
Anderson, A., 5, 14, 180, 185, 193.
Anderson, D. G., 148, 149.
Anderson Educational Institute, 5, 134.
Anderson High School, 185.
Anderson Homes, 185.
Anderson, J. G., 35.
Anderson, T. J., 36.
Anderson, W. J., 125.
Anderson, W. S., 154, 168.
Anderson & Co., 139.
Anglo-American Oil Co., 108, 140.
Anglo-Scottish herring station, 133, 155, 190.

Angus, James S., 186.
"Ant", 48.
A.Q.S. (Shetland) Ltd., 193.
Archangel, 103, 105.
Arcus, L., 18, 20.
Arcus, T. L., Ltd., 181.
Ash depot, 65, 190.
Auction system of sales, 44, 45, 48, 49, 50, 53, 59. *See also* Fish market.

Bain, A., 30.
Bain, J., 8.
Bain's Beach, 9, 36, 187.
Bain's Yett, 187.
Ballast yard, 65, 108.
Baltasound, 50, 51, 70, 76, 126, 174.
"Bard", mv, 184.
Barrel factory, 80.
Barron, Mr, 37, 54, 55, 57, 58, 61, 68, 86, 87.
Batteries, 8, 80, 92. *See also* Fort Charlotte.
Beattie, A., 166, 167, 182.
"Beaufort", H.M.S., 121.
Bell, F. A., 137.
"Ben Doran", st, 122.
"Bertie", 89.
Bessey & Palmer, 71.
Black, S., 111.
Blackwood, Commander, 75.
Blance, R. B., 153, 154, 168.
Blockade, 178.
Bloomfields, 79.
"Blossom", mv, 178.
Bluemull Sound, 179, 180.
"Blyth", ss., 134.
Blyth & Blyth, 138.
Board of Trade, 38, 56, 67, 85, 87, 102, 121.
Boatbuilding, 10, 11, 18, 20, 26, 27, 46, 50, 80, 81, 82, 118.
Boer War, 52.
Bolt, T., 5.
Bomschuit, 19, 51, 72, 187.
"Bonnie Dundee", 14.
"Boreas", 48, 49.
"Borgund", mv, 128.
Borrowing powers, 24, 25, 85, 115, 116, 124, 125, 175, 183.
Bovis, 175.
B.P., 173, 174, 175, 176, 193.
Brand, Rev. J., 3.
Brandal, K., 160.
Breakwater, 17, 84-91, 119, 144, 149; proposed, 144, 146, 147, 150.
Breiwick, 128, 131, 171.

Bremner's station, 170, 180, 192.
"Brenda", m.v., 188.
Bressay, 1, 5, 8, 36, 46, 67, 69, 72, 73, 76, 82, 90, 92, 95, 121, 130, 137,
    140, 151, 155, 157, 161, 167.
Bressay ferry. 179, 180, 188, 191.
Bressay lighthouse, 48, 72, 73, 135.
Bressay slip, 89, 151.
Bressay Sound, 1-3, 16, 113, 161.
"Brighter Dawn", mv, 184.
"Britannia", ry, 152.
British Ceca, 172.
British Steam Fishing Co., 70.
"Brother's Gem", 72.
Brown, J., 27, 80, 100, 105, 191, 192.
Brown, J. W., 105.
Brown, P., 89, 98, 107, 116, 124.
Brown, Sheriff, 75.
Bruce, R. S., 113.
Brunthamarsland, 3.
Buckie, 26.
"Budding Rose", mv, 147, 184.
Buoys, 73, 121, 140, 165.
Burgess, G. H., 142, 144, 153, 154, 167, 169.
Buses, 138, 146, 148.
Buss, 2, 4, 19, 49.
"Buttercup", 49, 76.
By-laws, 73, 74, 121, 123, 165.

Caithness flags, 90.
"Cambria," ss, 97.
Cameron of Garth, 24, 157.
Campbeltown, 51.
"Caspiana", st, 60.
Catfirth, 174.
Cay, Dyce, 22.
Channel Fleet, 93, 94, 95.
Charlotte Place, 15, 23.
"Cheerful", H.M.S., 99.
"Chieftain's Bride',, ss, 16, 17.
"Children's Trust", 76.
Church Army, 98.
Churches, 34, 77, 78.
Clark, I. R., 169.
Clark's Lodberry, 17.
"Claude Cecil Staniforth", 152, 188.
Clerks to the Trust, 30, 35, 40, 56, 88, 89, 98, 101, 116, 143, 144, 168,
    171, 172, 179, 184.
Clydesdale and North of Scotland Bank, 138.
Coal, 71, 72, 100, 129, 136, 192.
Coal hulks, 71, 72, 86, 129, 147. *See also* Lerwick Co-operative Coal Co.

Coastguard, 162, 186.
Cockstool, 2, 6, 17, 29.
Cod, 4, 11, 12, 20, 26, 48, 49. *See also* Fishing Industry and Smacks.
Coghill, A., 111.
"Columbine", 15.
"Comet", 82.
Commercial Road, 114, 133, 148, 166.
Commercial Street, 4, 6, 16, 17, 19, 23, 51, 52, 64, 135, 151, 188, 189, 191.
Commissioners of Northern Lighthouses, 72, 73, 121, 140.
Commissioners of Supply, 22, 24, 110.
Communications, 13-16, 22-24, 39-42, 45-47, 65, 66, 126, 127, 135, 170, 176, 177, 179-181, 185.
"Consolation", sd, 51.
"Contest", sd, 12, 48, 49.
Contract system, 44, 45, 48, 49, 50.
Convoys, 99, 100, 127.
Copeland, J., 9.
Costain Civil Engineering, 181.
"Courier", 15.
Craigie's Stane, 16, 84, 187.
"Creteground", 129, 147.
Cromwell, 3.
Crossan Oils, 190.
Customs & Excise, 5, 9, 20, 97, 147, 149, 177.
"Cuxwold", 49.
"Cyclone", 12.
"Cynthia", 12.

Dalziel, P., 154.
Danish fishermen, 51, 185.
"Danish Rose", 12, 48.
Danish Vice Consul, 169.
Davidson, J., 57, 61.
Defence of the Realm Act, 97.
"Defiance", 26.
"De Haan", 3, 113, 115, 147, 179.
Denmark, 10.
Dennison, Capt., 188.
Dept. of Agriculture & Fisheries for Scotland, 166, 167, 174, 177.
Dept. of the Environment, 174.
"De Reiger", 3, 113, 115.
"Destiny", 11.
Deufrika, 126, 128.
Deuk's Neb, 5.
Development Commissioners, 87, 115, 144.
"Diana", 13, 189.
Diana Fountain, 13, 17, 189.
Dogfish, 151, 158, 159.
"Dolphin", sd, 81.
"Doris", 14, 17.

"Dreadnought", HMS, 95.
Dryburgh, F., 138, 142.
Drydock, 137, 141, 142.
Dues, 23, 24, 29, 40, 41, 58, 61, 82, 86, 90, 102, 112, 115, 117, 143, 144, 145.
Duke of Edinburgh, 93, 151.
Duncan, W., 154, 182.
Dutch fishermen, 1, 2, 3, 4, 19, 20, 29, 51, 52, 72, 73, 74, 77, 113.
Dutch submarines, 132.
Duthie, A., 168.
Duthie, D. & A., 178.

"Eagle", HMS, 29.
"Earl of Zetland", ss, 16, 29, 30, 40, 46, 109, 124, 126, 131, 135.
"Earl of Zetland", mv, 126, 135, 150, 180.
Edwardson, C., 112.
Electricity, 73, 89, 123.
"Eleonore von Flotow", 192.
Ellerman's Wilson Line, 176, 177.
Ellesmere Buildings, 63, 189.
English fishermen, 70-75, 77.
"Equity", mv, 156.
"Eurylochus", ss, 126.
Evans, Lieut. Col., 96.
"Everline", ss, 122.

"Fair Maid", 12.
"Fairy", 14.
Faroe, 10, 11, 12, 20, 48, 49, 79, 120, 123, 163.
Faroese fishermen, 122, 162, 185.
"Fern", sd, 60.
Ferris, J., 185.
Fetlar, 4, 5, 36.
Feuars and Heritors of Lerwick, 56, 145.
Fines, 73-75.
Finnish vessels, 185.
Fishery Board, 115, 117, 118.
Fishing industry: haaf fishing, 4, 20, 48; haddock fishing, 46, 47, 83, 120; herring fishing, 2, 26, 48, 70-76, 96, 102, 103, 104, 105, 115, 118, 126, 137, 156, 161, 162; illegal fishing, 162, 185; industrial fishing, 162, 185; overfishing, 161, 162; seining, 120, 156; shell fishing, 157; smack fishery, 11, 12, 48, 49; "Spring" fishing, 26, 48; trawling, 46, 47, 96, 161.
Fish Markets, 54, 58, 66, 68, 71, 97, 112, 118, 120, 123, 137, 143, 147, 151, 158, 159, 166, 178, 190.
Fish processing: canning, 50; curing, 4, 5, 10, 11, 19, 20, 26, 27, 44, 49, 80, 103, 104, 121, 137, 187; freezing, 137, 155, 158; kippering, 59, 60, 104, 118, 155; manure, 81, 155; meal and oil, 137, 155, 162.
Fish salesmen, 70, 79, 80, 119, 120.
Fish stalls, 103, 146.

"Fitful Head", sd, 81.
Fleet Street, 47.
Flitboats, 16, 22, 29, 80, 118, 130, 191.
Floating dock, 68, 84.
Flying boats, 123, 126, 130, 132.
"Foam", 12.
Fog signal, 73.
Fordyce, S. W., 110, 111.
Fort Charlotte, 3, 6, 8, 16, 18, 23, 28, 31, 57, 83, 92, 96, 100, 105, 147, 190.
Forty Voyage Clause, 24, 30, 39-41.
Frame, A. P. & Co., 185.
Fraser, A. B., 182.
Fraser, A. S., 153, 158.
Fraser, J., 120.
Fraser, J. & M., 146, 157, 190.
Fraser, T., 142.
Fraserburgh, 26, 50, 51, 137.
Freefield, 10, 11, 20, 26, 27, 50, 53, 54, 72, 80, 82, 100, 106, 141, 192.
Free Masons, 6, 28, 124, 188.
French fishermen, 185.
French warships, 4.
Fresh fish trade, 26, 45-47, 103, 120, 146, 156.
Freshing, 50, 119, 126, 137.
Fyfe, J., 65.

"Gadus", ss, 50.
Ganson Brothers, 64, 108.
Ganson, R. D., 34, 110, 115, 123.
Ganson, R. J. H., 141, 143, 154, 167, 182.
Gardie House, 73, 157.
Garriock, F., 152, 153, 167, 169, 182.
Garriock, J., 111.
Garriock, L. F. U., 24.
Garthspool, 12, 20, 26, 27, 45, 50, 53, 67, 77, 79, 120, 192.
Gas, 18, 34, 65, 73, 89.
Gasworks, 18.
Gas Pier, 18, 22, 28, 31, 55, 67, 143, 147, 165, 178, 191.
Gatt, J., 81.
Gear, A. J., 119, 166, 167, 182.
Germany, 80, 93, 95, 126, 137.
German aircraft, 127, 128, 130, 131.
German fishermen, 51, 73, 185.
German prisoners, 128.
German Vice Consul, 94, 168.
Gibbs, R. P., 174.
"Gibraltar", HMS, 100.
Gilbert Bain Hospital, 9, 74, 78, 97, 129, 185.
Gilbertson Park, 115.
Gillie's Pier, 9, 36, 73.

"Girl Joey", sd, 118, 178.
"Glacier", sd, 118.
Glasgow, 82, 87.
Goodlad & Coutts, 89.
Goodlad & Goodlad, 109, 139.
Goodlad, J., 185.
Goodlad, J. B. Anderson &, 164, 185.
Goodlad, L., 18, 21, 26, 46.
Goodlad, P. S., 110, 124.
Good Templars, 29.
Gordon Highlanders, 129.
Gordon's station, 121.
Goudie, R. & Sons, 7, 17.
Goudie, W., 82.
"Gracey Brown", 81, 118.
Grand Hotel, 28, 61, 128, 184.
Granite setts, 65, 90, 140.
Gray, Capt. G., 69, 111.
Gray, G., 26, 82.
Gray, H., 154, 167, 182.
Gray, J., 81.
Greatorex, Rear-Admiral, 100, 105.
Green Head, 67, 129, 175, 183.
"Green Head", 113.
Greig's Pier, 145.
"Grey Sky", sd, 118.
Grierson's Lodberry, 18, 189.
"Grima", mv, 180.
Grimista, 1, 3, 5, 20, 172, 174, 193; Böd of Grimista, 5, 193.
Grimond, J., 144.
Grimsby, 45, 48.
Groat, Capt. R. J., 184.
Gunther's Station, 68, 191.
"Gustaf Reuter", ss, 130.

Haakon Haakonson, 1, 94, 153.
Haddock, 4, 6, 46, 47, 80, 83, 103, 159.
Haddock boat, 36, 83.
Half deckers, 10.
Halibut, 26.
Hall, A., 96.
Hall, J., 130.
Hall, Russell & Co., 181.
Hamilton, Sir R., 115.
Hamilton, W. R. T., 154, 167, 182.
"Hamnavoe" sd, 81, 104.
Hangars, 143, 144, 145, 146, 150.
Harbour limits, 76, 85, 116, 122, 145, 183.
Harbour Office, 63, 139, 151, 162, 189, 190.
Harrison, A. H. & Co., 44, 46.

O

Harrison, Captain G., 111, 139.
Harrison, G., 25, 53.
Harrison, G. & Sons, 12, 26.
Harrison, J., 12, 26, 111, 168.
Harrison, W. P., 123.
"Havana", 71, 129.
Hawick, P., 48.
Hay & Co., 11, 15, 17, 20, 26, 27, 35, 46, 49, 50, 54, 71, 80, 82, 121, 129, 152, 176, 182, 190, 192.
Hay & Ogilvy, 10, 11, 20.
Hay, G. H. B., 23.
Hay, Miss M., 91, 190; Miss Hay versus Lerwick Harbour Trust, 91, 102, 187.
Hay, Mrs J., 103.
Haynes, W., 119.
Hay's Pier, 17, 22, 24, 28, 56, 87.
Hay's Quay, 121.
Hay's Steps, 85, 89, 151.
Henderson, A., 115, 141.
Henderson, A. & Partners, 141, 146, 165, 180, 185.
Henderson, G., 185.
Henderson, T., 154.
Henderson & Nicol, 115, 125.
Henry, J. H., 183.
Herculeson, W., 48.
Herring, 2, 4, 10, 11, 19, 20, 26, 31, 44, 45, 49, 50, 51, 54, 63, 70, 71, 80, 102, 103, 105, 124, 126, 135.
Herring curing, 10, 19, 44, 49, 50, 51, 67, 137, 156, 161, 162, 187.
Herring exports, 80, 103, 137, 138.
Herring workers, 27, 51, 77, 78.
Herring Industry Board, 137, 155, 156, 158, 191.
Highlands and Islands Development Board, 166, 173, 177.
Holland, 1; Reformed Church of, 77.
Hollanders' Knowe, 2.
Holmsgarth, 107, 121, 129, 170, 174, 175, 176, 189, 192.
Home Guard, 129, 133, 134.
Howe, Rt Hon the Earl of, 152.
Hunter & Morrison, 181.
Hunter, P. B. A., 168.
Ice, 26, 120, 156, 192.
Iceatlantic (Frozen Seafoods) Ltd., 158.
Iceland, 147.
Icelandic vessels, 162, 185.
"Imogen", 15.
"Implacable", HMS, 100.
Income, 30, 31, 36, 37, 62, 101, 102, 112, 163.
Inkster, Capt. W., 139, 141, 169, 179, 184.
Ireland, 27, 51, 70.
Iron man, 27.
Irvine & Brown, 27.

Irvine, J., 27.
Irvine, J. C., 183.
Irvine's Pier, 18.
Irvine, R. B., 26.
"Isabella", 13.
Isbister, L., 48.
Isbister, Miss O., 50.
Isbister, T., 50.
"Isleford", ss, 105.
Isle of Man, 27, 51, 70.
Islesburgh House, 79.

Jackson, Major H. B., 79, 117, 119.
Jamieson Brothers, 63.
Jamieson, H., 190.
Jamieson, J., 85.
Jamieson, Mrs R., 65.
Jamieson, W., 131.
"Janet", 15.
"Janet Hay", 10, 15.
"J. M. Johansen", 160.
"Joey Brown", 81.
Johnson, Alex, 158, 191.
Johnson, Arthur, 145, 153, 167, 168.
Johnson, H. M., 120.
Johnson, Capt. J., 59.
Johnson, Inspector J., 165.
Johnson, L. H., 169, 184.
Johnson, S., 110.
Johnson, W., 30, 56.
"John West", mv, 156, 178.
Jones, Mrs A., 146.
"J. S. Sterry", 71.
"Juil", ss, 101.
Juliebø, Lieut., 128.

Kincairney, Lord, 38.
"King Arthur", 48, 49, 79, 121.
Kinnear, Moodie & Co., 87.
Kirkwall, 93, 94, 177.
Knab, the, 1, 5, 8, 105, 129, 130.
Kristiansand, 163.

"Lady Ambrosine", ss, 16.
"Lady Jane and Martha Ryland", 122.
Laing, J., 110, 115, 124.
Laurenson & Co., 98.
Laurenson, Allan, 131.
Laurenson, Arthur, 25.
Laurenson, Arthur (Clerk), 124, 144, 154, 168, 179.

Laurenson, Arthur B., 168, 171, 174, 175, 179, 184.
Laurenson, L., 79, 154.
Laurenson, T. W., 158.
Laurenson's Quay, 179, 191.
Laurie, J., 157, 159.
Leask, A. J., & Co., 27, 44.
Leask, D., 50, 80.
Leask, J., 11, 12, 25, 29, 54, 123, 124.
Leask's Jetty, 34, 108.
Leisk, J., 12, 25, 29, 54, 123, 124, 154.
Leith, 13, 14, 15, 46, 84.
Lerwick and Maloy Friendship Committee, 160.
Lerwick Boating Club, 147, 177.
Lerwick Coastguard, 162, 186.
Lerwick Co-operative Coal Co., 31, 65, 66, 71, 108, 190.
Lerwick Harbour Improvement Act (1877), 24, 29, 34, 40, 41, 56, 85, 182.
Lerwick Harbour Amendment Act (1903), 43.
Lerwick Harbour Order Confirmation Acts (1911-1976), 86, 117, 125, 140,
    146, 167, 180, 183.
Lerwick Lifeboat, 122, 126, 130, 131, 151, 152, 188.
Lerwick Lifesaving Company, 122.
Lerwick Sick Aid Society, 74.
Lerwick Town Council, 22, 24, 28, 57, 58, 63, 64, 88, 95, 103, 110, 115,
    125, 138, 139, 146, 154, 168, 169, 172, 175, 183.
Lerwick Town Hall, 29, 30, 46, 56, 61, 82, 88, 104, 124.
Leslie, G., 63, 110.
Lights and lighthouses, 33, 72, 73, 121, 131, 140.
"Lily of the Valley", 12, 48, 49, 57.
Lindberghs, 123.
Ling, 4, 20, 26, 48.
Linklater, J. R., 153, 168, 182.
"Linus", 80.
"Lion", mv, 181.
Lithgows (Holdings) Ltd., 191.
Livestock shipments, 18, 65, 66, 185.
Lizzie's Lodestar Cafe, 190.
Lochend House, 4, 6, 187.
Lodberries, 6, 16, 21, 29, 186, 187, 189.
Loeterbagh, Dr P. D., 20.
Loofa Baa, 73, 93.
Low, G., 113.
Lowestoft, 51, 174.
Lyall, G., 59.
Lyell, Sir L., 32, 93.

MacAlpine, Sir R. & Sons, 176.
MacBeath, A., 187.
MacDonald, H. & Co., 180, 191.
MacFisheries, 156, 157, 158, 159.
MacGregor, A., 30.

MacKay, J., 81.
MacKenzie & Kermack, 35, 38.
"Maid of Thule", sd, 130.
Mainland, Capt. L., 165.
Mair, J., 81, 142.
Mair, J. A., 110.
Malakoff, 18, 20, 26, 46, 80, 100, 120, 157, 158, 165, 167, 177, 191.
Malcolmson & Co., 65.
Mangan & Irvine, 64.
Manson, A., 111, 140, 168.
Market Cross, 5, 9, 63, 138, 151.
"Margarita", ss, 100.
"Marmion", HMS, 100.
Martin & Co., 185.
"Mary Rose", HMS, 99.
"Mary Watt", mv, 156.
"Matchless", 15, 16.
"Maud Evelyn", mv, 178.
"Mayflower", sd, 81.
Medical facilities, 78, 79.
Medical Hall, 20, 145, 189.
Merchant Navy, 92.
Merrylees, C., 17, 187.
Meteorological station, 121.
MFVs, 156.
Milchem (UK) Ltd., 172.
Mines, 130, 131.
"Minnie Hinde", 55, 65.
Mitchell, C., 58, 117.
Mitchell, J., 26, 44, 80, 117.
Mitchell's station, 67, 73, 121, 132, 161, 191.
Moar, J. P., 167, 179.
Moar, P., 109.
Moffat, McG., 79.
"Mona", ss, 40, 42, 66.
Moncrieff, T., 154.
Morrison, A., 157, 159, 169, 182.
Morrison, A. & Son, 25.
Morrison, L. D. & Partners, 185.
Morrison, M. H., 141.
Morrison's Pier, 9, 10, 17, 22, 29.
Morton Lodge, 6, 29.
Motor boats, 81, 82, 104, 118, 120, 126, 136, 164.
Mouat & Co., 58.
Mouat, Miss B., 15.
Mouat, H., 111, 117, 124.
Mouat, J., 17.
Mousa, 122, 124.
MTBs, 132, 133, 134.
Murray, G., 174.

"Myra", mv, 188.

Napoleonic Wars, 8, 92.
Nazis, 126.
"Nellie", mv, 127.
Neven-Spence, Sir B., 140, 151.
Neven-Spence, Miss A., 152.
Nicolson, Sir A., 78, 96.
Nicolson, Lady, 172.
Nicolson, W., of Lochend, 4.
Nimmo Offshore Services, 177.
Nisbet, Capt. R., 15.
"Norna" mv, 188.
Norscot, 174, 175, 193.
"Norseman", ss, 66.
North-Eastern Farmers Ltd., 191.
North Harbour, 5, 92, 127, 130, 141, 142, 171.
North Lodberry, 7, 18, 64, 190.
North Ness, 7, 8, 18, 26, 27, 67, 73, 80, 92, 129, 131, 141, 143, 145, 155, 158, 166, 177, 181.
North of Scotland Hydro-Electric Board, 175.
North of Scotland, Orkney & Shetland Shipping Co. Ltd., 15, 16, 23, 24, 30, 39-43, 64, 65, 89, 104, 122, 124, 126, 127, 128, 131, 135, 152, 157, 170, 181, 182, 189, 192.
North Road, 47, 67, 88, 171, 172, 173.
Noss, 9, 46, 157.
Norway, 1, 26, 127, 177, 179.
Norwegian fishermen, 36, 51, 160, 161, 185.
Norwegian refugees, 128, 129.
Norwegian servicemen, 128, 129, 132, 134.
"Novice", 11.
Numbering of stations, 119.
Number One Station, 148, 151, 158, 165-167, 177-179, 190.

Oceanex, 71, 172.
Ocean Inchcape (Shetland) Ltd., 176, 191.
Ogilvy, C., 10.
Ogilvy, T., 124.
Oil boom, 171-177, 185, 193.
Oil companies (local), 129, 140, 167, 190; (international), 173, 176, 193
Ollason, R., 188.
"Olive", mv, 127.
"Onward", 12.
"Ord", mv, 184.

P & O, 5, 174, 176, 180, 181.
P & O Ferries (Orkney and Shetland Services), 181, 189.
"Panther", mv, 181.
Parking, 109, 138, 146, 148, 165.
"Partridge", HMS, 99.

Paton, J., 167, 182.
Pearson & Tawse, 146.
Peterhead, 47, 51, 79, 104.
Peterson, J. G., 142, 144, 154, 157, 167.
Pilots, 121, 147, 153, 184.
Ployen, C., 10.
Police, 29, 34, 51, 109, 164.
Police Office, 64, 140, 190.
Polish fishermen, 161, 185.
Polson, Capt. D. I., 170, 184.
Pommer & Thomson, 192.
Post Office, 7, 17, 63, 78, 188.
Pottinger, F. H., 110.
Pottinger, J. J., 110, 111.
"Prince of Wales", 15.
"Prince of Wales" (smack), 48.
Provisional Orders, 22, 41-43, 85, 86, 116, 118, 125, 143, 145, 167, 175, 176
Public Works Loan Board, 31, 32, 33, 35, 57, 59, 90, 102, 118.
Purse seiners, 161, 162, 190.

Quarries, 36, 57, 87, 115, 193.
"Queen", ss, 14, 15.
Queen Elizabeth II, 151, 153.
"Queen of the Isles", 15.
Queen's Hotel, 17, 32, 91, 187.

Radio communications, 95, 121, 162.
RAF, 123, 126.
"Rangoon", HMS, 93.
Ratter, A., 110.
"Recovery", HMS, 105.
Refreshment rooms, 65, 190.
Rendall, Miss M., 190.
"Research", 49.
Reserve Fund, 33, 55, 101, 124, 125.
Retail system, 103, 120.
"Richelieu", 71.
Richmond Harrison & Co., 26, 46.
"Ringdove", HMS, 75.
R.N.L.I., 151. See also Lerwick lifeboat.
R.N.M.D.S.F., 78.
"Robert", 12.
Robertson, A., 49.
Robertson, Bertie, 119, 168.
Robertson, H. J., 13.
Robertson, John, 16, 17, 25, 187.
Robertson, John (Jun.), 17, 25, 26, 28, 69.
Robertson, John (Diver), 66, 113, 115.
Robertson, John J., 143.

Robertson, John W., 39, 66, 77, 78, 79, 80, 81, 83, 84, 85, 88, 98, 100, 104, 110, 112, 113, 116, 120, 130, 137, 142, 143, 144, 153, 154, 191.
Robertson, L., 154, 169.
Robertson, R. & C., 7, 29, 182.
Robertson, R. J., 140.
Robertson, S. & J. D., 191.
Robertsons (Lerwick) Ltd., 129, 163.
Robertson & Johnson, 114.
Robertson's Lodberry, 16.
Roll on-roll off terminal, 170, 180, 181, 182, 189, 192.
Rova Head, 73, 122, 193.
"Rova Head", sd, 81.
Royal Army Medical Corps, 129.
Royal Navy, 8, 92, 93, 94, 95, 131, 132.
Royal Naval Reserve, 92, 93, 95, 97.
Royal Naval Volunteer Reserve, 131.
"Royal Tar", 11.
"Royal Oak", HMS, 135.
Royal visits, 93, 151, 152, 153.
Russia, 80, 103, 105, 137.
Russian fishermen, 160, 185.

"Sage", 12.
Sales, J., 120.
"Salvador", 57.
Sandison, Alex, 12.
Sandison, Arthur, 23, 56, 89.
Sandison, W., 4.
Sailing drifter, 26, 31, 44, 49, 50, 53, 59, 71, 76, 79, 81, 102, 104, 119.
"St. Clair", ss, 15, 127, 135, 152, 157.
"St. Clair", mv, 170, 189.
St. Clement's Church, 77, 129.
"St. Fergus", 127.
"St. Giles", ss, 42.
"St. Magnus", ss, 15, 89, 104, 127, 128, 135.
"St Nicholas", ss, 15.
"St Pierre", 134.
"St Sunniva", ss, 122, 124, 127, 128.
Sandwick, 70, 71, 74, 94.
"Sapphire", 48.
Sargeant, T., 79, 119.
Scalloway, 1, 3, 46, 48, 49, 51, 70, 131, 132, 158, 171, 174.
Scapa Flow, 93, 120, 135.
Scapa Flow Salvage and Shipbreaking Co., Ltd., 115.
"Sceptre", HMS, 132.
Scollay, P., 6, 186.
Scotland, Bank of, 173.
Scott, J. H., 168.
Scott, W. A., 169.
Scottish fishermen, 26, 47, 77, 83, 157, 178.

Scottish Fishery Board, 87.
Scottish Home Dept., 143, 149.
Scottish Office, 143, 145, 146, 148, 174, 182.
Scottish Oil Agency Ltd., 108, 129.
Sea Angling, 163.
Seamen's Home, 8, 17, 34, 92.
"Sea Venture", ss, 126.
Secretary of State for Scotland, 123, 125, 143, 145, 149, 166.
Senior Naval Officer, 97, 100, 103.
Service bases, 172-176, 182, 193.
"Seventeen", sd, 73.
"Shamrock", sd, 72.
Shearer, J. & M., 156, 177, 186, 192.
Shearer, M., 115, 134, 153, 167, 168, 169.
Shearer, M. (Jun.), 174, 182, 183.
Shell, 173, 175, 176, 193.
"Shemara", 97.
Shetland Fishermen's Association, 118.
Shetland Islands Council, 183, 185, 189.
Shetland Islands Steam Navigation Co., 16, 30.
Shetland Islands Steam Trading Co., 39, 41-43, 65, 66, 67.
Shetland News, The, 68.
Shetland Seafoods, 170, 191.
Shetland Times, The, 22, 34, 67, 151.
Shewan, J., 80.
Sievewright & MacGregor, 23, 25, 30, 38, 56.
Sinclair & Buchan, 192.
Sinclair, Capt. G., 73.
Sinclair, J. T. J., 79, 98, 110, 111, 115, 117, 123.
Sinclair's Beach, 7, 17, 29, 34, 35, 37, 38, 63.
"Sir Colin Campbell", 12.
Sixerns, 20, 21, 48.
"Sixteen", sd, 74.
Skewis, Dr I., 179.
Slipway, 61, 68, 80, 120.
Smacks, 11, 12, 14, 15, 19, 21, 48, 49, 79, 121.
Small boat harbour, 16, 83-91, 101, 118, 163, 164, 178, 188.
Small, J., 111.
"Smiling Morn", mv, 122.
Smith, A., 25, 35, 38, 48, 53, 63, 67, 79, 105, 120.
Smith, A. & Schultze, 80.
Smith, Miss A., 120.
Smith, A. J., 79.
Smith, Capt. P. L., 18.
Smith Dock Trust Co. Ltd., 66, 75, 88, 97.
Smith, F., 79, 119.
Smith, I., 191.
Smith, J. R., 168.
Smith, L. W., 142, 143, 153, 168.
Smith, Sir M., 84, 87, 114, 115.

Smith, P., 154, 166, 179.
Smith, R., 153.
Smith, S., 74.
Smith, Mrs S., 103.
Smith, T. & Son, 150.
Smith, W., 153.
Smith, W. A., 168.
Smith, W. Spence, 13, 15.
Smith, W. Stevenson, 12.
Smith & Gear, 158.
Sound, 1, 3, 95, 101; Ness of, 183.
"Sound of Islay", mv, 175.
South Ness, 57, 73, 87.
"Sovereign", ss, 14.
Speed limits, 73-76, 109.
"Speedwell", mv, 182.
Spur jetty, 149, 150, 179, 180, 190.
"Star of Scotland", st, 127.
Stansbury, M. J., 172.
Steam drifters, 51, 58, 66, 68, 70-82, 90, 91, 102, 104, 115, 126, 130.
Steam trawlers, 37, 46, 47, 60, 90, 97, 122.
Stout, J., 145.
Stout, R., 186.
Stout's Pier, 36, 67, 186.
Stove Brothers, 18.
Stove, L. G., 25, 54.
Stove, T. W., 182.
Stove's Pier, 18.
Stove & Smith, 138.
Strikes, 89, 111.
"Strongbow", HMS, 99.
Submarines, 99, 100, 104, 126, 132, 134, 135.
Sumburgh Head, 37.
"Sumburgh Head", sd, 81, 120.
"Summer", 48.
"Superb", sd, 81.
Sutherland, J. & A., 15.
Sutherland, S. F., 85.
"Swan", 50, 51, 81.
Swedish fishermen, 27, 50, 51, 130, 185.
Swimming Pool, 147.

Tait, Capt. F. B., 154.
Tait, E. S. R., 110, 111, 118, 123, 124, 168.
Tait, G. R., 12, 21.
Tait, J., 30.
Tait, L., 12.
Tait & Peterson, 172.
Tait's Lodberry, 18, 189.
Tait's Pier, 28.

Tarry Beach, 18.
Tatton, G., 149.
Tawse, W., Ltd., 147, 149, 150, 167, 179.
Tedder, Air Chief Marshal, 134.
Telephones, 59.
"Tenby Castle", 100, 107, 114.
Territorials, 96, 97, 152.
"Thelma", mv, 82, 188.
"Thirteen", sd, 70.
Thompson, P., 114.
Thoms, Sheriff-Principal, 28, 29.
Thomson, C., 108.
Thomson, J., 154.
Thomson, W., 142, 154.
Thomson's Garage, 108, 109, 190.
Three mile limit, 47, 157.
Thule Bar, 18, 189.
Thulecraft, 190.
"Tjaldur", mv, 163.
Tod, J. & J. & Sons, 18, 108, 138, 190.
Tolbooth, 6, 17, 78, 187.
Torpedo boats, 80, 94.
Torrie, P., 6.
Traffic congestion, 109, 118, 122, 138, 146, 164.
"Trident", HMS, 132.
"Tigress", HMS, 132.
"Trojan", ss, 66.
Trucking & Shipping Ltd., 177.
Tulloch, A. I., 182, 183.
Tulloch, J. S., 111.
Tulloch, W. A. A., 73, 85, 98, 107, 111, 116, 124, 137.
Twageos, 67, 100.
"Twenty One", sd, 72.
"Tystie", mv, 180, 188.

Udal law, 38, 139.
"Ula", HMS, 38, 139.
Unemployment, 114, 123, 145.
Union Bank, 31, 32, 33, 55, 59, 87, 117.
Up-Helly-Aa, 21.

Vadill, 79.
Vehicular ferries, 167, 178.
"Venus", 11.
Victoria Buildings, 63, 189.
Victoria Pier, 16, 28, 29, 36, 37, 40, 42, 65, 66, 73, 83, 85, 87, 88, 90, 92, 94, 102, 115, 124, 125, 136, 141, 144, 146, 148, 149, 151, 157, 165, 180, 189.
Victoria Pier Arm, 152, 173, 176.
Victoria Warehouse, 17.

Victoria Wharf, 17, 18, 22, 23, 24, 28, 63.
Viet, K., 128.
"Vine", 26.
"Violet", 47.
Vista Clara C. A., 172.
"Vistula", ss, 126.
"Vyru", 161.

Waiting room, 64.
Wallace, Sheriff, 124, 139.
Wason, Sir C., 56, 84, 87.
Water supplies, 110, 139, 161, 163.
Watering trough, 65, 190.
Watt, A., 81, 104.
Watt, J., 118.
Watt, Joseph, 127.
Watt, J. T., 127.
"Wavecrest", mv, 183.
Weighbridge, 140, 190, 191.
West, J. M., 118, 178.
Whaling, 4, 12, 13, 19, 160.
Whalsay, 48, 55, 170, 179, 180.
Wheatley Report, 169.
"White Squall", 12.
Wick Radio, 162.
"William Hogarth", 14.
"William Martin", 49.
Williamson, D., 27.
Williamson, J., 185.
Williamson, L., 190.
"Willi Wilhelmsen", 160.
Wimpey, G., & Co., 146.
Wiseman, J., 182, 183.
Wood's Station, 192.
Workmen's Club, 123.
World War I, 96, 108, 129.
World War II, 126-135, 175, 192.

Yarmouth, 49, 51, 70, 81, 172, 174.
Yates, F., 187.
Yell, 27, 55, 103.
Yell Sound, 179.
Young's Seafoods, 159.

"Zeiten", 96.
Zetland County Council, 55, 84, 110, 125, 139, 147, 154, 163, 164, 167, 169, 179, 182, 183.